Dr Joyce J.M. Pettigrew is a Scottish anthropologist. Educated at the University of Manchester, she was a Research Associate at the School of Oriental and African Studies (SOAS) for three years before joining the staff of Queen's University, Belfast, where she is now Reader in Anthropology. The Punjab has long been the main site of her social research and she is the author of the highly acclaimed *Robber Noblemen: A Study of the Political System of the Sikh Jats* (Routledge and Kegan Paul, 1975).

THE SIKHS OF THE PUNJAB

UNHEARD VOICES OF STATE AND GUERRILLA VIOLENCE

Joyce J.M. Pettigrew

Zed Books Ltd
LONDON AND NEW JERSEY

To my mother in special memory

The Sikhs of the Punjab was first published by
Zed Books Ltd, 7 Cynthia Street, London N1 9JF, UK,
and 165 First Avenue, Atlantic Highlands,
New Jersey 07716, USA, in 1995.

Cover designed by Andrew Corbett.
Set in Monotype Baskerville by Ewan Smith.
Map on page vi reproduced, by kind permission of
Mark Tully, from *Amritsar* by Mark Tully and Satish
Jacob (London, Jonathan Cape, 1985).
Printed and bound in the United Kingdom
by Biddles Ltd, Guildford and King's Lynn.

A catalogue record for this book is available from
the British Library.

US CIP data is available from the Library of Congress.

ISBN 1 85649 355 5 cased
ISBN 1 85649 356 3 limp

Contents

Map vi
Preface vii
Acknowledgements ix
Glossary x
Abbreviations xii

PART ONE The Sikhs of Punjab: Place and People since 1984 1

1 State Terror 3
2 The Rise of Resistance, Political and Militant 30
3 The Guerrilla Movement 55
4 History and Organisation of the Khalistan Commando Force 82
5 Police, Guerrillas and Local Populations 103

PART TWO Children of Waheguru 135

6 Introduction 137
7 Profiles of Khalistan Commando Force Guerrillas: 'Sparrows into Hawks' 143
8 Concluding Remarks 187

Appendix One 199
Appendix Two 201

Bibliography 203
Index 207

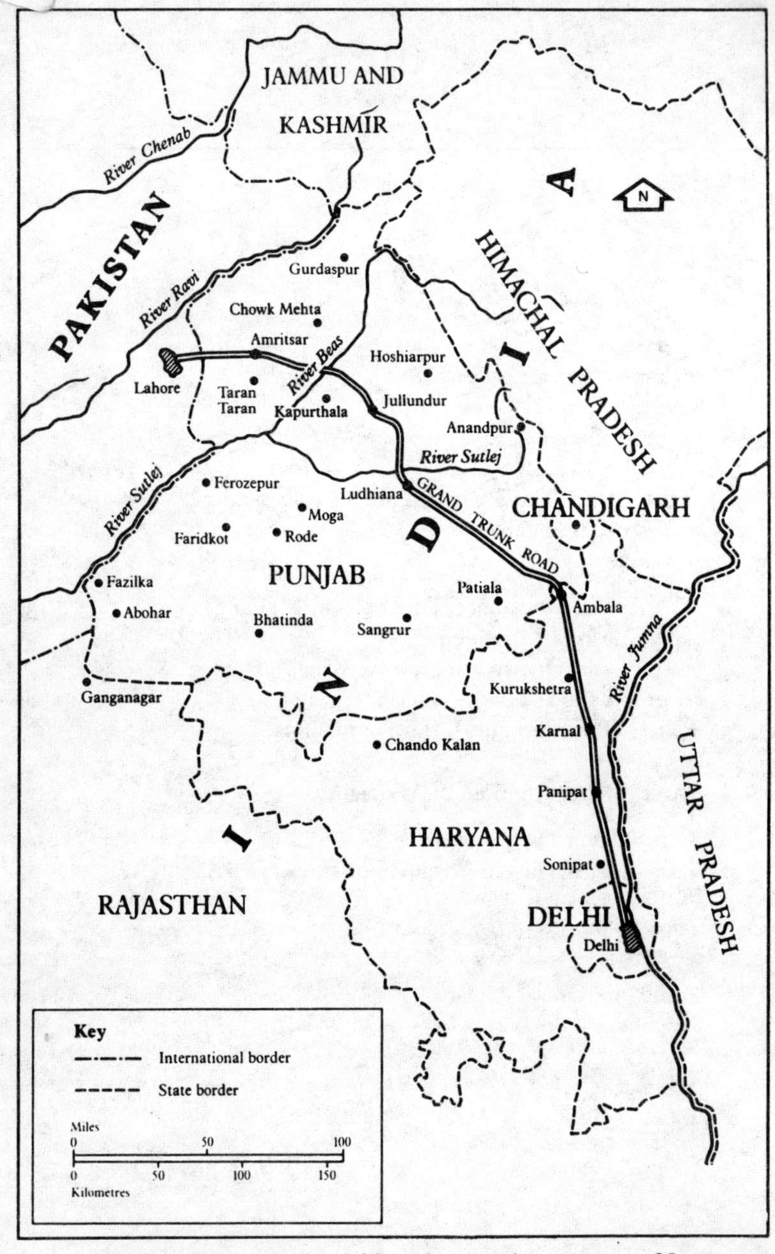

Indian Punjab and neighbouring provinces, post-1966

Preface

It seems a long time since the renowned South Asian poet, Faiz Ahmed Faiz, lamenting the division of the erstwhile Punjab, said to me 'Punjabis will always get together over *dharu* [country liquor] for, after all, a friend is a friend, whatever their personal politics.' Indeed neither the separatism of the Muslims, nor that of the Sikhs, has been particularly in keeping with the atmosphere of the Punjab plains. Yet both – one with a religious identity, the other with a national identity – have had their reasons for pursuing this form of politics, reasons which were determined beyond the land of the five rivers. This book deals with the nature of Sikh resistance to the Indian state in the years 1984–92. In times to come, if the self-reflection is deep enough and the dialogue broad enough, these years will be seen as the first phase of that resistance. Much of what is described can be regarded as behaviour under occupation: the familiar problems of very ordinary people in keeping themselves alive through times of terror, while attempting in some cases, but not all, to retain dignity as they know it.

Part of the book consists of interviews with a small number of ideologically committed people who are members of the Khalistan Commando Force, Zaffarwal (KCF), the original parent guerrilla grouping. These interviews are portrayals by guerrillas of their own movement. They may be seen as their diary of a particular time: 1984–92. By presenting these interviews in full, I am according their words no special sanctity. However, I am giving them prominence since their voices have not previously been heard at all.

The interviews were recorded on tape, and my main debt of gratitude is to Ajit Singh Khera, who made the recordings. There have been only minor amendments to ensure ease of reading. It is important to have this historical record, as all but two of those interviewed are now dead. Their words are preceded by the text of five chapters which seek to explain the conditions of life in the Punjab rural areas from 1984 onwards, the principal political developments, the history of the guerrilla movement, especially of the KCF (Zaffarwal) and the relations between people, police and guerrillas. These chapters present additional material in so far as they refer to events prior to a particular guerrilla's involvement or subsequent to his killing. The book details the effects of this resistance, together with the repressive tactics it has provoked, on the condition of the people. It is not purely an academic work. It has been impossible to keep it so. For the words of a dignified ex-serviceman remain in my heart: 'It is a relief to see that God has sent you to hear our gagged voice.'

The large amount of case material presented highlights the continuing savagery in the state. Unfortunately, because of the continuing civil war it has not been possible to analyse this with any investigative depth in the conventional anthropological manner.

Acknowledgements

Material for this book was gathered on three field trips to Punjab in September 1990, September and October 1992 and during the early months of 1993. During all trips movement was difficult and risky. On the last trip, particularly, the civil war situation in the state, with its many incumbent distrusts and suspicions, led to much personal isolation and fear. Threats were made against me in social settings, and suggestions that I could not be protected persuaded me to leave. It is in this context that I would wish to thank the many people who, in conditions that were certainly not easy and definitely not comfortable, gave me their co-operation. This was most tangible during my second visit. During my third and last trip in 1993, many, including those whom I had known well for over twenty years, wished to distance themselves from any research on the militant movement.

I am particularly grateful to Daljit Kaur, to Colonel Jamsher Singh Gill MBE, to the families of Bibi Gurdeep Kaur at Sarhali and Dr Shivinder Singh Sandhu in Amritsar, to Mrs Jasbir Singh Gill in Chandigarh and to Mrs Helen Khera in London for their extended periods of hospitality. Talks with former leaders of the All India Sikh Students Federation, writers, lawyers, army officers, judges, politicians and IAS officers were valuable. Meetings with the then Senior Superintendent of Police Amritsar, Hardeep Singh Dhillon, and Director-General of Police Karam Pal Singh Gill were frank. It was refreshing, too, to talk to many diverse members of the press and to Ajit Singh Khera, the press spokesman for the Council of Khalistan, London.

The trust with which I was received by many villagers in the districts of Faridkot, Bathinda, Amritsar and Ludhiana remains with me. A small grant from the Guggenheim Foundation, for which I am extremely grateful, enabled me to travel to meet them. Colin Irwin and Vida Zeruolis gave generously of their time in helping me with the manuscript. However, in situations of difficulty and danger it is inevitably those who give their sudden, unexpected and practical help who are remembered.

Glossary

Akali Dal: the main opposition political party to the Congress Party in Punjab until 1987

Akal Takht: the temporal centre of the Sikh people: a Sikh national institution

Akhand Path: continuous reading of scripture

Amritdhari: a Sikh who has been baptised

Ardas: the Sikh congregational prayer

Bandh: a total closure of all business premises, government offices and educational institutions

Bani/Gurbani: the words of the Gurus as recorded in Scripture

Bhog: last rites ceremony

Crore: million

Dam Dami Taksal: the religious seminary with which Sant Bhindranwale was associated

Darbar Sahib: the Golden Temple (also known as the Harimandir Sahib)

Dhadhi: eulogist

Granthi: scripture reader

Gurdwara: centre of Sikh congregational worship; a historic shrine in some cases

Gurmata: a collective resolution agreed upon by the Sikh people in the presence of their Holy Book

Guru Granth: the Sikh Scripture

Japji: the morning prayer

Jathebande: groups

Jhujharu: young freedom fighter

Khalsa: the Sikh nation; the Sikh people

Kharkhu: militant

Kesri: saffron

Kirpan: sword; one of the five Sikh symbols

Khalistan: a sovereign Sikh homeland

Kirtan: the singing of religious hymns

Lakh: one hundred thousand
Malwa: the area beyond the Sutlej river
Malwai: a person belonging to Malwa
Majha: the area between the Beas and Ravi rivers
Majhail: a person belonging to the Majha region
Misl: confederacies of equals formed to fight the Afghans in the eighteenth century
Pancayat: village council
Panth: the Sikh nation; the Sikh people
Panthic Committee: a five man executive council responsible to the Sikh people
Patka: a small piece of cloth which covers the topknot into which hair is tied
Sarbat Khalsa: general assembly of the Sikh nation
Sarpanc: head of the village council
Sewa/kar sewa: voluntary collective work for the Sikh people or any local representation of them.
Shahid; shahidi: martyr; martyrdom
Tehsil: a sub-division of a district
Thana: police station
Thanedar: person in charge of a police station
Waheguru: Almighty God

Abbreviations

AISSF	All India Sikh Students Federation
BSF	Border Security Force
BTFK	Bhindranwale Tiger Force for Khalistan
CIA	Central Investigative Agency
CJJ	Car jhujharu jathebande (the four groups of freedom fighters)
CRPF	Cental Reserve Police Force
DGP	Director General of Police
DSP	Deputy Superintendent of Police
EPW	*Economic and Political Weekly*
IAS	Indian Administrative Service
IB	Intelligence Bureau
IFS	Indian Foreign Service
IG	Inspector General
IPS	Indian Police Service
KCF	Khalistan Commando Force
KLF	Khalistan Liberation Force
MLA	Member of the Legislative Assembly
NSA	National Security Act
PHRO	Punjab Human Rights Organisation
RAW	Research and Analysis Wing
SGPC	Shiromani Gurdwara Prbhandhak Committee; the body controlling the historic Sikh shrines
SHO	Station House Officer, in charge of a police station
SSP	Senior Superintendent of Police
TADA	Terrorist and Disruptive Activities (Prevention) Act

ONE

The Sikhs of Punjab: Place and People since 1984

1

State Terror

A letter has been received from home today. It is from a friend and is about our situation.
He has written:
    All is well
The stamping of the soldiers' feet is not letting me sleep
    Otherwise all is well

He has written
Our labourer's daughter has been defiled by the government's gangsters with the connivance of the Congress *sarpanc*
    But all is well
    All is well

Yet not all are dead
Thousands are still alive
Heads placed on palm [i.e., accepting death]
    But all is well

In the courtyard we see only vultures
There is no nightingale
Flowers do not blossom
    Apart from that all is well

I received a letter from a friend in Punjab today
    He has written all is well

I have a letter from a friend in Punjab today
That the Moghuls have invaded the country
And yet again there is a price on our heads
    Apart from that all is well

For it makes so little difference how many they kill
The more they kill the more shall rise.

Buta Singh Rai

Thus a poet and farmer describes the violence that darkens people's lives in the rural areas of the Punjab in the years following the army invasion of the Darbar Sahib complex in 1984.[1] During those years Sikh nationalists have conducted a defiant struggle for an independent homeland for the Sikhs – Khalistan. They and the forces of the Indian state have been engaged in a bitter battle for the control of the Punjab. However, this is not just a battle for a strategic piece of territory adjoining an international border. It is a battle between two sources of authority, that of the centralised administration of the Indian state and that of the *Akal Takht* (the temporal centre of the Sikh people; a national symbol rather than a purely religious one). The first has its authority enforced by the paramilitaries – namely the Border Security Force (BSF) and the Central Reserve Police (CRPF)[2] both of whom, in the course of the conflict, have recruited increasing numbers of army personnel – by the various intelligence agencies and by the Punjab police. The second has its authority protected by small guerrilla bands.

Sikh guerrilla activity from 1984 onwards with the objective of achieving a national home can be placed within a number of contexts. The first of these is land relations and the agrarian situation. The second is the military recruitment policies of the Indian state, which have affected the employment opportunities of young people from the farms; smallholders frequently have had one or two serving army personnel in their families. The third is the reaction to the events of 1984 – the invasion of Darbar Sahib, the combing operations in the villages immediately afterwards, known as Operation Woodrose, and the November massacre – which has been permanent. The fourth is police activities in the villages, particularly against those civilians suspected of sheltering the guerrillas and who were often terrorised before they had given any concrete help, which antagonised many families in the rural areas. The first two contexts may be deemed to be predisposing circumstances leading to political violence; the latter two are its direct, immediate causes that have turned a farmers' movement, initially concerned with specific socio-economic issues, into a national struggle for freedom. Issues of religious identity and economic discrimination, important as they were, eventually became mere dimensions of the struggle as the Sikhs as a people faced the elimination of their young men. There is extensive literature on the first three points and I shall refer to them only briefly.

State policies in the agricultural sector

The movement for independence represents the politics of small farmers, many of whom feel close to financial ruin[3] due to lack of sufficient power and water, the high cost of electricity and diesel fuel and an inadequate support price for wheat. The Punjab is a wheat-growing state. Through a process of development that began first with land consolidation in the 1950s and then with seed improvement, use of fertilisers, mechanisation and the development of link roads in the mid-1960s, Indian Punjab became not only self-sufficient in wheat but a state with a wheat surplus. It is also a major rice, cotton and sugar cane producer. It is a land of owner occupiers who either work their land with the help of family labour or seasonal hired labour. The percentage of land under self-cultivation is now above 90% and there is hence very little absentee land ownership. In 1980 the area supplied 73% of the total wheat procured by the central government of India for its food grain reserves. However, the area experienced a high degree of centralised control over its resources, water, power and agricultural produce. This imposed a political brake on its economic and social development.

The central government regulated the amount of water Punjab could take from its own rivers, and it was calculated that 75% of available waters of riparian Punjab were allotted to non-riparian states. Over half of the land irrigated was irrigated by tube well as opposed to government canal and farmers in the ¾ acre group – i.e. small farmers – had the highest percentage of net irrigated area contributed by well and tube well.[4] According to one writer,[5] the cost of tube-well irrigation by electricity was three to four times more expensive than canal irrigation, and 'the uninterrupted supply of power from diesel or electricity is hardly assured'. Chadha (1985: 76) mentions the 'inadequate and erratic supply of power and its adverse effect on agricultural production'.

It was the scarcity of canal water, though also the desire to be independent on one's own land, free of as many outside controls as possible, that led to the exploitation of ground water. In any case, double cropping had increased water requirements, and the new strains of wheat needed a copious water supply. Canal irrigation lacks the kind of flexibility and reliability that can be secured by tube-well irrigation. It was not always available at the desired time and in required volume (Surendar Singh, 1991: A 153). Hence, farmers thought, why should the effective functioning of their farms be affected by state policy? Diesel-operated pump sets aimed to overcome this problem, though there was a shortage of diesel which affected not only transport costs but also the cultivation process during harvesting. Shortages of power, frequent cuts and a generally discontinuous supply ensured that farmers would never be free of state control. The shortages led to unremunerative farming for smaller farmers and falling profits for richer farmers, who, nevertheless, could still absorb the costs. Procurement prices offered to farmers for their wheat could not keep pace with increases in the price of inputs (Grewal and Rangi, 1981). Production costs were higher than procurement prices, reducing the farmers' profit in some cases and resulting in indebtedness in others. Kahlon and Kurian (1981) reported that the cost of wheat cultivation had increased by 84% between 1971 and 1978.

On account of the above, all agrarian interests saw the injustice of

Indian central government planning and policy and witnessed its effects on their production. Hence there began in the 1970s a non-violent campaign for autonomy that was conducted in the State Assembly and in the rural areas through peaceful mass demonstration. Its political expression was the Anandpur Sahib Resolution[6] of 1973 which sought to rectify many economic grievances of the Punjab as a region. It was supported by many government ministers and members of the state administration. Only as this movement for socio-economic redress went unheeded did it broaden to include other issues and developed a national colouring, so to speak, with the preachings of Sant Bhindranwale.[7] Socio-economic issues indeed emerge in a number of interviews with members of the Khalistan Commando Force.

Effect of state policies on army recruitment

Disaffection among Sikhs in the army was great. Surfacing principally through the views and activities of ex-servicemen, it initially emerged when the central government decided that each state and region should have representation in the army roughly in proportion to its recruitable male population. The text of an address at a convention in Amritsar on 28 April 1974 by Major-General Gurbaksh Singh pointed out how unwise a measure this was in the light of the fact that Punjabis in 1965 and 1971 had borne the brunt of land and air attacks. The ex-servicemen had presented a memorandum to the then governor of Punjab earlier, on 18 March 1974, in which they stated that:

> This new recruiting policy is all the more dangerous when allied with some other similar policies ... eg ... the Congress Governments of West Bengal and Maharashtra have forbidden the employment of outsiders in the public sector as well as private industries ... The effect of all this is to deny employment opportunities to the Punjabis on all fronts – the army, civil life and industry. Since the government of India would not establish any industry in the Punjab, being a border state, Punjabis ... would be reduced to total dependence on agriculture.

It is interesting that the Memorandum also noted the less than polite treatment that army veterans experienced, even then, at the hands of the civil and police bureaucracy.

Major-General Gurbaksh Singh's address drew attention to what was to become a serious problem in the Punjab, namely unemployment. In 1990 the two most militant affected areas – Gurdaspur and Amritsar districts – had the highest number of unemployed applicants for skilled and unskilled jobs, roughly three times the Punjab average. They were followed by Jalandhar, a district low in militancy. Gurdaspur and Amritsar districts also had the highest number of both educated and uneducated unemployed, followed by Jalandhar and Ludhiana. Overall unemployment was highest among matriculation passes, postgraduates and agricultural specialists. Among the latter it had trebled in the decade 1980–91. Postgraduates who were unemployed had almost doubled as had unemployed matriculation passes.[8] However, even as unemployment had grown, the number of government employees had increased in all districts of the state. Not much can be deduced regarding the role of unemployment in creating militancy in the border districts. However, the dramatic rise over the entire state in educated unemployed may have played a role in the rise of militancy. Hence the early relevance of the Major-General's comments, Punjab being a smallholder economy.

'The income of a typical cultivating household is derived from both farm and non-farm sources … Non-farm income constitutes about one fifth of total household income for cultivating households in general. For marginal farmers (2½ acres and below) it is about 65% of the total household income.' (Bhalla and Chadha, 15 May 1982: pp. 831–2). Hence there is a very real dependence on service pensions and salaries, as well as on remittances from abroad. It is estimated that small farmers' households are in difficulty in the sense that 'they are obliged to mortgage land … or else become tenant cultivators of another's land while still retaining their own … or while holding on to land to mortgage their jewellery or other assets' (Bhalla and Chadha, 22 May 1982: p. 874).

The complaints surfacing in the 1970s, which the Anandpur Sahib resolution might have remedied, persisted. Central government investment in the Punjab, which was 2% in 1980, fell to 0.8% over the next ten years, and the central government continued to return to Punjab as investment only one-third of what it borrowed. Summing up, one may say that the state's centralisation policies, particularly its control over the productive process, were an important source of gathering discontent. Then, when there was also a decrease in army recruitment at a time when surplus labour could not be released to the Middle East, pressure and conflict within the rural sector of society began to build up.

It was during the 1970s that the bonds of the Sikhs with the state began to loosen. Geertz (1975) has noted that identification with the nation as represented by cultural tradition, religion, history and language remains unorganised and latent among minority nationalities if their élite have strong ties with the dominating nationality, and if the mass of the people are not greatly affected in their daily lives by state activity. This accurately describes the Sikh position at the beginning of the 1970s. In the course of the next ten years the élite's mental and emotional ties to the state perceptibly weaken, though they make no practical commitment to change that is not within the limits of the constitution. After 1984, the masses took to new political alignments with the élite participating from the sidelines when it was safe to do so. However, a radical change in the Sikh position had occurred. The Sikhs had ceased to be integrated in Aron's terms (1972: 90): 'A national minority is integrated when those of its members who serve the state are neither condemned by members of their own group nor held in suspicion by members of the majority.'

The events of 1984

On three successive occasions in 1984 Sikhs as a people were attacked. On each of those three occasions, their social class, their family background, their service to and positions in the structures of state signified nothing. The fact that they were Sikh removed their status and their rights from them. Resistance began soon after, and was formalised as a freedom struggle when Khalistan was declared on 26 January 1986 at the Akal Takht.[9] It is pertinent to note that allegiance to modern political institutions was replaced by armed conflict only after the attack on the two central Sikh institutions, the Darbar Sahib and the Akal Takht, followed by the army's mopping up operations in the Punjab rural areas, when it removed Sikhs in the 15–25 age group from their homes and villages,[10] and the murder of four thousand and more Sikhs in the cities of Northern India, though specifically Delhi.[11]

These three developments in which the Sikhs encountered the reality of state power gave rise to a defiant and participatory resistance. The considerable violence to which ordinary civilians were to be subjected in the years following stems from these events when the state treated the Sikhs as a collective entity for the first time in post-independence India as well as attacking their institutions. These attacks were crimes, and as Foucault (1979) has remarked: 'the injury that a crime inflicts upon the social body is the disorder that it introduces into it ... the example that it gives, the incitement to repeat it if it is not punished and the possibility of becoming widespread that it bears within it.'

The initial crime was celebrated and indeed had been planned for a full year beforehand. The Darbar Sahib complex, a place of great beauty, the spiritual and political centre of the Sikh way of life and of the Sikhs as a people, their historic home through years of invasion from the west, had its sanctity shattered. The army went into Darbar Sahib not to eliminate a political figure or a political movement but to suppress the culture of a people, to attack their heart, to strike a blow at their spirit and self-confidence. The second crime, the penetration into the heart of many rural homes by non family members in search of the young and fervent, gave rise to the early forms of resistance in the rural areas. The third crime, the systematic and planned attack on the Sikh settlements in the trans-Jumna area of Delhi in which neighbourhoods were surrounded and their Sikh inhabitants set alight and burnt alive, was a massacre in the true sense of the term.[12]

High officials of the then ruling Congress Party were named in forty affidavits as having been involved in incitement to murder, as were two MPs and one Union Minister. No protection came from the police. Indeed the police first seized the licensed weapons of the Sikh inhabitants of these areas and, the Sikhs disarmed, the mobs were free to enter. The army was confined to barracks. When eventually an enquiry was commissioned it was very reluctantly publicised. The judge concerned, Judge Mishra, said in his report: 'The riots after spontaneous origin got into channelised methods in the hands of gangsters' (cited in Amiya Rao, 1987). He described the death of more than four thousand people as 'unpleasant episodes of the cloudy days' (as cited in Harji Malik, 1987). The comment of the then Prime Minister, Rajiv Gandhi, was 'When a great tree shakes, the earth trembles.' With the exception of Lalit Maken[13] the guilty remain unpunished and the general feeling in Delhi and Chandigarh was that the Sikhs had got what they deserved.[14]

In 1990 an Indian Intelligence team went to the home of one of the MPs (Sajjan Kumar), named in innumerable affidavits as having been present when whole families were set ablaze by mobs, to arrest him. Neighbours surrounded the house and prevented the team taking him away. An *Economic and Political Weekly* (*EPW*) report (15 September 1990: 2024), described the scene thus:

> Within an hour the crowds swelled to thousands. Girls came out from a nearby college blocking traffic ... Buses were parked across the road leading to Sajjan Kumar's house and were turned into road blocks to prevent police reinforcements from coming ... It was really intriguing to find the police – always ready to lathi charge, fire tear gas shells, or even resort to firing on the slightest pretext – all of a sudden turning into non-violent spectators while all this was happening. It seems that Congress I politicians even out of power enjoy the same immunity from the law enforcing machinery as in the past.

For what Delhi 1984 meant to the Sikhs I leave it to a *dhadhi* [eulogist] to express, since the *dhadhis* have been the customary voicers of protest against injustice.

> I can forget all my personal sorrows but not the massacre in Delhi
> The rest of the world thinks it all forgotten but the Sikhs have been sawn
> in two.
> Oh Government!
> You surrounded the defenceless [Sikhs] and set them alight.
> To those Sikhs who had sacrificed their lives for you this is the reward

you gave to them.
Oh Delhi Darbar!
Don't forget that Sikhs always return their debts.
You placed burning tyres around the necks of innocent children
Look at what persecution you have inflicted upon a peaceful sacrificing nation.
Oh Oppressor!
Those whom you have burnt they have been reborn.
Oh Delhi Darbar!
Those gruesome bodies you can never hide
Their wails will haunt you to the end of time and bring your end.
They will set Delhi alight.

As one reads these lines the degree of alienation is clear: Delhi, the central government and oppression are interchangeable.

These three crimes against the Sikhs were events of like order, all equally involving the institutions of the state. Since then, they have been repeated many times over in the third degree methods that police have employed in all districts of the Punjab against the supposed sympathisers of the Khalistan movement. Both police excesses and, as one report puts it (*EPW*, 3 May 1986: 759), 'the apathy and inaction of the non Sikh masses during the anti Sikh carnage in the national capital' contributed to a rising sense of political difference among the Sikhs as a whole.

Police activity in the villages

A condition of *zulm* exists in the rural areas. *Zulm* is oppression directed against an entire people and so intense that it has to be resisted. One of the interviewees uses the word *tashaddar* to describe the cruelty to which he and others were subjected. Some indications of the meaning of *zulm* for those who live in rural areas are found in the three case studies at the end of this chapter. Briefly, *zulm* covers a whole range of behaviour inflicted on the innocent, such as the disappearance and torture of sons, death in false encounter, illegal detention in false cases, harassment of witnesses and of the relatives of the militants both near and far and the creation of an atmosphere of terror so that people are driven out of their homes and villages.[15]

It was common in the present Punjab situation for persons, both suspected and innocent, to be abducted, not produced before a magistrate and no records kept of their arrest and detention or interrogation, irrespective of the duration of that detention. During the period December 1992 to mid-February 1993 one small political party alone registered 98 affidavits which, in the main, concerned cases regarding illegal detention, torture, kidnapping and false encounter. *Amritdhari* (baptised)[16] Sikhs were especially targeted. Once in custody, torture was especially severe for the following categories: those who were members of the Mann Akali Dal,[17] the only opposition political party regarded as a threat; those who were long-standing political activists and who had registered judicial complaints against the police in the past, appealing to higher authority; members of the All India Sikh Students Federation; those who had close kin in custody; those who had been army deserters. Additionally, those who came from key militant areas such as Batala, District Gurdaspur or Tarn Taran, District Amritsar[18] were given harsh treatment in order to create a general feeling of terror among the populace in those areas. Having had a responsible position in no way alleviated one's treatment once in paramilitary or police custody, as the first of the three case studies at the end of this chapter illustrates. Nor did even membership of the police force.[19] In nearly all cases, the families of those abducted and detained and eliminated were harassed, that is, they were involved in false cases. In some instances they left their homes out of fear or indeed because their homes, crops, costly agricultural implements and businesses had been destroyed. In these types of situation, families suffered considerable financial loss and had to move to the *gurdwara*. Those who were involved in democratic politics were also the targets of paramilitary and police attack.

For example, Kulwant Singh Saini, a lawyer at the District Courts Ropar and District Secretary of the Mann Akali Dal, disappeared along with his wife and small child while making a legal representation to the police on behalf of a girl from his village. His father's statement to the court records that the family had no rivalries and was not engaged in any village feud. Children would be penalised for the long-time political activity of their parents. For example, Jathedar Lakha Singh, District Secretary of the Mann Akali Dal, Bathinda had one son killed by the police, another kept intermittently in detention for five years through repeated involvement in false cases and a third son was forced to abandon his studies due to the police constantly picking him up. If parents, or their children, were politically involved or even if their relatives through marriage were politically involved they could expect some sort of police activity *vis-à-vis* their family. Usually people were at a loss to know why their sons had been picked up and would assume that it was because it was they were *amritdhari* and were young. I encountered a near universal belief in the rural areas through which I travelled, on both my trips to Punjab in 1992 and 1993, that 'Mr Gill's men', as the people put it, that is, the police under the direction of the Director General of Police K.P.S. Gill, were eliminating all young, aware Sikhs. An editorial comment in *EPW* (1990, 6 January) records that 'No action has been taken against police personnel named by several civil liberties groups as responsible for tortures and extortions.'

Suspicion was enough for the most brutal retaliation, often of a generalised nature. For example, if a guerrilla cell attacked in the vicinity of a CRP or BSF picket, the villages in a five- to ten-mile radius of the attack would be surrounded, combed and every Sikh male, irrespective of past service to India, dragged out of their homes, beaten and in some cases arrested, tortured and eliminated.[20] This harassment, torture and killing by paramilitary and police forces was against the constitution. Quoting Simranjit Singh Mann, leader of the Mann Akali Dal (see note 17, Chapter 2):

> Article 19 [of the constitution] says people must be brought to trial speedily. Yet people are in jail for years at a time. Article 22 says that you cannot keep a man in custody for more than 24 hours. There are many cases of illegal custody for more than three years. They are in violation of their own constitution. If the young fighters say they have no faith in the constitution or in the political process, are they to blame, when the majority does not support its own laws? (interview September 1990).

Likewise his party's memorandum of the same year notes:

> In effect India stands constitutionally partitioned between Punjab and India proper. Different laws apply to Punjab than the rest of the country. The people of Punjab are denied any legal or administrative redress, thus while in Punjab people can be shot by the police on the vaguest of suspicion without any process of law, those guilty of killing Sikhs in 1984 freely roam the streets of Delhi.

This was the context for the resurrection of the Khalsa *pancayats* (councils of the people at village level) for 'If the Indian judicial system has two yardsticks, one for Indians and the other for Sikhs, are the Sikhs then unreasonable in pursuing, redefining, motivating and evolving their own system?'[21]

In a democratic system, courts provide a constitutional check on executive power. However, in the Punjab, the executive dominates the judiciary. A judge of the High Court can be superseded without reference to seniority. A Supreme Court Judge can also be superseded and the government, when making legal appointments, no longer need consult the Chief Justice of the Supreme Court and, if consulted, his advice need not be accepted. Allurements are given to judges to comply with the state.

After the events of June 1984 the government introduced the Special Courts Act which tried detainees *in camera*.[22] These courts could keep the identity of witnesses secret and the accused had no right of appeal to the High Court though an appeal could be made to the Supreme Court. Many of the provisions contained in the Special Courts Act were incorporated into the Terrorist and Disruptive Activities (Prevention)

Act or TADA as it is known (1985, 1987). TADA allows confessions extracted under torture to be admissible as evidence. In normal law the statement of the accused before the police has no evidential value. Under TADA a statement made before a Superintendent of Police (SP) has evidential value. TADA shifts the burden of proof onto the accused, who is presumed guilty; and the National Security Act (1987) or NSA provides for detention without trial for a two-year period and continued detention beyond the two-year period on the production of fresh detention orders. Trial is *in camera* and without legal representation. The NSA also allowed the government to detain those suspected of having certain views. One lawyer summed up:

> There is no constitutional protection of ones rights. Suspects are tried in designated courts. Each district has a designated court and there is no provision for bail unless the court is satisfied the man will not commit the crime again. In cases where bail is denied, the right to approach the High Court is also denied. The case then goes to the Supreme Court which is expensive and time consuming and there is difficulty getting advocates to take on the cases. The innocent are detained under TADA for there is a vast difference in the mode of trial under TADA and the mode of trial under normal law. He has to prove his innocence.

The former State Advocate-General, Gurdarshan Singh Grewal, believed TADA was responsible for increased militancy, since if an innocent person is confined to jail he becomes hardened and joins the movement.

> We have not had a single conviction of a known militant under TADA. If arrested an ordinary and innocent person cannot get bail unless the police agree and they don't have to put his paper for trial (*challan*) until a year has elapsed. Ordinarily there are no witnesses and confessions are admissible. No evidence is forthcoming because the police threaten witnesses.

He pointed out the difficulties even when bail is granted:

> The engineer son of Mr Multani, an Indian Administrative Service (IAS) officer who was holding then the position of Joint Development Commissioner Chandigarh, was kidnapped. When he asked for bail the court issued a notice for a particular date on which it would be considered. On that date we were informed he had escaped from custody. Escaped from custody means 'escaped from this world'.

There are various references to this sort of happening in the text. TADA was the subject of much early adverse comment[23] and all aspects of TADA have been challenged in the Supreme Court, New Delhi.

The case studies[24] which follow truly reflect the horror and the terror for the ordinary person of living under these conditions. They describe the sudden disappearance and furtive killing that has become part of the fabric of the ordinary citizen's life in the Punjab. They are in no way unique and reveal the nature of police practice. The disrespect for the old which emerges in the two ex-servicemens' cases is a regular and common occurrence. There are many such cases, involving either ex-servicemen or their children, some of which are cited in Kumar and Sieberer.[25] One should also take note of a statement made by the Indian Ex-Servicemen's League as contained in a letter to the *Tribune* (13 October 1992):

> The Indian Ex-Servicemen's League therefore voice concern that a large number of cases of police harassment and bad behaviour towards ex-servicemen and serving defence personnel were taking place in Punjab ... Colonel Dhillon (retd.) ... alleged that a number of ex-servicemen were being kept as hostages by the police for the waywardness of their wards.

Age, previous position, high social standing or loyalty to the state provided no guarantees of personal safety and right to life. The first case, the most recent, deals with a fifty-year-old ex-soldier from District Amritsar and the harassment, torture and threat to life under which he lives. The second is from District Faridkot and concerns the extra-judicial killing of the son of an ex-serviceman. The third concerns the victimisation of a well-to-do farmer from a well-known family in District Amritsar. They are typical happenings of everyday life in the rural Punjab during the years that have followed the invasion of the Darbar Sahib.

Typical happenings of everyday village life

Case 1: Surinder Singh s/o Teja Singh village Fatehabad, tehsil Tarn Taran

'This is an account of the happenings in my life from 27 May 1986. These happenings relate to government terror, state oppression and false implication in cases. They are my own personal experiences.

'I am an ex-soldier and I have fought in two wars (1965 and 1971) for India. Despite this, the state has chosen to implicate myself and my family in false cases and thereby shown them little regard or respect. I am giving in writing the details of these cases and the reasons why I am in hiding, rather than living normally, with my family, as indeed would be expected of an old soldier.

'In 1984 this Congress government attacked what is for us our most beloved and precious place, the *Akal Takht.* After the death of Mrs Gandhi they carried out a massacre of the Sikhs in order to please the majority Hindus and by appeasing them to give the political office of

Prime Minister to Rajiv Gandhi. In the Punjab, with such a small percentage of votes behind them, our not so very far seeing Chief Minister and his Director General of Police are involved in the killing of their own youth. TADA is used excessively to imprison young people who are often innocent yet kept in illegal custody for many months and then killed in false encounters. The police have imprisoned even the most respected of citizens. Even freedom fighters' families have become the victims of this murderous regime.

'On 27 May 1986, I admitted my Father, who was ill, at the Jalandhar army hospital. I was returning to my home at Fatehabad during the night of 27 May–morning of 28 May when the Punjab police with the CRP surrounded my house. They took me to Fatehabad police post. There were already five young boys sitting there from village Kawaspur [he names them]. I became the sixth person. Our hands were tied behind our backs and we were taken to a house in a neighbouring village where they tortured us and then to a Central Investigative Agency (CIA) staff centre at Amritsar. They treated us very badly there. We couldn't even stand up. This continued until 8 June. We were charged on 9 June at *thana* [police station] Verowal under TADA. We were sent to jail in Amritsar. The village *pancayats* [councils] of our respective villages gave character references.

'When we were at Amritsar jail, the then Deputy Commissioner issued orders that we remain in jail under the NSA. This was on 1 July 1986. As we had been charged innocently we appealed. On 22 August a judge, after listening to our case, lifted the NSA ruling. The case continued until 1988 and we won it.

'In 1989 I was re-arrested and taken to Mal Mandi [the CIA centre, Amritsar] which is called the butcher's yard. Many different types of torture were inflicted on me and they asked 20,000 rs for my release. My family arranged 15,000 rs. I was released and started living normally again. My only crime was that I had rented out a room to the local cell of the All India Sikh Students Federation (AISSF). Then in 1991 when there was a call for elections I too became part of the political process and joined the Sant Sipahi Front[26] of Colonel Kahlon. I became a member of their central committee and the election agent of Bibi Darshan Kaur in Khadur Sahib. In that election we promised redress for those who suffered from police injustice. One day before the elections were due to be held they were stopped.

'On 18 August, 1991 one of my wife's relatives was kidnapped. His name was Sirdar Bachittar Singh, *sarpanc* of his village. He was kidnapped by SHO Surinderpal Singh[27] in charge of Goindwal *thana*. I went to Goindwal *thana* to inquire about his whereabouts.[28] The SHO arrested me also. I and Bachittar Singh were beaten by this SHO when he was drunk. On the 20th we were taken to Khadur Sahib. There our legs were pulled apart and we were given *ghottna*[29] and hit with sticks on our feet. We were unable to walk. The next day we were sent to Sarhali *thana* and on the 23rd to Valtoha. On the 24th Sirdar Bachittar Singh was separated from me and I was handed over to the BSF.[30] They took me up to a camp near the Pakistan border. Electric currents were passed through my penis and I became unconscious. I was beaten badly and my entire body became swollen. I became deaf in my right ear. The doctors have written it off. Due to these beatings my eyesight has also been adversely affected and, too, my ability to remember. My arrest was reported in the 22, 23 and 25 August 1991 editions of *Ajit* [a Punjabi vernacular paper with a high circulation]. On 27 August I was sent to Verowal *thana* where my case (FIR or first information report) was registered. I was shown to have been in possession of certain types of hand grenade. On 28 August I was sent to Amritsar high security jail. Due to ill health I was admitted to the hospital after two months but owing to lack of proper facilities there I couldn't get appropriate treatment.[31] I organised my bail after eight months and on 20 April 1992 I left jail on bail. However, that does not appear to mean anything here. For on 27 April the SHO Goindwal came to my house and started beating me up. In my case the judiciary was fair. But these police people who claim to be the protectors and guardians of the law are just the opposite. SHO Surinderpal Singh's words from his very own mouth were 'which sister-fucking judge has allowed you out on bail and which daughter-fucker has paid your bail'. He dragged me at gunpoint to Fatehabad *chaunki* [police post]. There they beat me up and gave me the usual treatment, hanging me upside down. I was there from 27 to 30 April 1992 and they threatened me that if I did not cancel my bail and return to prison, then they would link me with the murder of a lady in village Dhunda. The important thing to note here is that the woman was murdered while I was in Amritsar Security jail. I was able to escape being blamed for that murder, therefore. Then they said they will charge me with being in possession of an AK-47, so I wouldn't be able to secure bail. In the meantime my wife sent telegrams to the Chief Justice of the Punjab and Haryana High Court. The SHO found out about this and on 30 April sent me back to *thana* Verowal. My relatives and friends had no idea of my whereabouts. I was shut in Verowal *thana* for fourteen days and the same SHO returned to beat me up. He tore my legs apart. I was hung upside down every one of those fourteen days and then transferred to Sarhali police station. Then on 26 May I was brought back to Fatehabad. Here Assistant Sub Inspector (ASI) Balbir Singh asked me for some money and said he could help me out of my misery. We had to give him some money and on 28 May I returned home. At the time my life was saved by the intervention of the military commanding officer Fatehabad unit.

'This SHO had detained me illegally for thirty-two days. We were on the alert all the time. Ten days later, raids on my house began at night. I stopped coming home at night. They carried out eighteen attacks against me but due to God's protection I escaped. Five of the attacks were well orchestrated and I became convinced after two of them had nearly resulted in my death that this SHO was out to kill me in a false encounter. So in order to save myself I talked to the GOC 15 Infantry Division. They recorded what I had to say and on 25 September sent me to my village in army transport. I stayed at home for nineteen days. Then on 13 October the SHO came from Sarhali to where he'd been transferred along with ASI Balbir Singh and invaded my house at 5.15 in the morning. I succeeded in escaping and by daybreak I arrived in Fatehabad. I went to the army barracks there and told them what had happened. Fatehabad was no longer in the SHO's jurisdiction as he had been transferred and the army people were furious with the police. After taking their assurances that I would be safe, I returned home. But I still did not trust that SHO or take my safety for granted. Sure enough, on 8 December the SHO sent some people to my house and they tried to foist a false case on my wife. On 9 December she came to see me in Amritsar. On the night of the 10th Surinderpal Singh invaded my home with a whole platoon. Some were in uniform, others were not. Surinderpal Singh was in civilian clothes. They manhandled my wife and children and abused them. When I visited one of my daughters, who is a student in Tarn Taran, she told me what had happened. She advised me to escape far away, for the SHO had said to her: 'He can run wherever he likes, I'm going to kill him anyway. We don't obey the orders of the army or of anyone else.'[32] The same day my wife was arrested from home. The Amritsar police picked her up. They also took our television and refrigerator. On the 12 December I was informed that the respectable Punjab police had kidnapped my wife and stolen all our belongings, as though we were *dacoits* [thieves]. Then, on 13 December when I myself was coming to Tarn Taran, at the Tarn Taran–Jandiala crossroads, two jeeps belonging to Surinderpal Singh arrived. With the help of police commando units, they kidnapped me. They blindfolded me and took me to some police station. I was given nothing to eat or drink and not allowed to speak to anyone. There, conditions were very sad and sorrowful. Many were screaming with pain. This dark, dangerous and cold night I did not sleep. Next day I also spent without food or water. Then on the 14th night I was taken to Chowla Sahib police post and from there in the direction of Kharka village. Then, it seemed, they started going in the direction of the river bank where there were reeds. They took off my blindfold and tied my hands behind me with a towel. I started moving my arms to loosen the towel but left it in place. There were six others.

I was the seventh. They were beaten to pulp, dragged like animals, blown to bits with bullets and thrown in the river.[33] All of the police were completely drunk. I pushed a *hawaldar* [sergeant major] forward and succeeded in escaping. They started shooting but I managed to dodge their bullets. I hid until they were gone, then started walking, and by daybreak I reached Tarn Taran. Then I went by mini bus to Amritsar and then on to Chandigarh. I informed the relevant bodies what I had witnessed and undergone.

'By God's grace I am alive and in high spirits. I have informed a colonel in the 15th Infantry Division of my escape from police custody. I received a letter from my wife from *thana* B division, district Amritsar. It was written on 15 December. She is still in the hands of the terrorist police and the goods in my house are still in the possession of the uniformed police terrorists.

'I appeal to the democratic peace loving countries of the world to stop giving economic aid to India, for this money is being spent on killing and on the oppression of minorities. I would appeal to the UNO to send their investigative team to the Punjab to listen freely to the people without government interference, so that truth may prevail. In present day India tyranny has surpassed that of Mir Mannu.[34] No democracy is left and no rule of law. Surjit Kaur, my wife, remains illegally detained and has not been presented to any court. She is kept as though she is a person without roots and without a home. Meantime my children are with their maternal grandparents and my home in Fatehabad is locked up. I myself am underground. I am reciting this story of recent happenings in my life in all humility' (signed Surinder Singh, 12 January 1993).

Case 2

Report by Subedar Gurdip Singh, village Chahal, P. O. Tehna, District Faridkot, on the murder of his son Bharpur Singh and his friend Bobby on the Moga-Talwandi road at bus stop Khukhrana on 27–28 December 1990.

'On the night of 27–28 December my son Bharpur Singh, aged 21, along with his friends, was returning from Ludhiana. Bharpur had been to see his brother who worked as a telecommunications engineer for a company owned by a Congress MP. They were searched thoroughly on the outskirts of Moga near the Nestle factory and cleared to continue their journey. On approaching Khukhrana bus stop on the Moga–Ferozepur GT road, the car was signalled to stop by a police party who flashed their torches.[35] The driver slowed down, lit the interior car light and stopped alongside the police. The police immediately opened fire without warning or challenge. The driver of the car opened the right door and came out raising his hands and shouting 'We are innocent, please check us.' However, the firing, which was coming from the left side and from behind the covers of a tea shop, continued. My son was killed on the spot but Bobby remained seriously injured. The police allowed no one near the car and Bobby bled to death. The driver of the car was asked to crawl towards the police. The police gave no first aid to the victims and Bobby died after bleeding profusely for two hours. My son's body was not removed from the rear seat of the car until daybreak. It was removed from the car only for a post-mortem examination. Subsequently the police concocted a story that the car in which the boys were travelling had come into cross-fire[36] between the police and the militants.

'I am sad and utterly dismayed that, although it was confirmed to me by the Governor of Punjab Mr O.P. Malhotra during his visit to Faridkot that the police party under ASI Mangal Singh were in the wrong, no action has been taken against the killers of these innocent lives. Not to speak of action, not even a word of condolence has come from any quarter. Aside from a sympathetic hearing from the Governor, not even an acknowledgment has been received of the three petitions sent to his office on 29/12/1990, 21/1/91 and 25/2/91. When I wrote to the Governor on 25 February I told him that:

> I being an ex-serviceman, PA to GOC 20 Mountain Division remember that in 1965 Major General J.I. Sataravala MC court martialled three soldiers for the rape of a married woman and sentenced them to three years in jail ... Hence I hope you would kindly realise what type of shock waves are passing through my own body and those of my family members when observing that the killers of this innocent son of an ex-soldier ... are enjoying their lives whereas I, the ex-soldier, am the one who has to request justice from a General of the Indian Army.

'I have sent letters regarding the circumstances of my son's death and that of his friend to twelve members of Parliament. Of these twelve MPs, George Fernandes raised the matter in Parliament and Syed Shahabuddin wrote to the Home Minister twice, once on 16 September 1991 and then again as a reminder on 5 February 1992.

'I have been given to understand that these policemen who fired on my son and his friends were drunk – three Punjab policemen and three homeguards with a CRPF party – and that they sought to hide their arms. In a hearing into the case before the SSP Faridkot (at that time Swaran Singh) and the Deputy Commissioner, on 21 September 1991, I was at pains to point out that all the bullet marks are on the left hand side of the car and none are on the rear of the car, thereby proving that the car did not speed beyond the police *naka* [check point] as was alleged by the police. Nearby villagers mentioned the heavy firing, while the affidavit of the car driver and the bullet marks on the car gave the proof. In the inquiry I also reported that when I reached Moga hospital to collect the dead body of my son, a police inspector retorted that 'our DSP was killed yesterday'. Another police officer on the SSP's personal staff said 'we want to kill all the militants' relations'.

'I was offered 50,000 rs in compensation for my son. I would not take it as that would have implied my acceptance of the police story that he and his companions had been killed in cross-fire between the militants and the police. With twenty-five years in the Indian Army, during which I was personal assistant to high military dignitaries, and having the distinction of meritorious service, I ask for justice against the murderers of our innocent children.'

Case 3

Maninderjit Singh, close to the Akali Dal leader, Simranjit Singh Mann. He has 56 acres of land near the border, close to village Sarhali (a good holding in this part of Punjab) and is the youngest son of Bibi Gurdip Kaur, a strong, religious-minded lady of 80 years of age, respected in Amritsar district and beyond for her piety. She and her sister were great admirers of Sant Jarnail Singh Bhindranwale. Maninderjit Singh was educated at a good public school and an American university and he married the daughter of an Air India pilot. His family had owned 2,000 acres of land in what is now Pakistan and his father had been personal secretary to Lord Wavell. The family is both traditional and modern. They are traditional in the sense that they adhere to their religious values. However, by virtue of their education, lifestyle and associations, they are completely modern. In this context, the events that Maninderjit Singh relates are especially interesting, showing the unbridled power of the police in the Tarn Taran area and the disrespect shown by the paramilitary and police forces for those whom ordinary villagers would respect.

'It was in the October of 1986 at about 6.30–7.00 in the morning and I had just got up to attend to my duties in the village. I was *sarpanc* of village Usman. I picked up my scooter but, as I was leaving my house which was a remote farm house on the outskirts of village Usman, my workers came to me and said there were a lot of policemen who were running through the farms. I thought it was just a factional fight or a feud between neighbours, one trying to be one up on the other by calling the police and getting them harassed. So I carried on and went to village Usman and came back after forty minutes or so. In the meantime, I felt more and more the presence of the CRP and they were passing through my fields. I was in my traditional kurta pyjama dress [straight white trousers and long white shirt] with my saffron *patka*[37] and I decided that I should walk towards them and speak to them and ask them what the hell they think they're up to. They were approximately two acres away from my house and I had walked about one acre towards them. When they saw me walking towards them, these people in single file would fall down, take position and aim their rifles at me. So for a moment I stopped. I thought there must be something terribly wrong with these people. While walking, whichever side I looked, they would immediately stop running, fall to the ground, take position and start aiming their rifles at me. So it just struck me that perhaps I should not move any further in their direction and I about-turned and walked back to my house. Then my workers came again, rushing. They said there was a very large contingent on the east side of my farm and along a dry canal on the north side. A very heavy contingent of paramilitaries was advancing towards the house and certainly they are surrounding it, they told me. I stopped the talk. I still thought they were only passing through my fields and I told my people not to mind and that they were terrified for nothing. So I as a solitary figure walked out again, this time in the direction of the canal. As soon as I stepped out, immediately I heard shouts "Put your hands up! Put your hands up!" I was a little amused by that because I thought that nowhere along the line should I be the target of any form of state inquiry, least of all of any form of state oppression. I put my hands up. The CRP surrounding the house by now were at least a few hundred strong and the forces that were asking me to come out with my hands high must have been at least 250 strong. They were walking shoulder to shoulder and on seeing me would fall in unison into the canal, like it was a natural ditch for them. "Put your hands higher," they shouted. I came out with my hands high and they kept asking me to put them higher, higher! I stated to them, "Don't panic, no one is in my house, neither am I armed and please don't let your rifles go off accidentally." I was petrified that they would let off one of their rifles accidentally and then in a chain reaction before anyone knew what had happened a few rounds would be exchanged in the air. They frisked me and found nothing. Then they told me that a few days earlier there had been an encounter between villages Lalpura and Dugri and this was a traditional route Manochahal[38] used to take walking past our fields. Manochahal had had an encounter with the CRP and been hit on the thigh and they felt that he had been taken to my house and was receiving medical treatment there. They also had an informer with them who was handcuffed and whose face was hidden. You could only see his feet. They put a big sheet over him. His identity was totally concealed. He was saying "Yes, this is the house" to the person concerned and the person concerned was SP operations who became SSP Majitha. As he was muttering they were pointing their AKs at me. They also had SLRs [self loading rifles] and were wearing bullet-proof jackets. Three or four of them pointed their weapons in my back as I walked back to the house, all the while trying to pacify them. I recognised the SP and I told him, just a few days back I came to visit you in your office. He was rather startled. I made sure I was speaking English so that he understood I was not just some local rustic, but had a certain educational background and that I was a person of some little consequence in the environment in which I was living. They took me to the house and then started searching it. And how they search your house! They start throwing everything down no matter what it is. It is as though a tornado has hit it. They pick up everything from a cupboard and it is thrown down. One fellow started watching my colour TV so I had to remind the DSP concerned, that you are searching my house, so why is it your constable is watching my colour TV. What has that got to do with searching my house. He had to reprimand that fellow. All the constables were so angry with me. "You just watch it," they said. "Once we take you to the police station we'll thrash you." I decided to calm down and they ransacked my whole house. And what they found was a two and a half foot colour photograph given to me by the ABC reporter John Mills of Sant Jarnail Singh coming out of the Darshani Deorhi [the gate to the Golden Temple]. That confirmed to them that I was involved. And this fellow, the SP, became very uppity. Then the DSP Narinderpal Singh (SSP Tarn Taran, SSP Sangrur and SSP Kapurthala subsequently) who had informed no one of their raid since they were sure they were going to capture Manochahal himself, said we're going to take you to Mal Mandi and once we hang you upside down you're going to come out and confess all that you've been up to.

'They found nothing. I did not even know Manochahal, nor was I politically involved at the time. After studying in the USA my close involvement was in developing the village. Into this I'd put my heart and soul after returning from there, getting government grants for the village to tarmac the roads, opening a veterinary hospital and a dispensary. But these people were least interested in all of that and they continued with their threats of torture. All the while that informer kept on saying "Yes, he's the person involved; this is the house we came to." He was being taken aside from time to time and he was being briefed what to say. So God knows who he was. He was perhaps someone taking a breather from his torture so at least he could get relief for a few hours. So I was a victim of that and these people were out to gun me.

'Short of looting my house, whatever came their way, whether it was money that was lying around or even a pair of cheap plastic slippers from Bata, they walked away with it. At least fifteen jeeps stood next to my house and the buses parked at village Sehron in which these paramilitaries involved in this operation had come were enough for 800–1,000 people. So it was a traumatic thing. And after that, through my friends in the bureaucracy who were with me at public school, I went to the then Director General of Police, Ribeiro. I tackled him that there were very few people in this country who would return to it in their twenties with an educational background from an American university and who would settle in the villages. The SSP Amritsar, Izhar Alam,[39] called us to meet him at his house after this whole business. I thought let bygones be bygones, what had happened could just be a minor error. My mother came along and also my elder brother. We were very courteous. He was sitting playing with his 38 special [revolver] and his AK was nearby. He simply stated "Next time we come to your house", and he tapped with his right finger on the table, "we will come with a group and if a single shot is fired from that house, I am the one who gives the orders here and I've told them to blow that house apart." "What is he saying?" my mother asked me. And when I interpreted to her in Punjabi she started crying. So we quietly got up and walked out. After that I decided to move home and hearth because vigilante groups were already operating in the area. They would come in unmarked cars, youngsters, barely with their moustaches coming and no beards. Three or four times they had gone through my farm. And, in any case, imagine the SSP telling me he'd kill me outright. So I was not going to be a fool living there. I was so disenchanted that I'd left America to come back and the government is hounding me for nothing. That is the time I decided to move my wife and family to a quieter part of the earth – New Zealand. We had much harassment from Alam. He would not leave us alone. On my last meeting with him I said to him "I'm a Jat, and as a Jat I'm speaking to you truthfully and with the grit that I've got in me. That grit is that I'm looking you right in the eye instead of the other way around where you as the conqueror should be looking me right in the eye and I'm simply stating to you I'm not involved at any level and if you want to check it out, you can do so with Gurbachan Jagat, IG Intelligence (who was number two to Ribeiro in those days)." This fellow spoke to Jagat. I asked Jagat later what did you say to him. He replied "All I said is don't plant anything on him, don't frame him, if he's not involved." Because the majority of people are just framed in this country. So Alam got the message and this is how I was saved.'

Notes

1. Known as Operation Bluestar, the army invasion of the Darbar Sahib, or Golden Temple as it is popularly known, as well as of other historic *gurdwaras* in the Punjab, is described by Mark Tully and Satish Jacob (1985) and by Har-

minder Kaur (1990). The Darbar Sahib complex houses the most important institutions of the Sikhs, namely the Darbar Sahib itself, the centre of the Sikh faith, the Akal Takht, which is the temporal centre of the Sikh people and a national institution, and the Langar, or community kitchen. These institutions reflect the central values of the Sikh faith: work (for justice and equality among all members of mankind), worship, and giving in charity.

2. India has a long border with Pakistan – 3,310 km – and also a long border with what became Bangladesh – 4,095 km. Most of the commanders of the BSF have belonged to the armed forces and its personnel have received army training. The only difference between the BSF and the army is that they have no heavy weapons such as tanks. The BSF was created to deal with the threat, real or alleged, from Pakistan and in that capacity it has an intelligence gathering role. The CRP was supposed to handle internal disturbances such as riots.

3. Whether they were, in fact, close to financial ruin, is difficult to tell. Sucha Singh Gill (1989: A83) comments that there is little to suggest the large-scale sale of land by small or marginal farmers.

4. Chadha (1985) reports that in 1984, 58.65% was irrigated by tube well as opposed to 41% by government canal.

5. Daljit Singh (1992: 218).

6. The Anandpur Sahib resolution of 1973 demanded autonomy for the Punjab in all matters except those relating to external affairs, defence and communications. It was not secessionist.

7. Sant Bhindranwale was the charismatic preacher, much beloved of the youth of Punjab, who was killed when the army entered the Darbar Sahib complex.

8. Statistical Abstract, government of Punjab.

9. The most important parts of the text of this declaration can be found in Gopal Singh (ed.), 1987: pp. 387–91 and pp. 173–5.

10. It is difficult to assess casualties, either for Operation Bluestar or for its aftermath, especially because of the curfew enforced in the period after Operation Bluestar. However, civil liberties organisations, such as the Movement Against State Repression, have claimed that the total number killed in Operation Bluestar exceeded ten thousand. Thousands of young men also went missing in the period after Bluestar.

11. The *Indian Express* of 2 November 1989 lists the names of those killed in Delhi under the heading 'Blessed are those who die for their convictions. In sacred memory of the 3870 men, women and children who were killed in an organised manner in Delhi during the first days of November, 1984.' Killings of Sikhs travelling on trains also occurred during those days and the names of those killed at Kanpur according to statistics collected by the Punjab Union of Civil Liberties from families of the dead, social workers and from *gurdwaras*, total 172.

12. Descriptions of the Delhi massacres are contained in many publications, but notably in Chakravarti and Haksar 1985. Moving accounts are presented in the work of Veena Das (1985, 1990). All accounts mention the partisan nature of police behaviour.

13. A Congress I trade union leader and metropolitan councillor, killed by the Sikhs for having reportedly incited mobs to indulge in arson. He was identified by survivors.

14. Das (1990: 15) notes that 'Many Hindus felt that violence against the Sikhs expressed an anger that had been building up against acts of terrorism against Hindus in Punjab.'

15. The Amnesty International reports of 1988, 1989, 1991 and 1992 list innumerable cases of what Punjabis refer to as *zulm*, that is, they reveal cases of extra-judicial killings, disappearances, arbitrary and unacknowledged arrests, torture, encounter killings and deaths in custody. A very pointed description of encounter killings is contained in a report presented to the American Congress on 19 January, 1993:

> In Punjab there were credible reports that police in particular continued to engage in faked encounter killings. In the typical scenario, police take into custody suspected militants or militant supporters without filing an arrest report. If the detainee dies during interrogation or is executed, officials deny that he was ever in custody and claim he died during an armed encounter with police or security forces. Afterwards the bodies reportedly are sometimes moved to distant police districts for disposal, making identification and investigation more difficult. Indian human rights groups estimated that 1,350 people were killed in fake encounters during the first nine months of 1992 ... There was no indication that any police officers were held responsible and punished (unclassified US State Department document, 19 January 1993).

16. An *amritdhari* Sikh is one who has taken *amrit* or baptism. Under present social and political circumstances the taking of *amrit* is not a purely religious act and neither is it so regarded by those who participate in the struggle as guerrilla fighters or their opponents. For both, amrit is an oath of allegiance to one's Sikh identity. It especially took on that characteristic in the light of how *amritdhari* Sikhs were described in *Baatcheet,* July 1984 no. 153, which is an army communication letter published by Army Headquarters. What was said in that particular issue of the journal is quoted by Harminder Kaur (1990: pp. 47–8).

> Although a majority of the terrorists have been dealt with and a bulk of the arms and ammunition recovered, a large number of them are at large. They have to be subdued to achieve the final aim of restoring peace to the country. Any knowledge of the *amritdharis*, who are dangerous people and pledged to commit murder, arson and acts of terrorism, should immediately be brought to the notice of the authorities. These people may appear harmless from the outside but they are basically committed to terrorism. In the interest of all of us, their identity and whereabouts must always be disclosed.

17. The Akali Dal had been the principal opposition party to the Congress until the signing of the Punjab Accord from which ultimately it was to suffer discredit. It split into a number of factions after 1988, one of which eventually came under the leadership of Simranjit Singh Mann.

18. In Districts Gurdaspur and Amritsar, the entire populations of certain villages have been targeted. Villages known for their militancy such as Sursinghhwala (tehsil Tarn Taran, District Amritsar) and Sultanwind (tehsil and District Amritsar) have suffered badly at the hands of the police with upwards of fifty young people having been killed in each of these villages.

19. Reference may be made here to the case of Amrik Singh of village Sihaura, Payal, a retired policeman, with a son in police service who was tortured for 5–6 days from 14 August 1989. The case of another retired policeman is recorded on p. 125.

20. An Amnesty International report mentions an incident at the end of August 1990 when 200 residents of five villages near Kathunangal district Amritsar were rounded up and taken by the CRPF to their local station. The report quotes one journalist as saying 'Many of them could not walk and showed injuries on the limbs. Electric shocks were given to some of them' (Amnesty International, 1992: 31). This sort of incident was common following an attack on paramilitary forces by the guerrillas. For example, information contained in innumerable affidavits refer to an incident at Chatmala on 26 May 1991, where an encounter occurred in which the police suffered heavy losses. In retaliation the paramilitary forces started picking up people at random from a barrier erected 4km away on the Chandigarh–Ludhiana road. Affidavits also reveal that when any government or police tout is eliminated in the villages, police pick up people at random from neighbouring villages within a radius of ten miles. The fate of all such picked up is the same – torture and elimination.

21. Harminder Singh Sandhu, 'Note on Khalsa Pancayats', contained in documents given to me by his father in October 1992.

22. Those who were tried in Special Courts were usually youths with no previous criminal conviction. It is not known how many Special Courts were set up, how many people had been arrested and brought before them, how many were convicted and how many remained in custody.

23. In an editorial, 'The Insecurity Act', the *Tribune*, 25 August 1988 reported: 'The Centre knows that these enhanced powers do not in any way add to the security of citizens ... In fact the security services in Punjab have devised their own methods of dealing with the terrorists, some legal, some arguably within the law and some patently extra-legal.' In the same vein a news report in *EPW*, 23 April 1988, remarked: 'While newspaper headlines keep assuring us that "terrorists" of all grades and categories are being arrested every day in Punjab, one wonders how many among them are really terrorists. The difference between suspicion and sure knowledge has been blurred by the catch-all provisions of the Terrorist and Disruptive Activities (Prevention) Act which whet the subjective inclinations of any policeman who wants to settle old scores or impress his bosses with the greatest number of catches.'

24. The first case, that of Surinder Singh, takes the form of a letter which he wrote to a civil rights lawyer Navkiran Singh. It is a translation by the present author. The second case is reconstructed in the first person from an interview, letters and related documents. The third case is an interview recorded on tape in the month of September 1992.

25. Kumar and Sieberer list cases on pp. 300–3, 324–6, 372 and 374. There is the well-known case of Amandeep Kaur, whose father was a retired sergeant-major and a veteran of three wars. The entire family was taken into custody due to the juvenile involvement of her brother with one of the militant groups, an involvement unknown to the family. Amandeep Kaur was murdered after witnessing the torture of her father and husband and on the orders of the SSP Sangrur, Harkishen Singh Kahlon, whose own son had been killed by militants.

According to one reporter (Ravi Sidhu of the *Hindu*) the SSP reportedly said to the father and husband of Amandeep 'Here is a photograph of my son. Now I take my revenge.' The SSP has died since of a heart attack.

26. The Sant Sipahi Front is an organisation founded in 1989 which besieges police stations to get the police to declare arrests. Its founder, Colonel Kahlon from village Kishengarh, District Ludhiana, resigned his commission in 1984. The organisation was politically close to a former Chief Minister of the Punjab, Parkash Singh Badal. It was involved in finding shelter for those who were hiding from the police. However, its political role and its position on the issue of Sikh sovereignty is not clear.

27. Surinderpal Singh, the SHO who figures throughout much of this story, is a notorious figure. He is, at the time of writing (May 1993), in charge of Sarhali police station. I was in Sarhali at the time of the *pancayat* elections in January 1993. An affluent government contractor reported to me how Surinderpal Singh regarded himself – 'I am the god of my district' he said in conversation. One incident in the village at that time displays the brutality of the man, though it also shows how villagers are prepared to tolerate that brutality. This concerns the case of a keeper of a roadside stall (called a *dhaba*) selling *pakoras* and *samosas* – Punjabi savouries that one usually eats with tea – who showed an interest in becoming *sarpanc*. During the pancayat elections the police were stopping nominations from anyone who had ever known the militants or who had offered them food. The said *dhaba* owner, knowing the power of the police, was using the name of the SHO to get elected and was taking bribes. When he was not elected one of the persons who had given him 2,000 rs went to the SHO complaining, 'I've given your man that sum and yet he is not elected. So I want my money back.' Several other complaints of a similar nature surfaced. Hearing this, the SHO resorted to both traditional and modern punishments. He blackened the man's face and paraded him naked around the village. Then he severely beat him over several days and shaved off his pubic hair. He then thrust a burning candle up his anus. His relatives approached respectable landlords to intervene on his behalf to the SHO. They would not do so, knowing the strength of public feeling against the *dhaba* owner. They did feel the brutality was excessive but their feelings were productive of little action since, as mentioned by the contractor whom they knew socially, the SHO was god of Sarhali.

28. The missing lawyer, Kulwant Singh Saini, also went to the police station accompanied by his wife and small child to inquire about a prisoner on the request of her village council. See reports in the *Pioneer*, 6 and 10 February 1993. Likewise the unforeseen subsequently fell on him too. Eyewitnesses record the family's arrival at the police station but none has been seen since. Lawyers of the Punjab High Court were on strike for more than a month in protest. Mr Saini was the third advocate to disappear. Jagwinder Singh of Kapurthala was picked up by the police on the morning of 25 September 1992. He was practising at Jalandhar. His whereabouts are unknown. A third lawyer, Mr Manaahi of Bhatinda, is also missing. All three lawyers are said to have been fighting the militants' cases. In Saini's case, he is said to have sheltered the wife of Jagrup Singh Kalak, a former area commander of a guerrilla unit who had a high reputation in the Dehlon Ahmedgarh area of Ludhiana.

29. *Ghottna* is in widespread use throughout the province's interrogation

centres. Early reference is made to it in Rao, A. et al., 1985, *Oppression in Punjab*, New Delhi, Citizens for Democracy, and on pp. 4–5 of the *Tiwana Commission Report* (unpublished), which describes it as follows: 'It involves the use of a thick pestle of wood like a mini log which is placed on the thighs of the *détenus* with one person or two standing on it. The *détenu* is made to lie on the floor prostrate or supine. The pestle with load thereon is rotated over his thighs.'

30. This moving around of arrested personnel from police station to police station, in this case Goindwal, Khadur Sahib, Valtoha, a BSF camp on the Pakistan border, is common police practice. It results in prisoners being uncontactable by relatives and reduces or prevents any form of intervention in the interrogation process.

31. In this connection a Senior Medical Officer (SMO) reported to me that there appeared to be a controversy over whether the prisoner's medicine should be provided by the jail or by the hospital. This controversy resulted in many prisoners being neglected by both jail and hospital authorities and a delay in the supply and provision of medicine. He reported that many had been forgotten in hospital and that the treatment is delayed for as long as it can be. Therefore there is much malnutrition. The hospitals state that according to the jail manual the prisoner is the responsibility of the state. According to the state, medicines and diet of prisoners should be provided by the hospitals. The same SMO mentioned that tincture of opium is provided to patients to suppress their complaints.

> In fact it is bought in bulk and has taken a major chunk of hospital expenditure in — District. Also, prisoners have been tortured so much that afterwards they need muscle relaxants. Frequently they are given so much treatment for musculo-skeletal disorders because their torture has been so great that the entire muscle degenerates and becomes pus since the substance administered contains a chemical damaging to the muscle.

32. This statement is not exceptional. Those who were out with the civil structure, and who could complain to the army and were given protection by it, incurred police ire.

33. See also Naveen Garewal's article 'Watery Grave for Punjab Militants' (*The Pioneer*, New Delhi, 26 March 1992), in which he mentions that dumping the bodies in the canal is the safest way of preventing identification. The article refers to bodies which surfaced when the water inflow into the Sirhind canal was stopped in order to allow repair work. The report mentions that 'Senior Punjab government officials admit that the Rajasthan government has complained to the Punjab government and expressed serious concern over the increase in the number of bodies flowing into that state through the Rajasthan and Abohar canals.'

34. Mir Mannu was a feudatory of the Afghan king during the second and third Afghan invasions.

35. This was normal police practice when requesting the driver of a car to slow down and stop. The driver was then obliged to switch on his interior light so that the police could see the occupants. Having been through this procedure a number of times myself it always seemed to create a degree of ambiguity since

the police did not always signal whether one was to remain stationary or whether one was free to move on.

36. Gurdip Singh is using crossfire in the ordinary sense of the term – that is, between two bodies of men who are shooting at each other. Normally when crossfire is mentioned in press reports it refers to the occasion when 'a militant is taken for recovery of weapons by the security forces. The party comes under fire of the militants and in the cross fire providentially everyone escapes except the escorted militant' (letter to the Prime Minister by the Movement Against State Repression, the Punjab Human Rights Organisation and the Punjab Union of Civil Liberties, 15 January 1992). An editorial in the *Pioneer*, 26 March 1992, mentions that 'in the last three months of 1991 over forty persons died in what was euphemistically termed "crossfire".' The Movement Against State Repression lists twenty-seven cases from 5 January 1992 to 23 April 1992 and fifty-one cases from May of that year until the end of September.

37. *Patka* is the small piece of cloth which covers the topknot or *jura* into which the long hair of the Sikhs is tied. Saffron is the colour of sacrifice.

38. Manochahal was one of the more prominent militant leaders from the Tarn Taran area. His village – Naushera Pannuan – is close to Sarhali.

39. Izhar Alam had founded a special unit known as the Alam Sena, his own private force, which used discredited policemen to eliminate militant sympathisers.

2

The Rise of Resistance, Political and Militant

It is an irony that the Sikh people, after fleeing the establishment of a religious state in 1947, should be murdered in such large numbers, almost forty years on, in what they, until the army entry into the Darbar Sahib, had regarded as their own home – secular India. Reacting to these events and the way in which they affected the political future of the Sikhs, the young Harminder Singh Sandhu,[1] former secretary of the All India Sikh Students Federation, wrote:

> When they asked him about goals, Sant Bhindranwale used to say 'What are you willing to give? We put no demands. We are not beggars. We have been giving our blood and our lives for India. Now we are giving it bread. And what have we been given in lieu? There is a different set of laws for us. Our water is being stolen. Our capital city has been taken away ...' And Santji used to ask 'Will you allow us to live with dignity or not? And if your answer is no, then why ask us what we want in the first place.' When someone says they want the implementation of the Anandpur Sahib resolution, Rajiv Gandhi calls him a traitor. So what our goal is, is being evolved through the discrimination against us, by the injustice meted out to us. It is being dictated by the damaged Akal Takht. It has been proclaimed by the cries of thousands of Sikhs who were butchered just because an evil dictator has been punished for her misdeeds.[2]

My own data shows that it is primarily the violent happenings of everyday life and the daily experience of terror which have continued to interest ordinary farmers in having their own home (*apna ghar*).The brutal police killings, affecting primarily the young population, have proved Sirdar Kapur Singh's words prophetic: 'Let the Sikhs make no mistake about it that, unless they delve deep into their own soul to rediscover the direction the Guru gave them, they are facing mortal danger of being pushed out of the mainstream of history and of eventual extinction' (Kapur Singh, 1971: 48).

In fact, state violence has been no more than a propelling force for the political expression of a distinct and separate historical and cultural tradition. Much closer to the heart of affairs than we can ever be now, since he was writing at the start of British rule and was nearer to the events concerned, Cunningham, who died in 1851, recorded that distinctness in the following words:

> So Nanak [the first Guru] disengaged his little society of worshippers from Hindu idolatry and Muslim superstition and placed them free on a broad basis of religious and moral purity; Amar Das [the third Guru] preserved the infant community from declining into a set of asceticists; Arjun [the fifth Guru] gave his increasing followers a written rule of conduct and a civil organisation. Hargobind [the sixth Guru] added the use of arms and a military system and Gobind Singh [the tenth Guru] bestowed upon them a distinct political existence and inspired them with the desire of being socially free and nationally independent (Cunningham, 1966: 80).

At this particular historical juncture it is the Dam Dami Taksal[3] that has expressed the cohesiveness of Sikh tradition and articulated the difference between Sikh and Hindu traditions. Quoting a Taksal spokesman:

> We are quite different from the Hindus. We believe only in the merit of the person. A good person is one who works and shares. By contrast the Hindus have a caste system based on separation, hierarchy, hate and intolerance of others. They practice untouchability. They are polytheists, whereas we believe God is one and all human beings are one. It is the difference between *ek* and *anek* – the one and the many (that is the Sikhs with one God and the Hindus with many).

It is the guerrillas who have defended the Sikh way of life. Zaffarwal, head of the Khalistan Commando Force, when asked about the ideological basis of the freedom struggle, said simply 'Our history and *bani* [scripture] inspires us. Whatever government we set up in Khalistan will have to be based on the principles of Sikhism as contained in the *bani*. We will not create a society where one human being is poor and sleeping on the street and his neighbour is in a palace or luxurious building.'

Thus, it was not merely the happenings of daily life that encouraged people to take to arms to resist the state. Certain aspects of Sikh religious tradition have been the source of the idea of resistance: particularly the right and duty to use force to restore justice in society as well as to resist in high spirits, cheerfully, and to offer unyielding resistance. Resistance is seen as the honourable response, the moral response, to specific acts of wrongdoing and to overall oppression. One can cite as examples the murder of General Vaidya, in overall charge of the invasion of Darbar Sahib, and Beant Singh's killing of the Prime Minister, Mrs Indira Gandhi, who had ordered that action in Darbar

Sahib. The moral and ultimate meaning of the action is recorded and celebrated by Professor Harinder Singh (1990: pp. 826–8) in the poem 'The Murder of Sleep and the Wonder of the *Shahid* [martyr]' A translation of the poem can be found in Appendix One. Resistance is also underpinned by a cultural inheritance centred on the tradition of the *dhadhis*.[4] Hence, although, as stated in the first chapter and as mentioned again in Chapter 3, mobilization for the cause of autonomy and then of sovereignty proceeded through the concerns of the masses – the concerns of these masses being the control of the development process by New Delhi and the never ending and extensive abuses of human rights – nevertheless, the cultural and religious contexts of this resistance are significant. All those involved in the militant movement believed Sikhs to be a nation as from 1699, the date on which the Khalsa was founded on 13 April at the Baisakhi fair.[5]

The years before the declaration of independence

'May the Rider of the Blue Horse [a reference to Guru Gobind Singh] now Himself redeem the promise he has made of coming to the aid and rescue of the Khalsa whenever grave danger threatens it' (Kapur Singh, 1971: 51).

The youth who rallied to Sant Bhindranwale in the years after the events of 1978 undoubtedly saw him in the above mould and bonds of fascination and attachment held them together. The memory of the Sant lives!

The militant movement and the beginnings of resistance can be dated to 1978 when on 13 April – i.e. Baisakhi day, the day when, according to Sikh tradition, the Khalsa had been founded almost four centuries ago – a breakaway and heretical Sikh sect known as the Nirankaris[6] had gunned down sixteen people at the government colony railway estate, Amritsar. As Dilbir Singh,[7] at that time a correspondent of the *Tribune* and formerly of the *Patriot*, New Delhi, pointed out:

> They could have chosen somewhere other than Amritsar to commit such a crime and some other day than the 13 April. For we have two tasks – to keep the purity of *gurbani* [the Sikh scripture] intact and to see that there is no change in the writings of the Guru Granth. Faithfully the Dam Dami Taksal have been looking after this job. The Nirankaris had wanted to totally distort the Sikh faith and an attack on one's ideology is a very dangerous phenomenon for those who believe in it.

Dilbir Singh recalls how Sant Bhindranwale's handling of the dead bodies impressed him.

> For it was a situation of terror and pessimism and that man was physically

> with his own hands carrying the dead bodies and placing them in his vehicle. Afterwards, at Amritsar Medical College he and Bhai Amrik Singh[8] personally received the bodies after the post-mortem examination. The next day the dead bodies were brought to Guru Ram Das Serai[9] and placed there. I could not help but notice his sincerity and in politics that is a very dangerous thing to have.

The next day, as large crowds gathered from all over the Punjab for the cremation, it presented a difficult situation for the Akali Dal government of Parkash Singh Badal to handle.

> After all, this was the cremation of mass murdered victims and although the entire cabinet showed their respects by attending, the youth were burning with fire. There were the inevitable clashes and some were killed which caused still further outrage. The Chief Minister made no effort to arrest those who had fired upon the Sikhs on the 13th April even though the real culprits and their weapons were still around. Sant Bhindranwale had wished moral values to be placed at the centre of life in a rapidly changing society. He was essentially a religious person who wished the principles of the Guru Granth to be translated into social and political life in whatever way was relevant for the times. One of these principles which he constantly reiterated was that the Guru Granth was leader. Sikhs bow before the *Shabd Guru* alone [the written word] and not before any person. They are thereby not entangled in relationships of false social bondage. To preserve this and other values he held that Sikhs would have to give their lives.

Sikhs had tried to use the democratic system to tackle their legitimate socio-economic grievances which, briefly put, concerned the control of the development process – water and electricity distribution and the price of wheat – by New Delhi. In 1982 over a hundred thousand had courted arrest for the achievement of those rights. When the government of India did not listen to the voices of the mass of rural people peacefully organised, there was no remaining political alternative. They were ripe for new political mobilisations and they came under the spell and umbrella of Sant Jarnail Singh. Walter Benjamin's words close to 1940 appropriately describe this situation. 'To articulate the past historically does not mean to recognize it the way it really was. It means to seize hold of a memory as it flashes up at a moment of danger.' (Benjamin 1973: 257)

As a former Akali Minister describes him: 'Bhindranwale was a young man with honest intentions, a novice in politics. He was a *sant sipahi* [saint warrior]. He attracted the support of Sikhs of all hues.'

Dilbir Singh in conversation remarked on how physically attractive he was and how he teased him many times about the adulation he received. He too agrees that he was non-political. However, he states that: 'Starting from the 13 April incident he was angry with the Sikh

Chief Minister, Badal, for not arresting the real culprits, and that during the period of a predominantly Sikh government, the Nirankaris had dared to come and hold their gathering.' Dilbir Singh continues:

> Then a situation came about when the President of the SGPC,[10] Gurcharan Singh Taura and Gurdial Singh Ajnoha, the then Jathedar of the Akal Takht[11] went to the USA, and Lala Jagat Narain wrote an article about them in the three language editions of his newspaper - Punjabi, Hindi and Urdu. Sant was a regular reader of the Punjabi edition *Jagbani*. For other newspapers he depended on his followers. Lala's articles he would always personally read. And in one edition Lala had written in an editorial comment that Taura and Ajnoha are traitors. On that day in a great fury he called upon someone to read out aloud what Lala had said. There was quiet. 'Our turban has been torn from our heads' he proclaimed. Then one of his followers asked 'What are your orders?' Again in anger, he said 'Orders, you need orders! What orders? Are you blind?' Now you see he did not say anything. And they said it. 'OK' meaning thereby, we'll finish this man. So, then, 3–4 days later, Lala was coming from Ludhiana and they fired upon him.

The government arraigned him in what came to be known as the Lala murder conspiracy case. However, his support among the Sikhs was massive and when he offered to surrender, a large gathering collected to prevent that from happening.

> It appeared that it was the Congress game to woo the Sant. But then the Sant came to the conclusion that the responsibility for Sikh troubles lay with the Congress party. First he would address Indira Gandhi as *bibiji* [a respectful term for a woman]. But later on when Indira Gandhi said in a public speech in Calcutta that they are an insignificant minority outside the Punjab and compared them to salt in flour he flared up. He came to Manji Sahib. I well remember being present on that occasion, and instead of calling her *bibiji*, he altered his tone and said 'This daughter of a Brahmin should understand that if this quantity of salt is increased in wheat flour it becomes irritable. It's not that simple that Sikhs are an insignificant minority', and addressing her directly he said '*Bibi* we want to tell you that every Sikh has a share of thirty Hindus in the country!' In other words, if things do come to such a pass one Sikh can kill thirty Hindus and that will balance us. It was a very bitter thing to say and from then on there was no meeting. Earlier she had written him a letter in her own hands which went unanswered.

The public became very emotional when he eventually surrendered himself for arrest. And there were many deaths and still more anger. On the recommendation of the intelligence agencies he was released after very intensive interrogation. It was still hoped they could woo him. They followed his activities closely. He involved himself greatly in protests over the killing of Sikh youth.

At the beginning of their friendship, the Sant had asked Dilbir Singh what he would predict on the basis of a three hour discussion they had together. Dilbir Singh, as it turns out, had correctly predicted: 'You'll be surrounded by the masses from whom you'll get a response no Sikh leader will be able to equal. They will adore you.'

They did! There was a very close association between the Sant and the people, as I myself witnessed on a visit to meet Sant Bhindranwale in Guru Nanak Niwas.[12] He generated great excitement and optimism. This close relationship is touchingly recorded by Dilbir Singh himself. 'He said to me that if he was killed his body should be cremated in front of the *Deorhi* [entrance gate] on the road at Chowk Mehta[13] because "I wish to receive the touch of the feet of the people as they pass over my cremated ashes".'

Concluding, Dilbir Singh says that

> In the ultimate fight at the Darbar Sahib only the Babbars [a guerrilla group who then numbered about twenty and who owed no loyalty to the Taksal] left the Darbar Sahib. About two hundred fighters remained and one Indian army general was heard to comment that 'with the strength and conviction of such men, I could have won any war with Pakistan'. In the fight Bhindranwale was injured on the right side of his temple. A government doctor verified he was captured alive. Permission from Delhi was sought as to what should be done with him. He was tortured to death. Before that, General Shubeg Singh had been wounded outside the Akal Takht. Amrik Singh was shot outside the Akal Takht. Rachpal Singh [Bhindranwale's secretary] first shot his wife Pritam Kaur (who unfortunately did not die and remained in Jodhpur jail for five years), and his small son of 2–3 weeks. He then shot himself.

Dilbir Singh commented that 'They made it a point to burn the Sikh library. This was a well thought out calculation of a government which knows what Sikhism means and where its sources lie.'

Without any plan in mind, groups of Sikhs were to be seen moving towards Darbar Sahib. The army blocked the roads and flew overhead in helicopter gunships. Likewise in the army itself Sikh units moved, as if by impulse, in the direction of Amritsar. Hindus were seen to dance on the dead bodies and distribute sweets and whisky to the army. The government used Hindu class IV employees to remove the dead. Most persons I have talked to listed the dead as around 2,000 but some think the figure of 5,000, inclusive of army deaths, to be more realistic. The SGPC listed names only of those who received compensation and only 353 post mortems are on record. The bodies were not individually cremated and the stench was such that the municipal cleaners were given whatever was on the body in order for them to have the incentive to remove them. The bodies were cremated *en masse*. The practice of not returning the ashes to the families may be said to date from that time. When Sikhs were allowed to enter the Temple they were horrified by what they saw. One doctor's mother, a headmistress in Amritsar reported 'People were hugging the pillars of the Temple, weeping. It was our heartbeat, you see.'

One Akali Minister remarked:

> Operation Bluestar left a deep scar on the Sikhs, and the Indian polity was damaged. For the first time there was a revolt in the army. For the first time IFS, IAS and IPS officers resigned. People returned their medals. Army people simply rebelled, retired or left the country. Then during the follow up operation, Operation Woodrose, the youngsters crossed over to Pakistan for safety and for the first time Sikhs started seeking asylum in western countries.

As one guerrilla who had been in the army expressed it: 'We felt there was no use our remaining in the regiment. We had joined for the service of the country. If the same country attacks our home, it is a very bad thing.'

What happened in the immediate aftermath of events in the Darbar Sahib is best described in the words of General Narinder Singh – a retired general, vice-chairman of the Punjab Human Rights Organisation – in September 1990:[14]

> The real scar was Operation Woodrose. It was Operation Pacification. The men were taken out of the houses by a predominantly non-Sikh army. They then searched and removed many precious things from the homes. Systematically, everyone wearing the saffron *patka* or having a flowing beard was branded a terrorist and eliminated. This went on for three months. It occurred primarily in the Majha region but throughout other districts they searched pockets of marked influence which were given the same treatment. The only exemptions were some Hindu villages in Pathankot tehsil. The army took the help of the Hindu population. So a certain amount of polarisation between the two communities, Sikh and Hindu, did occur at that time.

Many *amritdharis* were killed during this period and the Sikh Students Federation was badly bruised. Whatever resistance was left was scattered, in hiding, with a few weapons and very little money. The organisers of the federation and those politically close to Sant Jarnail Singh went underground. Some, such as Harinder Singh Kahlon, General Secretary from 1985 to 1986, had been underground for two years (1983–85). Warrants were issued for the arrest of Dilbir Singh under the NSA, and the police arrested his wife in lieu of him and put her in an out-of-the-way jail. During the year 1985–86 the federation under Kahlon was well organised and most of his immediate team were well educated, with MA degrees. Kuldip Singh Kahlon, the finance secretary, had an MSc in mathematics. Mukhwinder Singh Sandhu, the office secretary, was an MA, LLB. Kahlon himself had an M.Ed. at the time. Dilbir Singh comments that it was largely with the help of Kahlon that they reorganised the federation and put new life back into the Taksal. The Taksal, he adds, was very conservative.

> I thought there should be a *shahidi samagam* [martyrs' gathering] for those killed in Bluestar. Thakur Singh [the head of the Taksal] wanted this kept quiet. However Harinder organised this at mass level. On this occasion 36 lakh rupees came from England, of which the federation received and distributed 9 lakh to the families of Bluestar victims. On the occasion of the *samagam* we decided that the *kar sewa*[15] of the Akal Takht be undertaken by the Taksal. Thakur Singh resisted. This was not the Taksal's role, he said. but with great effort and threat, he agreed.

There was a representative gathering at Mehta Chowk and it was decided to hold a Sarbat Khalsa (a meeting of the entire Sikh people). 'Sikhs believe that when selfless persons sit in front of the Guru Granth Sahib and speak their thoughts, this is democracy.'

Cunningham reports that the first Sarbat Khalsa took place in Amritsar in 1747. Usually at that time Sarbat Khalsas were held twice yearly, at Baisakhi and at Diwali, the Hindu festival of lights. Gurbachan Singh Nayyar says: 'During the middle years of the 18th century, the Akal Takht served as the most important centre of the political activity of the Khalsa. It was only in the latter part of the 18th century and during the time of Ranjit Singh that the importance of the Akal Takht began to decrease' (G.S. Nayyar, 1979). He suggests that this was because co-operation was considered necessary only if they faced a common danger. They were discontinued in the period of rule of Maharajah Ranjit Singh when power and authority were concentrated in the person of the Maharajah. From him it passed to the British Empire and from them to the Indian Congress Party. The sovereign ruler, the Empire and the political party, in turn, became the instruments of political administration. By resurrecting the tradition of the Akal Takht and the Sarbat Khalsa, what was, in fact, being stated was that social and religious justice was not attainable without political freedom, i.e., it was not obtainable through the institutions of others. A new claim to legitimacy was made on behalf of a tradition that had had no connection with any form of political administration.

In 1986 over two hundred thousand attended the Sarbat Khalsa. They came from all parts of the Punjab and represented many of its organisations and villages. A document, authored by Dilbir Singh, on the basis of which the Declaration of Khalistan was subsequently framed, and which described the principles and values that should rule Sikh life, was issued as a *gurmata*.[16] It was formally presented to the world on 29 April 1986. Dilbir Singh insists that the intent of the meeting was only to form a political network to achieve the reorganisation of society in the light of Sikh principles: 'I was the author of the document, the creator of its basic fundamentals and I thought it the wrong slogan and the wrong path to take and that too at the wrong time.'

Yet how such social re-organisation in accordance with Sikh principles was to take place when Sikhs had no control over the material bases of their life, and could not even control what was taught in the local village school, remains unclear. There is thus some inconsistency in Dilbir Singh's position. Those who put forward the Khalistan resolution asked him to guide the movement politically, but he refused. He told them 'I am the person who put you where you are. I cannot function as your junior.' He says 'On the night of the 25th January the Sarbat Khalsa resolution had been approved. On the same night the Khalistan slogan was raised. Shortly past midnight a messenger came to me and I returned to Chowk Mehta. There I saw Dr Sohan Singh [see pp. 48 and 77]. He it was who brought up the issue of Khalistan and said it should be raised the next day. I walked out.'

Harinder Singh Kahlon also opposed the declaration of Khalistan, because no constitution had been drawn up and no detailed plan as to how to achieve it worked out and presented. However, those who were fighting in the movement had asked for a statement of the goals to which they were moving. The account of a fighter – Zaffarwal – on the convening of the Sarbat Khalsa and what this meant to those fighters around him is recorded on pp. 151–2.

Ideas were put before the Sarbat Khalsa concerning the nature of a future Sikh society. Although these ideas were couched in a cultural idiom, they were undoubtedly secular in their import. (See Gopal Singh (ed): pp. 387–94 and 172–4.) They outlined an alternative socio-economic structure which allowed growth but which also encouraged social responsibility. It was after much discussion that Khalistan – an independent and sovereign homeland – was declared the legitimate goal of the Sikhs. A five-man executive body or Panthic Committee was elected, the SGPC, hitherto the governing body in control of the Sikh *gurdwaras,* disbanded, and Jasbir Singh Rode, a relative of Sant Jarnail Singh Bhindranwale, in jail in Bharatpur in Central India, appointed guardian of the Akal Takht. Those parts of the Akal Takht which had been destroyed by invading shell fire in 1984 and rebuilt by the government were demolished for, as one journalist, not noted for his sensitive religious feeling, had remarked regarding the government rebuilding of the Akal Takht: 'It is like if one's daughter is raped and afterwards they come to drape her in fine clothes.' It is now being rebuilt by the *kar sewa* or voluntary service of committed Sikhs who belong to the Dam Dami Taksal.

The fate of the Federation's leadership

The state created and sponsored division, both within organised political groups and among those politically active, rendering them ineffective through a combination of killing, incarceration, and harassment of their personnel. Its treatment of Kahlon and the political leadership of the Panthic Committee and of members of the Mann Akali Dal, especially in the rural areas, are examples of this. It also attempted, for its own purposes, to break any solidarity that potentially could have emerged in the wake of the events of 1984, by compromising a large number of the Sikh political leadership of the Akali Dal. The Accord may be cited as one instance of political sabotage of the struggle and the agreement with the Rode family as another. Much later, when it had eliminated or otherwise tarnished guerrillas of all hues in the winter of 1992, it held the *pancayat* elections in January 1993 to resurrect politics of a kind that it could manipulate, in order to control the rural areas.

The political leadership of the movement and its most able personnel were neutralised very early on in the struggle. Harminder Singh Sandhu remained in Jodhpur jail for six years. A reward of one lakh was placed on Kahlon's head and when captured he was imprisoned for four years, 1986–90, in Jammu, Amritsar and Nabha. While in jail he was given electric shock treatment a number of times and three out of the four years were spent in solitary confinement. He felt it was the daily psychological torture – living in the same space alongside defecated material, eating food containing too many chillis or only half cooked, with no light either from a bulb or the sun, that had more continuous long-term effects (interview, village Dhakoa, District Jullundur, January 1993). He came out of jail in 1990, having completed a second MA in political science, and returned to his profession as a teacher. Of the other people on his team Mukhwinder Sandhu was also in jail for a time and Kuldip Kahlon was shot at, though he survived. Dilbir Singh, as the author of the Sarbat Khalsa document, was harassed for years, a harassment that has led to much ill health. His house was raided innumerable times over the years by some of Punjab's most ruthless police officers, even when technically they had no jurisdiction in District Jalandhar, where his house is located. When he was arrested, the President of the Punjab Union of Working Journalists put pressure on the government and he was released, but several false cases, such as bomb blasts and murder, remained pending. He had to resign from the *Tribune,* and his right to a journalist's house in Bathinda was cancelled. The government also confiscated his private property in Jullundur. The cases against him were withdrawn by the Barnala government, though his house is still raided periodically. The latest raid, he told me in an interview in October 1992, was that of the Ludhiana SSP who came to his house on the pretext that Dr Sohan Singh was consulting him. He now lives out in the fields in a one-roomed house on sixteen acres of very poor land in the Bet: land close to the river and liable to flooding. He lives proudly, cheerfully and has indomitable spirit.

The Mann Akali Dal

Simranjit Singh Mann, an ex-IPS officer who had resigned his service after the invasion of Darbar Sahib, had been incarcerated on a number of charges until November 1989.[17] He had shared the fate of many in the rural areas, namely imprisonment and torture. As a friend noted: 'He was a product of the sentiments of the people, particularly their feelings after Bluestar.' Hence, when the government held elections in the Punjab in November 1989, he won a massive majority in the Tarn Taran constituency. During that election, those who were relatives of the *shahids* likewise gained massive sympathy votes. On 26 December 1990, Mann managed to unite the various factions of the Akali Dal under his own leadership. The party then passed a resolution that the Sikhs had a right to self-determination. This sealed the fate of the Anandpur Sahib resolution in a forum other than that of the Sarbat Khalsa. Four months later, the Akali Dal split into several factions, and has been ineffective ever since. The Mann organisation itself, however, was the only Akali Dal that had an office which had a local organisation and which made serious attempts to document police activity in the villages. Precisely because of that, the state attempted to render it impotent. The local level organisation in the various districts had contacts with militants in the sense of giving them shelter, knowing their views and their relationship to the village population. They were a direct source of information for the leadership in Chandigarh, the state capital, primarily Mann himself, who was called by those around him 'President'. The state, in fact, regarded the Mann political organisation as a wing of the militant movement and over the years it eliminated innumerable persons important to the workings of its local organisation: in 1992 this included the senior vice-presidents of Amritsar, Gurdaspur and Hoshiarpur, and in 1993, the District President Rupar, Kulwant Singh Saini. Others were kept in jail: for example, the Senior Vice-President Sahnewal. If it could not find them, it arrested their aged parents, keeping them in custody over long periods and ruined their businesses as well as removing all things of value from their houses and their land. The lives of those working for the organisation at local level suffered greatly because police extended their terror to the entire family network. Within its organisation there were those who were internally politically committed to Khalistan. They had been picked up during Operation Woodrose, suffered great economic loss and subsequently turned to political work. They were much respected. Others had long political experience or were ex-servicemen. Both these categories kept in touch with the militants. Due to the experience of some of its members at the hands of the police, it was, for a period, close to the rural heart of the Punjab and this was why the local level organisation, more than Mann himself, was seen as a threat. However, Mann was very far from militant thinking, involved as he was in the stunts of conventional politics. For example, in protest against the hanging of Sukhdev Singh Sukha and Harjinder Singh Jinda on 9 October 1992, he said Sikhs should not cook food that evening and sleep on hard floors. This smacked of ritualism and was an inappropriate response to the action of the concerned men who had purposefully done what they thought to be their duty. A more dignified, and in that sense more fitting, response came from the international wing of the Panthic Committee, the Council for Khalistan in London.[18] The telegram simply said, 'Sikhs throughout the world are thinking of you both and praying for your *chardikala* [high spirits]. Dear beloved sons of the Sikh nation, you will be remembered in our hearts forever. The *Waheguru's* [Almighty God's] blessing is with you.'

A letter by the two men themselves said, 'Dear Sikh people ... We've been awaiting this auspicious moment which will finally arrive at 4 am, 9 October. The everlasting God has bestowed good fortune and we consider our fate a very happy one. Your brothers' weddings have been formalised. For love and justice we accomplished our mission and await union with the Almighty' (extracts of a letter printed in the daily *Akali Patrika*, Amritsar, 16 October 1992).

At the most, the Mann organisation could remain in contact with the militant movement. He was appreciated as a man of sincerity and integrity who had stood firm for Sikh sovereignty. The government saw him as a threat because he was a vocal and distinguished voice against injustice. Therefore he and his organisation were constantly under attack. In fact, they were marginalised more by their own failure to evolve policies for the future and their lack of concentration and thought on the process of building an underground government. The most intelligent of all the remaining political leaders, Mann's fatal flaw was judged to be a lack of co-ordination with sympathetic political forces. Kahlon was to note that 'he was eager to see the back of those whose sacrifice is equivalent to or approaching his own', the reference here being to Bimal Kaur Khalsa, the wife of Mrs Gandhi's killer, and Mrs Bulara, the wife of Professor Gill. In an interview with the author in September 1990, he criticised Bimal Kaur Khalsa for having accepted government housing and accused her of being a police 'cat' [spy].

The state terror on the organisation weakened it and necessitated several non-stop and exhausting mass contact campaigns. Also, despite the fact that the Mann organisation had contact with the militants, the overall impression I gained from his Chandigarh team[19] was that they had contempt for the young guerrillas for their lack of education. Ultimately villagers were left alone to face the wrath of the state as was seen in Rataul (see pp. 117–18), Latala[20] and Biro Majri,[21] to mention but a few instances, and political and human rights organisations alike could only inform the outside world what had happened after the event.

The Punjab Human Rights Organisation (PHRO) and the Movement Against State Repression

These are very small bodies, some of whose personnel are very dedicated. PHRO has units in all districts. They are usually composed of professional people. Their activities are not as extensive as those of the Mann organisation, as they have limited resources. The Movement Against State Repression has somewhat broader functions in that it deals with issues of economic and religious repression and gives support through the legal process to militants and their families in court cases. Their activities were co-ordinated until mid-1992. The government has targeted both organisations as subversive. Both keep in touch with human rights organisations outside India such as Asia Watch and Amnesty International, and their personnel also send reports to the UN Secretary General and interested foreign embassies. As with the Mann organisation, their district secretaries suffer periodic arrest and detention. In one case, that of Ram Singh Billing, a reporter for *Aj di Awaz* and *Ajit* arrested on 3 January 1992, he is presumed dead. Another activist, Dr Sukhjit Gill, remained out of the country for a year and a lawyer active in human rights cases, Navkiran Singh, was shot at. The chairman of the Movement Against State Repression, a retired judge of the High Court, Justice Ajit Singh Bains was detained in April 1992. Despite his distinguished position, his age (71), and the fact that he was a heart patient, Justice Bains was handcuffed by police on the Chandigarh golf course, illegally detained for 52 hours and thereafter imprisoned under TADA.[22] His treatment, as he himself acknowledged, was no different from that of any other person arrested by the police. Jaspal Singh, formerly a tea estate manager in Assam and a devoted worker, was imprisoned in August 1993 but, after a harrowing time in custody, released.

The police see human rights workers as being part of the militant team, and some did indeed work closely with militants, albeit as part of a network or through intermediaries. Certain members of the PHRO had great respect for those militants who were educated. On the basis of the information they received, which reached them through Daljit Singh Bittoo (see p. 48) who met them frequently, the Chandigarh team seemed predisposed towards those involved with the Second Panthic

Committee of Dr Sohan Singh (see p. 48). Together with certain intellectuals in Punjabi University, Patiala, they maintained contact with certain militants and sought political influence through them. According to one informant, they were led into believing that they would have important political positions in a new state. In consequence, when rivalry between guerrilla groups developed after 1988 and intensified during 1990 and 1991, they raised no voice of protest over some of the killings, for example those in the All India Sikh Student Federation who remained aligned to the First Panthic Committee.

In 1990, the PHRO monitored police activity in the villages and advertised disappearances in the newspapers to try and ensure that the person concerned would be produced eventually in court. Only rarely did such advertisements prevent the death of the detained person in a false encounter. They also attended the *bhogs* [last rites ceremonies] of those killed by the police. *Bhogs* at that time drew large rural attendances because the population believed the boys concerned had been gunned down arbitrarily. Now, however, attendance at *bhogs* is frequently prohibited by the government. People wished to attend these *bhogs* as a mark of respect for their families and to show solidarity. For example, according to Ravi Sidhu of *The Hindu*, at the death of one militant leader (Sukhdev Babbar) police had to construct a barrier 20km from the *bhog* site, on all sides, to prevent people from attending, and fifty thousand would have gone to the *bhog* of another slain militant (Gurjant Singh Rajasthani) had it not been for the police presence. 'The Punjab police have admitted that people wanted to go' he stated. By March 1993, the rural work of the PHRO had been severely curtailed as it was too dangerous for them to travel to the villages.

Political sabotage (I)

The Punjab Accord was stage one of a process which was concerned with fragmenting the unity of political purpose among the Sikhs. The Sarbat Khalsa meeting took place when a Sikh government belonging to the Akali Dal, whose Chief Minister was Barnala,[23] ruled the Punjab with a two-thirds majority. It occurred because ruling interests among the Sikhs – both landlords and businessmen – could not guarantee the sovereignty of the Sikh people. On 24 July 1985 these interests had signed with the New Delhi government what came to be known as the Punjab Accord. The Accord came about because those prominent in the Akali Dal could not retain their power in any other way. Theirs was a power base grounded on collaboration. They went back on innumerable promises to the Sikhs. For example, statements had been made to the effect that unless an enquiry was ordered into the November 1984 riots in Delhi and elsewhere, the arrested innocent Sikhs released, special courts abolished and the victims of communal violence rehabilitated, there could be no talks with the Delhi government. These promises were disregarded and not even the Anandpur Sahib resolution was stated to be a precondition for talks. The Accord also committed the Akali Dal to complete the controversial Sutlej Yamuna canal link,[24] despite its earlier opposition in 1982 to the construction of the canal. There was evidence to suggest the canal would cause waterlogging in Punjab.

All controversial issues, whether over river waters or over those unjustly imprisoned by Special Courts, were passed on to Committee. The two chief architects of the Accord were subsequently murdered. However, at the beginning of November 1985, a committee under the High Court Judge, Justice Ajit Singh Bains, advocated the release of those detained under the National Security Act and of a further eight thousand boys imprisoned under the Special Courts Act. Under the Barnala Ministry a judicial investigation was begun under Justice C.S. Tiwana (retd.) of the Punjab and Haryana High Court in January 1986. It concluded that torture of National Security *détenus* had been rampant at Ladha Kothi jail. The former state Advocate-General, Gurdarshan Singh Grewal, remarks that Tiwana's report[25] ignored the IAS officers who were involved in the torture in that they had arranged the jail in the first place and signed orders permitting the taking of prisoners from Nabha to Ladha Kothi. He mentioned particularly the then additional Home Secretary. The Chief Minister, Surjeet Singh Barnala, was trying to win over some people, yet it nevertheless was during his period in office that an order was given to eliminate sixty boys in District Gurdaspur.[26] Abraham writes 'Repeated requests for an amnesty for Sikh army deserters and for the release of the Sikh *détenus* in Jodhpur were of no avail. What, then, did Barnala have to show for his much touted accord with the Centre?' (*EPW*, 3 May 1987: p. 838).

It was against this background of broken promises that the Sarbat Khalsa had been called in January 1986. On 29 April of the same year, Khalistan was declared to have come into being. The Barnala government had not tackled the central economic issues nor what became a central political issue after 1984, namely the arrest of those with no previous criminal conviction and the behaviour of the police towards those in its custody. As General Narinder Singh commented, 'Their very position rendered them useless to the people, especially to the small farmers. Theirs was a government in name only. The actual administration was run by Delhi. The Sikh bureaucracy and police were pro-establishment even in the face of the attack on Sikhism.' How different were the attitudes of the guerrillas, all of whom, when interviewed, showed a marked love for Darbar Sahib as a place over which sovereignty could never be conceded. Inevitably those who had suffered could not identify with those who had compromised.

Resistance began to establish itself throughout the rural areas, albeit in a very dispersed form and under no central direction. These were days when a new sort of struggle was developing, while the old struggles amongst families and between factions had not yet been resolved. There was an intermixture of criminal elements and personal vendetta-seekers among those with genuine political motive, and that would not go away. During this period the first crop of important guerrilla leaders, for example Sukhdev Singh Sakhira, Manbir Singh Chaheru and Harjinder Singh Jinda, were killed or captured. Manbir Singh Chaheru was captured from the house of a retired army officer who was a relative, Major Baldev Singh Ghuman. The Major himself was later killed. Other boys, it was claimed, used official bungalows as hideouts and one state minister was accused of having connections with 'terrorists'. Protection and justice were cliquish in their implementation, based on family connection and not principle. For example, the Chief Minister knew the whereabouts of a certain IAS officer who had been close to Bhindranwale and who had been declared a proclaimed offender. Yet no effort was made to apprehend him. The number of such incidents enabled Rajiv Gandhi to impose President's rule in May 1987, and allowed him to claim that 'The Barnala Government had become part of other groups'. For Gandhi, the Akali leaders may have been folding back into the structures of Punjabi rural life. Rural Sikhs saw matters differently. Barnala and his ministers were thought to be irrelevant as the number of false encounters rose and the number of arrests and detentions of the innocent by the police increased. The period of the Accord was essentially an interregnum in which the forces of resistance to the state and the repressive forces of the state gathered strength.

Political sabotage (II)

The view of the then Director General of Police, Ribeiro, was that 'the terrorist operation is being co-ordinated by the committee of five men [a reference to the Panthic Committee] based inside the Golden Temple complex. Terrorist killings really began after they took charge of the Golden Temple on January 26th 1986.'

As the strength of the guerrilla groups grew during 1987 and 1988, the government put into operation plans to sabotage both their strength and co-ordination. Initially it did so politically, by making an agreement with the then convenor of the All India Sikh Students Federation, Gurjit Singh, and Jasbir Singh Rode (see Pettigrew, 1991). Rode was to become the guardian of the Akal Takht, but at that time was lodged in Tihar jail. As one political leader informed me: 'Rode was won over in Tihar jail. He could not suffer the consequences of his imprisonment.'

Chaman Lal, the former Inspector General (IG) of Police, Border, also revealed in a note to the President of India on his resignation that Rode did indeed have connections with intelligence personnel.[27] Members of the Bhindranwale family such as Rode and Gurjit Singh were in any case, irrespective of their personal ambitions, ripe for exploitation by the government because the Bhindranwale family and the Taksal had opposed the convening of the Sarbat Khalsa and the resolution for independence passed by it. They hence had very little power or confidence and so they started doing deals. The Zaffarwal interview records the reasons for this.

Darshan Singh Ragi's account of these times is especially interesting. Although it is an account of one who was appointed Jathedar of the Akal Takht twice, first by the Taksal and then by the SGPC, he shows some sort of neutrality towards the happenings of those days. Bemused and astonished he relates how, in his view, Sikhs were contributing to the strength of New Delhi. For example, at a meeting on 26 January 1987, he recalls how certain guerrillas wanted Khalistan reaffirmed. He asked them to amend this to the effect that 'we will support this because of the *zulm* against our people'. He wondered why this reaffirmation was necessary. He wondered too why Sikhs should be asked to support Pakistan in the event of a war, which was another resolution. He says:

> I must say that from early 1987 the movement was taking a direction away from all the basic tenets of Sikhism and we didn't know from where this thinking was coming. The planning was most certainly that of the government but it was executed through many of these militant groups. For example, the Babbars were by no means an effective force in 1987. Yet SSP Suresh Arora was commenting favourably on them saying that when they are arrested they don't speak, or the police are convinced that when they do speak, they are telling the truth. In other words they were being praised by their enemy. Their enemy was building them up. Many times as I was talking to people I thought to myself the traitors are sitting within.

Darshan Singh Ragi says that many times while he was Jathedar, he received letters from Canada saying 'Support the Congress Party to win power'. Then he says, 'there was Dr Sohan Singh calling all intellectuals traitors and saying that all the harm that exists comes from them', presumably so that he would be dissuaded from ascribing any importance to their views.

> Many Sikhs came to me from the city and elsewhere, saying they had received letters asking for money and on which even the room number was mentioned. No one knew who was giving these directions. Sikhs were being killed and Sikhs were taking responsibility for the killings. So something was wrong! Then in May 1987 Sushil Muni[28] came. He said to me that 'I've come from the government, can you get your people together in two days for a dialogue with our people'. I replied, 'Look, I can't. Your people are in houses and

ours are underground.' Then he said: 'Leave arrangements for contacting the *kharkhus* [militants] to us. We'll send two people who can contact all of them. We've the man who can contact them'. [This is a very clear and explicit reference to the fact that the government already had a group among the militants collaborating with it]. I was instructed by Sushil Muni that some sort of a dialogue be initiated. It was suggested, for example, that all those political prisoners from 1978 be released. Gurjit Singh opposed this since Harminder S. Sandhu was one of these *détenus*. He made a statement that the *kharkhus* are not involved in any dialogue with the government [just as earlier he had adopted a confrontationist stand over the raising of the Khalistan issue and the support for Pakistan]. This prompted Sushil Muni's PA to say to me 'There are Sikhs within the organisation who are not wanting their release'. The government had their people inside posing as *kharkhus*. Then Rode carried on the sabotage further, saying that they would review the decision of the Sarbat Khalsa.

Rode put forward a confusing and ambiguous plan of '*puran azadi*' [full freedom] for the Sikhs within India and endeavoured to win their support. Panthic Committee member Jagir Singh and several others of note broke with Rode as his statement was not in accordance with the wishes of the Sarbat Khalsa as enunciated by the Panthic Committee on 26 January 1986. In an effort to discredit and destroy the Panthic Committee, the government then launched Operation Black Thunder in May 1988. Accusations much the same as were hurled against Sant Bhindranwale by the Akali Dal were now made by the Dam Dami Taksal against those sheltering in Darbar Sahib and who opposed Gurjit Singh and Rode in their talks with the government, namely, that people were being murdered in Darbar Sahib and that loose women were being brought in.

Under an agreement that the central government reached with Gurjit Singh in New Delhi, they promised him the Chief Ministership of the Punjab in return for promoting division within the military wing of the Panthic Committee, namely the Khalistan Commando Force (KCF). For Gurjit Singh, it was easy to divulge information on the KCF – the only active militant organisation at that time – as well as on its chief, Labh Singh (Pettigrew, 1991) since the AISSF and the KCF had such close connection. Moreover Labh Singh had not agreed to Rode's plan to have elections. While Operation Black Thunder was in progress, Rode had been removed from Darbar Sahib and held protectively by the police. Some time after this the Dam Dami Taksal withdrew their support from him and when he attempted to return to Darbar Sahib he could not muster many followers and had to be given police protection *en route*. The Zaffarwal interview mentions that

Two months after Operation Black Thunder Jasbir Singh Rode came back to the Golden Temple with government body guards. He had totally sold out. Many were working quite sincerely for the Taksal but when Rode came out of jail he saw to it that two prominent members of the Taksal were released with him. These two were Mokkam Singh and Malkiat Singh and they, on an individual basis, did much to disrupt the Taksal as an organisation.

The military wing of the Panthic Committee, the KCF, under its commander Labh Singh, would not agree to Rode's plan to hold elections, and Gurjit Singh issued a statement against the Panthic Committee, which was condemned. Shortly afterwards Gurjit Singh escaped to Pakistan. Zaffarwal says:

> When it became clear to all the groups that Rode and Gurjit Singh were not supporting the struggle we disassociated ourselves from them. Only the Babbar Khalsa kept their channels open. We reorganised the federation after Gurjit's departure with Dr. Gurnam Singh Buttar [a medical doctor] as its head ... then after Labh Singh's death the Babbars announced a new KCF and a new Panthic Committee.

Gurjit Singh went to Pakistan along with Daljit Singh Bittoo, a postgraduate student of veterinary science at Punjab Agricultural University, Ludhiana where his father was Professor of Entomology. Bittoo became convenor of the Sikh Students Federation (in other words the Federation was now split, the Buttar Federation keeping its link to the first Panthic Committee). Together with a breakaway element of the KCF under Panjwar and a group that came to be known as the Khalistan Liberation Force (KLF) they formed an alliance with the Babbars and were from that time on known as the *car jhujharu jathebande* (the four groups of freedom fighters). Their figurehead was the aged Dr Sohan Singh, a former director of health services whose son, an IAS official, was married to the daughter of a former Foreign Minister of India, Swaran Singh. He gave his name to the new Panthic Committee. At the time of my visit to Chandigarh in September 1990, journalists, political personalities and civil rights workers were convinced that the four groups represented the authentic face of the Sikh resistance. Many were still convinced in 1992 and 1993. A typical remark was 'The only group ideologically committed to Khalistan were Sohan Singh, Daljit Bittoo and the groups affiliated to them. Bittoo was superbly intelligent.'

Yet the countryside had never been so convinced. For undoubtedly one of the principal events of 1988 had been the split in the resistance movement achieved together by government intelligence and Sikh opportunism, in collaboration and in equal measure, and the restoration of the credibility of a guerrilla group that had been against Bhindranwale, against the Declaration of Khalistan and opposed to the Taksal, i.e., the Babbars. Those who joined Gurjit Singh were the unprincipled on the make and they allowed the Babbar Khalsa, which in 1988 had numbered only twenty to thirty boys, to rise to a position of prominence in the movement.

From the summer of 1988 to the spring of 1991 when its leadership was dispersed, the Car Jhujharu Jathebande (CJJ) held sway and carried out a programme which suited Delhi's interests, wittingly or unwittingly. This will be related in detail later. Suffice it to say, it was symbolised by their statement, 'Anyone who wants to talk of Khalistan must be able to take up the AK-47.' Excusing itself thus from political dialogue and debate, it threatened anyone who surfaced to political prominence. The climax of this was the aborted June 1991 election when thirty-two candidates were murdered, twenty-seven of them Akalis. Before that many political figures who were intelligent, popular or truthful were eliminated. Thus Jagdev Singh Khudian, the MP for Faridkot elected by a large majority in the 1989 elections, was murdered in January 1990 as was Akkanwali, a Sikh youth federation leader who was working in the same district. Dr Rajinder Kaur, forthright in her condemnation of the police and the daughter of the renowned Sikh leader, Master Tara Singh, as well as president of the Women's Akali Dal, was murdered after giving a speech in Moga as she left the meeting. Her husband, retired Wing Commander Kanwaljit Singh, blamed her murder on government collaboration with 'selfish interests among the Sikhs', a reference to the Rode group.

A most vicious killing was that of Harminder Singh Sandhu, who was murdered only a month or so after his release from jail. He had been working on the outlines of a phased programme for introducing a new society. Neither the CJJ nor the government, each because of their own interests, had liked his ideas. His mother describes his murder:

> On the previous night three boys had come to our house in Court Road [Amritsar] inquiring about his whereabouts and at five in the morning a telephone call came for him. I told those who were calling that he had gone to bed late so they should come a little later if they wanted to see him. Some other guests had been sleeping in the drawing room. At 7.10, those who had telephoned earlier came to the house. The very moment they arrived there was a call for them. They said they wanted to receive it privately. They went into Harminder's room and shot him in the head. Shortly afterwards my guests left. They were never questioned by the police.[29]

The plans, programmes and actions of the CJJ at its high point during 1990 and early 1991 were of such a nature that others portrayed the movement as fundamentalist and sectarian. Certainly the political movement was derailed by them. And as the KCF saw its social and economic programmes distorted and its ideologically committed cadre decimated, it reacted violently. The movement was then portrayed as internecine and fratricidal, which it was, precisely because of the individual ambition of some of its leaders and government subversion. The purpose of the Accord and the agreement with the Rode family had been to thwart any emerging national perspective. This was not so easily done. It was a continuous project which required other than political action.

Notes

1. Initially Harminder Singh Sandhu, who had a law degree, had been General Secretary of the Federation for Amritsar District. Many *gurmat prchar* camps (training centres on the Sikh way of life) were organised under his leadership and he was responsible for removing the communists from positions of authority within the universities. According to his father:

> In 1982 he fled bail and was declared a proclaimed offender. From then on, he remained in the Golden Temple and started dispensing justice from the Darbar Sahib to people who could not afford to go to court, especially in land disputes and family altercations. He was arrested with many other federation workers and tortured after the Darbar Sahib invasion, being first placed in Ajmer jail and then in Jodhpur jail. Many times the government tried to bribe him with political office He spent five years in Jodhpur jail and six months in Sangrur High Security jail. When the Congress Party lost the elections he was freed on the 3rd December 1989. He was assassinated on the 24th January in his own home. He had been planning the foundation of a parallel government for the people through the formation of Khalsa *pancayats* [peoples' courts], but he could not fulfil the dream he had when he emerged from prison of fulfilling Sant Jarnail Singh's programme (from 'The Contribution of Harminder Singh Sandhu to the Struggle for Freedom: An Outline Written by his Father').

The words of Sandhu's *Shardanjali Samagam* (Gathering to Pay Homage) show considerable affection:

> For Bhai Harminder Singh Sandhu, 24 January 1990
>
> To the memory of our renowned Secretary of the All India Sikh Students Federation, close friend of Sant Bhindranwale and martyr Bhai Amrik Singh and our youthful learned leader. He is the present struggle's ideologue, the federation's life and soul and our ever living martyr.
>
> Signed, slaves of the People, Rajinder Singh Mehta, Amarjeet Singh Chawla on behalf of the All India Sikh Youth Federation.
>
> In order to keep his memory fresh there will be a gathering at his home village of Matthian, tehsil Ajnala, District Amritsar. We appeal to all to attend this gathering.

2. 'Problems of Sikh Politics'. Documents given to me by his father on 17 October 1992.

3. The Dam Dami Taksal, frequently just referred to as The Taksal, is centred at Chowk Mehta, Baba Bakala tehsil, District Amritsar. It is the religious seminary with which Sant Jarnail Bhindranwale was associated and which, before 1984, was engaged in extensive religious preaching in the villages. These activities have now been curtailed somewhat, though it engages in other social service

work such as the building of hospitals. It is currently repairing the damage done to the Darbar Sahib by the army invasion. Its present leader Baba Thakur Singh is in his eighties. Sant Kartar Singh, who had nominated Bhindranwale to succeed him, had been a much respected figure who had opposed the declaration of a state of emergency in India and taken out processions against the state in all parts of Punjab.

4. For a full discussion of the *dhadhi* tradition and its dynamic effect on the militant struggle, see Pettigrew (1992).

5. *Khalsa* is a word generally used to denote the Sikh people as a collectivity and is used interchangeably by Sikhs with the word *Panth* which also, in a political context, means the Sikh people.

6. The Nirankaris were a sect who believed that their guru or teacher was of divine descent – the Almighty in human form.

7. Nobody's account of this particular period in Sikh history is totally free of bias. I have incorporated the more generally agreed upon points made by Dilbir Singh as well as fresh insights that he gave of Sant Bhindranwale. Dilbir Singh, who was also Public Relations Advisor at Guru Nanak Dev University for seven years, first came into contact with the Sant during the clash with the Nirankaris in 1978. I have given some prominence to his report because he was with the Sant constantly from 1978 until the last week of his life, and because of his own prominence in Sikh affairs in the 1984–86 period.

8. Bhai Amrik Singh was President of the All India Sikh Students Federation. He died in the army attack on the Akal Takht.

9. The Serai is a place within the Darbar Sahib complex where pilgrims usually reside when visiting the Darbar Sahib on the birth and martyrdom days of the Gurus.

10. The Shiromani Gurdwara Prbhandak Committee is the governing body of the Sikh historic shrines (*gurdwaras*).

11. The Jathedar of the Akal Takht is a largely symbolic position but one of honour, denoting the significance of the Akal Takht as the pre-eminent Sikh national institution.

12. Guru Nanak Niwas is a building close to the SGPC offices which is used as a meeting place.

13. Chowk Mehta is a place, but the *gurdwara* there, Gurdwara Gurdarshan Parkash, is the headquarters of the Dam Dami Taksal. When referring to the Gurdwara, the name Mehta or Mehta Chowk is frequently used.

14. General Narinder Singh, born in 1920, retired from the army in 1974. He served in the North West Frontier Province (NWFP) and Burma during the Second World War. He became a brigadier in 1963 and in 1965 had a pivotal appointment as director, military operations. As such he was responsible for the preparation and implementation of the overall operational plan of the army in the Indo-Pakistan war of 1965. He became a major-general in August 1966 and in 1971 accepted an invitation from the then director-general of the BSF to be its inspector-general, operations on the eastern border. He retired from the BSF in 1975. He is from an ordinary farming background in village Thatha close to Jhabal, District Amritsar.

15. *Kar sewa* means the voluntary and committed service of the Sikhs on behalf of the Sikh people or on behalf of some local community project connected with

the interests of the Sikh people. The government did not allow the *kar sewa* of the Darbar Sahib conducted by the Dam Dami Taksal to be conducted on its premises and, according to one IAS officer, allowed only four people to be involved in this *kar sewa* outside the precincts of Darbar Sahib. A spokesman for the Taksal said their work was hindered severely by the fact that the original workmanship on many of the destroyed buildings had been the work of Muslim craftsmen.

16. A Gurmata is a resolution endorsed by the Guru. The Guru (Spirit of God) was believed to be present within the Panth or Sikh people when they collectively deliberated on political matters.

17. Simranjit Singh Mann was a former Indian Police Service (IPS) officer. After being SSP Faridkot he was sent as deputy inspector-general (DIG) Central Industrial Security Force Bombay. When Operation Bluestar occurred he resigned his post on 18 June and on 3 July the government dismissed him from the IPS. In November of the same year he was arrested on charges of high treason, waging war on the state, sedition, and inciting Sikhs in the armed forces and the constabulary to revolt. Kept in solitary confinement in Bhagalpur, Bihar, he was also tortured. He came from a distinguished family which had also possessed over 8,000 acres of land in Sheikhupura district. They now have 100 acres of land in village Talaniyan, District Fatehgarh Sahib. His grandfather was made an OBE by the then rulers of India, the British, and his father, Sirdar Joginder Singh Mann, had been a member of the Legislative Council of the united Punjab and a speaker of the Punjab Assembly. Sirdar Joginder Singh was an honorary colonel in the British army and an MBE. Mann's wife's sister was married to the Maharajah of Patiala.

18. The International Political Wing has assumed increasing importance in the military struggle because of its role in communication between groups within the one guerrilla organisation, the Khalistan Commando Force (Zaffarwal). Juergensmeyer (1993: 68) describes politically involved groups of expatriate Sikhs as marginal. However, in this particular case they are more at the centre than on the margins. They maintain telephone contact with Zaffarwal, are in regular contact with Simranjit Singh Mann by fax and actively take up human rights cases (through the Sikh Human Rights Internet), many times successfully, together with Amnesty International. There have been many official attempts on the part of Indian intelligence to curb the direction and support they manage to give to the KCF Zaffarwal.

19. His office team principally comprised persons from his own class background some of whom had studied with him at University College Chandigarh or who had been his classmates. No great respect was felt by the public for some of these persons, as they had made no political sacrifices.

20. At Latala a woman by the name of Harjinder Kaur was beaten to death by the police on the night of 11 August 1992. Her husband, who had been taken into police custody, was not released to attend the *bhog* ceremony. He succumbed to his injuries in the police station. The police pressurised the villagers not to highlight these killings as they assembled before the DC's office and a magisterial enquiry was ordered. The head of the village council was kept in illegal custody and tortured from 28 August until 3 September according to a report in the *Tribune*, 15 September 1992: p. 3.

21. On the night of 24 December 1992, the villagers of Biro Majri apprehended six Punjab police commandos who had reportedly raped three women. The villagers' night vigil was at the behest of the army. They returned on 6 January with the same intent and the villagers locked them in the *gurdwara.* A report in *The Pioneer* states that the police 'instead of registering a case against the culprits ... registered cases against eight persons of the village who were on guard duty that night and had apprehended the culprits. The police beat up the entire village. Since that day only the old have returned to the village and at night they sleep in one place.'

22. Advocates in the High Court were on strike for one month against the detention of Justice Bains in April 1992 but in a letter dated 1 May 1992 Bains requested the Bar Association to end the strike because 'How can we forget the ordinary man fighting his heroic battle through the courts? My cause should not extinguish his cause.' Bains received very little support from his fellow judges. The former State Advocate-General Gurdarshan Singh Grewal mentioned to me in an interview the judges were scared of being branded anti-state. He mentioned the case of Justice Sodhi who had been made Acting Chief Justice, rather than Chief Justice as his seniority required, because he had expressed sympathy for the Sikhs, which in the government's eyes was 'sympathy for the traitors'. Justice Sodhi believed that interrogated youth be given bail rather than shot arbitrarily. Likewise Bains in a letter dated 20 April 1992 said that

> when the state chooses the easier alternative of forgetting the actual killer and killing anyone it feels like, to claim a prize and close the case, then I think I ought to raise my voice ... if an innocent is killed today either by an AK47 or in custody my turn is bound to come ... it fills me with anger when a citizen is denied [the] basic protection of the law (*Bulletin of The Committee for the Release of Justice Ajit Singh Bains,* 17 May 1992: p. 2).

23. Surjit Singh Barnala, a large landlord from District Sangrur and a lawyer by training, had had a lifetime career in Akali Dal politics. He came to power in October 1985 and remained in power until Rajiv Gandhi dismissed his government and reimposed presidential rule in May 1987. Presidential rule was in force uninterruptedly until the February 1992 elections.

24. The controversial Sutlej-Jamuna canal link project was supposed to carry 7,000 cusecs of water to arid areas in the adjoining state of Haryana. For a full discussion of the river waters issue see Singh, Mansukhani and Mann (ed.) (1992: pp. 196–237) and Dhillon (1992).

25. The most important judicial record of torture was that contained in a report to the Punjab government of a visit to Amritsar Central jail in February 1989 by Justice Sodhi in which, referring to the condition of the detainees, he mentioned that they were tortured, that money was extracted from them, and that when granted bail they would be re-arrested under some new case.

26. The former director-general of police, Ribeiro, remarked, 'Barnala himself gave me the names of some terrorists from Gurdaspur. He said, neutralise them, the situation will change. We did and things did change but only for a while.' (*India Today*, 31 October 1989)

27. *EPW* (15 October 1988, p. 2136) spoke of Chaman Lal going on leave in protest against his superiors granting permission to Rode to enter the Golden

Temple with a band of 100 armed followers. Chaman Lal felt that official policy was sinister and that it would be 'counterproductive to be harsh towards the people. People as a whole must be respected and only the minority of diehard militants should be dealt with firmly.'

28. Sushil Muni was sent to Punjab in the summer of 1987 by Rajiv Gandhi to participate in talks to bring militants to the negotiating table.

29. Dhal Singh, Harminder Singh Sandhu's father, who was president of the State Services Federation in 1992, places responsibility for his son's murder on the differences he developed with Labh Singh, the KCF guerrilla commander in Jodhpur jail. However, the fact of the matter is that Labh Singh was in Jalandhar jail, not Jodhpur jail, from where he successfully escaped to organise two very important bank robberies which funded the KCF's purchase of arms. There was a certain amount of distrust for Sandhu in KCF circles. Harinder Singh Kahlon mentioned that in his view this arose because 'he was too intelligent for the ordinary person to understand. He was years ahead in his thinking and so jealousy arose.' My own recollection is of his articulate speech. Additionally, the government planted much disinformation that Sant Bhindranwale distrusted him so that regrets over his murder would not be too vocal.

3

The Guerrilla Movement

General comments

The story of the rise and fall of the guerrilla movement is essentially and materially a story of what happened to a community of farmers as they experienced the effects of a process of economic change known as the Green Revolution. However, this farming community (the Jats) were part of a people – the Sikhs – who had a religious and historical tradition of being a nation. The resistance that arose to the state from 1978 onwards occurred because the ways of life associated with both the dominant Jat farming community and the traditions of Sikhs as a people were undermined. Not only was their economic viability threatened but assaults on their national institutions took place in 1984 and on innumerable individual lives since. Sant Bhindranwale, who became a martyr in the attack on Darbar Sahib, had wished religious values to be placed at the centre of life in a rapidly changing society. Yet in saying so I must remark that in the democratic societies of the West, these values would not be termed religious but rather would be described as civil libertarian and socialist. His primary objective was to undercut the spread of consumerism in family life. There was no one to whom this appealed more than the small farmers who were struggling hard under the impact of the Green Revolution.

During the 1970s the Green Revolution's promises had turned to menaces. The cost of implementing the new agricultural technology became punitive for the small farmers and the government of India failed to support a realistic procurement price for wheat which would allow the farmer to cover his production costs. The low price for wheat was combined with a high cost for consumers. Unrest began to grow[1] and became a permanent feature of life after the imposition of a quota system on army recruitment in 1974, since many small farmers could afford capital investment on their farms only by virtue of the employment in military service of one or two of their family members (see Bhalla and Chadha, 1982). Indebtedness was at its height due to the purchase of agricultural implements. Sucha Singh Gill reports (1989:

A83) that a sizeable proportion of land was being leased in by larger farmers, but he also notes that there was little evidence to suggest the large-scale sale of land by small and marginal farmers. Nevertheless, for rural Sikhs an intolerable level of economic polarisation was occurring. Distinctive unease began to accumulate with Delhi over the way in which it used the Punjab as a producer of raw materials and made precious few returns by way of investment in the Punjab. A decade of economic undermining was followed by the army attack on the Darbar Sahib complex. After 1984 the unease turned to rejection – explicit rejection of *Brahmin Bania vichar*, the hierarchical structure of power and wealth based on the belief of the caste system as divinely ordained.[2]

The Green Revolution was creating a hierarchy unacceptable in Sikh life, hierarchy being synonymous with injustice. Of the politically committed cadres involved with the KCF, none save two came from families of status. Yet from a historical point of view, their role in the struggle for Sikh freedom may be pivotal, for they were prepared to give their lives for concepts central to the Sikh tradition, namely social and economic justice. For a farmers' movement, this tradition meant individually the right to own that for which one has worked. Alienation of land was not acceptable, and thus whichever government introduced measures whose effect was a low cash return on crops, they had to take appropriate measures to avoid rural revolt. Collectively this tradition meant that the rights to the fruits of one's labour must be guaranteed; and they were not. This was the heart of the matter. Surpluses were transferred to the institutions of the government in Delhi at a cost too low for the farmer to sustain himself. Above all, the means of production, namely, irrigation, water and electricity, were controlled not by the government of Punjab but by New Delhi.

There is widespread owner occupation in the Punjab and the small business sector also is dominated by Sikhs (Statistical Abstract of Punjab, 1980: 383). Both reflect the individual's desire not to be subject to any other. Therborn (1978: 121) has noted that 'If a society were wholly composed of independent producers, it would contain no classes and this would require no state apparatus.' This is the Sikh ideal. The state has always been alien, referred to by the word *sarkar* (government). *Sarkar* is never prefixed by *sade* (our). Before the independence of India and Pakistan, the state did in fact have minimal functions and Sikhs always tried to evade the state even while some developed close relationships with its structures – especially, for example, with the military, for reasons of family pride and tradition. Government penetration through control of prices and water has broken the consensus between state and society.

There is, in fact, a historical way of regarding this rejection of hierarchy and dependence and its protectiveness of the small space of one's own farm and that is to see it as the modern equivalent of the area claimed by each associate of the *misl*[3] chief who, likewise, through his efforts had obtained a stretch of territory over which he had rights of control.

For whatever reason, farmers were tenacious in holding onto their land, however small a piece it might be. Even the monarchical rule of Maharajah Ranjit Singh felt compelled to recognise the Sikh principle that work entitled one to ownership. Banga (1978: 171) for example, notes that 'the Sikh regime did a good deal in some places to restrain the growth of landlord families' while in their dealings with tenants, they tended to treat them as proprietors so long as they could pay their share of the revenue. Thus there was no class of exploiters as against the mass of the exploited. In contemporary times, too, these terms have no relevance. Many who own a small farm also take land on a *bathai* (half share) basis while many of the larger farmers are in debt.

Who resists? The social composition of the movement

In Wolf's terms the participants in this insurgency are middle peasants.[4] The rich are compromised by local power involvements while the poor and landless have no resources to sustain a revolt. His term 'middle peasant'[5] refers to a peasant population which has secure access to land of its own and cultivates it with family labour. He also says that 'Middle peasants are also the most exposed to influences from the developing proletariat ... The middle peasant ... is caught in a situation in which one part of the family retains a footing in agriculture while the other undergoes the training of the cities ... It is the very attempt of the middle and free peasant to remain traditional which makes him revolutionary' (Wolf, 1973: 292). In this respect the contents of the Zaffarwal interview make interesting reading for Zaffarwal, the head of the Khalistan Commando Force, worked in a mill in Dhariwal for some years.

In an interview (September 1992) the SSP Amritsar similarly drew attention to the objective economic category[6] from which 'the boys', as the guerrillas are called, came, though he also stressed that the insurgency was a Sikh national problem:

> And I will say that with the Darbar Sahib attack, emotions came into the situation and it became a Sikh national problem. Our psyche was badly hurt. Vengeance also came into the situation. They [the government] should have known that one doesn't hit a Sikh without repercussions. By and large all have had a justifiable reason to start their armed activity. I will go this far and no further. Sikhs didn't feel secure, but the problem of having Khalistan was the large Hindu majority. More specifically the guerrillas were the

> products of the effects of the Green Revolution on the Punjab as a whole. The dividends of that had been TVs, access to city life, and a city education in some cases. They were lured by that life, yet couldn't pay for it from their earnings on the land. Rural education was pretty bad and one could not think of getting an IPS, IAS or army position if one came from a small farmer's background and had just been to the local school. Then there was curtailment of emigration as the construction boom in the Middle East subsided. So not only was there not enough expertise, there was also no money for starting businesses. However, they did have enough to eat. They ate three meals a day but had nothing for their higher needs. In that sense a two acre farm was not a viable unit. So, half educated, with little land, attracted by city life, they could not go back home to the farm to work.[7] Those young people had tasted affluence yet had nothing to sustain it. Such young people were fit to be exploited by anyone.

He was implying 'by Sant Bhindranwale'! Shiva (1991: 185–6) comments more positively on how many lives were rehabilitated because of the Sant and how eternally grateful were many mothers to the Sant for stopping the addiction of their sons and husbands to alcohol and drugs, usually opium, thereby saving their families. She is worth quoting:

> The most ardent followers of Bhindranwale in the first phase of rising popularity were children and women both because they were relatively free of the new culture of degenerative consumption and they were the worst hit by the violence it generated. In the second phase of Bhindranwale's popularity, men also joined his following, replacing vulgar movies with visits to *gurdwaras* and reading the *gurbani* in place of pornographic literature. The Sant's following grew as he successfully regenerated the good life of purity, dedication and hard work ... These basic moral values of life ... had been the first casualty of commercial capitalism.

Regarding the problem of drug addiction, the former State Advocate-General Gurdarshan Singh Grewal said to me 'Yes, there may be more wheat production, but at what cost? And after the Land Reform Act made our holdings so small and put nothing in their place we had the problem of drug addiction, for our boys were not working.'

However, it is interesting to read the statements of those guerrillas who are committed and motivated. All guerrillas are not, as the SSP and Grewal imply, the disaffected products of the Green Revolution. The SSP Amritsar has mentioned what he considers are the conditions that create militants:

> There is the problem that Sikhs have been tortured. However, if we let them out on bail, they rejoin their old circles. At the very least they will be asked to keep the weapons of their former comrades. Besides that, a certain awareness has been brought to them by those fighting for human rights and they see the tables can be turned.

However, police activity creates militants. As Dilbir Singh, the journalist, reflected 'If I cannot compromise with the arrest and imprisonment of my wife, how can others compromise with the killing of their sons?' The SSP's statement did not openly acknowledge that sometimes the police picked up innocent persons. However, as a local doctor, who was a social contact of his, put it, in the event that they did:

> then, if some powerful or influential person does not intervene, and that too provided they know, of course, they are unlikely to get off with their life. Even in the event of intervention they'd have beaten that man black and blue before help could reach him. I put it to *you* will that man be the same afterwards, either in his attitude towards the police or towards society?

In this manner police practice created militants. Very frequently, in the course of apprehending one person, they would pick up other non-involved persons in the family. Yet having done so, their involvement with the movement would be secure forever. Quoting Sarabjit Singh, the former Deputy Commissioner Amritsar District 1987–92:

> I used to tell people in the villages, you keep an eye on your young sons. Make sure they don't spend the night away and if you find they go off from time to time, or you find any change in them, talk to them. Parents in Amritsar district have had a horrible time. If one son became a terrorist it was a source of anxiety but then also in that case, the police would require the other son for interrogation. This was dreadful for the family. They'd think both sons were gone. And there were in fact many families where a son became a terrorist and his brother followed him and they both were killed.

Sarabjit Singh was referring here to the fact that very often the brothers of the man picked up would have no choice but to go underground to escape police harassment.

Certain features characterised the typical profile of those guerrillas who were prominent in the early stages of the insurgency and whose families I met in February 1993. All their families suffered in the past from harassment or are still suffering from it; all had had contact with Sant Bhindranwale; and, with the exception of one, all lived in the typical smallholder's house. Sukhwinder Singh Sangha, a small farmer, used to attend the lectures of Sant Bhindranwale. Sital Singh Matthewal, the vice-chairman of a cooperative bank, owning 22 acres, had come into the movement after meeting and being influenced by Bhai Amrik Singh in Gurdaspur jail. Harbhajan Singh Sursinghwala had done *kar sewa* for the Sant. Kanwarjit Singh of Sultanwind, a BA student from a totally different background – his family owned 80 acres of land – used to go and visit Sant Bhindranwale regularly. Sukhdev Singh Jhamke, a truck driver, had also met the Sant. They are all now dead. Since their involvement their entire families have suffered. In Sangha's case, two of his brothers have been killed and two are in hiding. All Jhamke's brothers are now in police custody. Of Matthewal's three brothers one was killed by the police and two are in police custody. His wife and child have been killed. Harbhajan Singh's family are taken repeatedly to the police station and beaten with rifle butts. A dull and sullen pain shows in their eyes, as well as fear. Upwards of forty-five men have been martyred in their village of Sur Singh. The two brothers of Kanwarjit Singh were taken before his death in August 1989 to the CIA centre in Mal Mandi and to BR Modern School, the site of another torture centre. They were given electric shock treatment and hung upside down. The memory of the eldest brother was affected for months. All families saw their sons rarely after they went underground. Harbhajan Singh's family saw him twice in four years. Kanwarjit Singh escaped with the help of his friends from Amritsar judicial courts and never went back to his home afterwards. In all cases their families and communities respected their ideals. The eldest brother of Kanwarjit is setting up a small library in his village on the *shahids* (martyrs) and their ideals. Kanwarjit Singh was only 23 when he died. Jhamke's village had constructed a gate; his was 'a sacrifice for the almighty' his mother said. In Sangha's village, a tall *nishan sahib* (Sikh flag) commemorates his memory. Harbhajan Singh's family adored him. 'He was in Labh Singh's mould' they said, weeping, and producing the photograph of an exceptionally handsome young man, they remarked, sadly, how fair he was. In all families they had lost the most able. However, perhaps in this family, more than in some, they felt that the state had taken their best, and the pride of their life. Harbhajan Singh, who was the youngest in the family at twenty-five years, had had twelve years of schooling, while his brothers had had none. Also he had been in the police. He liked the police, his mother told me.

These few examples illustrate what the interviews show in greater detail, namely that the boys did not become resistors by conscious deliberation alone. As noted for France during World War II there were many jobs represented in the resistance simply because it was a question of character (Kedward, 1978: 275). This is certainly true of the rural Punjab in the post-1984 period. Such political leadership as there was relied very heavily on the ability and willingness of young people to sacrifice, though many in the villages of Tarn Taran criticised 'the old men whose lives were past' who encouraged the resistance of the young. What had happened inside Darbar Sahib in 1984 had released its opposite, a creative energy to be free. Obviously only young people could engage in armed struggle because of the activities, and habits that sort of life required.

Type and nature of the resistance: some issues

Jim Scott has argued that a history of the peasantry which focuses only on uprisings would be much like a history of factory workers entirely devoted to major strikes and riots (Scott, 1990). Other earlier writing contrasts everyday resistance with open direct confrontation. (Scott, 1985). The Punjab data does not encourage such a contrast. The entire area has been saturated with police and paramilitary forces over a continuous stretch of time – eight-and-a-half years – and day-to-day life involves struggle, as the data already presented has shown. Depending on what is tactically feasible, open, repeated and direct confrontation may occur. Guerrilla activity has been persistent and regular over this time span and every district of Punjab has been affected by it. The accumulation of such actions has succeeded in bringing the army into the state and vast sums are spent yearly on the maintenance of the police and of border defences. Every electricity and power generating station, every railway, dam and canal, and any public building has to be guarded. The state is financially crippled. Every government servant travels in a state of fear. Their police guard is frequently mixed (an acknowledgement of the dangers they face from a Punjab policeman who may have a brother who is a militant) to include CRP and ITB personnel. A car with one armed bodyguard is usually preceded by a jeep-load of six policemen, heavily armed, who clear away the traffic as one proceeds on the roads, particularly through towns, so that the car with its important personage can pass unhindered. 'It is a war for the police' commented one IAS officer. 'A continuous armed battle.'

Relatives of government servants and politicians are guarded at home, whether they be from the husband's or wife's family. Their children are guarded at school and their parents are guarded in their villages. The police budget has jumped from 20 crore to 300 crore.

This state of affairs has been achieved because everyday resistance and open direct confrontation are one and the same. The farmer who at night lets his sugar cane fields be used or who provides a meal or shelter to the guerrillas, his brother who informs on police patrols, his other brother home on leave from the army who drops a few useful hints, all physically sustain the one who carries the AK-47 to further engage in open direct confrontation. There is an acknowledgement of this in several of the interviews with KCF personnel. The state also acknowledges that continuity by its efforts to disrupt the guerrilla relationships with the local population.

Writers such as Wolf and Scott say that the issue of localisation is frequently a problem in rural revolts. That, too, is not apparent in the Punjab. Scott says 'The individual, often anonymous, quality of such resistance is ... suited to the sociology of the class from which it arises. Being scattered in small communities and generally lacking the institutional means to act collectively, it is likely to employ those means of resistance which are local and require little co ordination.' (Scott, 1986: 28) 'Peasants function within a local setting rather than an inter-local or non local basis' (Wolf, 1955: 455).

Wolf (1973) mentions that, due to their heavy workload, peasants remain on farms, uneducated and unused to decision making and that continuity of membership in a resistance movement may not be possible because 'Momentary alterations of routine threaten his ability to take up the routine later' (Wolf, 1973: 289).

However, in the Punjab case, members of rural families have not been hindered from either joining or remaining in the resistance since they merely pass over their share of the farm or the working of the land to a father or to a brother. Wolf is correct in saying that 'the decisive factor making a peasant rebellion possible lies in the relations of the peasantry to the field of power which surrounds it' (Wolf, 1973: 290). This statement is of direct relevance to the rural Punjab. There, even in the traditional structures, the units that were mobilised in dispute had no reference to locality. There were no mechanisms available for containing conflict within the unit within which it initially occurred. In a situation of guerrilla war this led to disastrous escalations. An example of this are the events at Behla described in Chapter 5.

All rural areas of the Punjab are accessible and no village is isolated. The farmers of the Punjab are integrated into the socio-cultural whole through the structure of the market rather than the structure of the community. Additionally, they are recruited into professions which have a Punjab-wide, if not India-wide, basis: the civil and police administration, transporting, smuggling, the army. The absence of silence and of any sign of passivity to state terror has to be seen in the light of the good positions people occupy in civic life. The government is also attacking the group who have been the traditional rulers of Punjab. All families belonging to this social group (Jats), even if they are widows of little education, with small acreages of land, protest at the police treatment which leads to the disappearance of their sons. Many are the cases of telegrams sent to the Governor, the Director General of Police by ordinary small farmer families. They might know that their son is dead but they stress their right to be heard when unjust acts fall upon them and they feel no inhibition about exercising that right.

Turton and Scott make statements to the effect that the type of resistance relates to the type of repression: 'Forms of peasant resistance are not just the product of the social ecology of the peasantry. The parameters of resistance are also set in part by the conditions of repression' (Scott, 1986: 28). 'Forms of resistance are a response to everyday forms of repression' (Turton, 1986: 37). These everyday forms of repression in the Punjab rural areas are detailed throughout the book.

Although there have been many changes in their formation over the past eight and a half years, guerrilla groups have always been small. The hidden, local means of organisation, as Scott calls them, should not be so deprecated since it was when there was a command type structure in existence under a single unified command (1986–88) that infiltration was greatest and losses were highest in the KCF. Prior to that, in the early days immediately after Operation Bluestar and Woodrose, when resistance was a matter of resurrecting the honour of the Sikhs, considerable open defiance had been displayed, characterised by the principle of 'inform and challenge'. Physically at that time, groups were freer and more mobile, because they had an escape route across the border. These actions did not cost the KCF the same number of men as did the infiltration that subsequently occurred. In 1990 a cell, type organisation was introduced to minimise infiltration and with the erection of formidable border defences and the drenching of the state with military, who co-ordinated their activities with the police in the border areas, there came to be more emphasis still on group activity rather than on individual exploits. The group activity itself is subject to overall policy requirements and innumerable expulsions have taken place of those individuals whose actions do not conform to the organisation's policy. This has been going on for quite some time.

After December 1991 and the concentration of the army in the Punjab, the KCF guerrillas' actions ceased being dramatically personal (see Pettigrew, 1992) and became more anonymous, working through bomb blasts. In this phase there was less of an emphasis on martyrdom for the struggle. However, these were matters of tactics and responses to the organisation's overall policy and to the presence of government forces in large numbers. There are few problems relating specifically to limited co-ordination, though due to the decentralised cell structure operating right across the Punjab and the fact that the local leadership is in Pakistan, control over the organisation by its leadership is not always possible. Additionally, the police seize the letter pads of the organisation and start carrying out robberies and rape in their name. Therefore, the problems faced have little to do with individual as opposed to collective resistance, local or non-local means of co-ordination. The problems are of a totally different nature. They relate particularly to the fact that decentralised means of organisation are seen in a cultural light by individual guerrillas rather than as tactical responses to a war situation. Also, there were problems caused by the limited understanding of the young recruits. Quoting a political worker: 'A lot of lumpen elements had AKs. Now if I'm a Khalistani surely there must be a different criteria for friendship and enmity than the mere possession of an AK-47.' He was suggesting that certain leaders had doled out weapons merely to enlarge the size of their respective groups and had not looked into the background of the persons concerned. The statement also draws attention to the fact that the recruits had been through no ideological training. The events that occurred in 1984 were events of considerable magnitude. Yet all that certain guerrilla leaders could think of was securing their own local power base. Others with little education found themselves used. So, limited and parochial ambitions aided government efforts to destabilise the movement. Overall, this limited understanding of both guerrillas and their leaders showed itself by attacks at different times on the police as a force. For it was the police themselves who had killed those among them responsible for atrocities, for example, Gobind Ram SSP Faridkot and then Batala. The two attempts on DGP Mangat's life were organised by the police, although he was not guilty of any atrocity. And it was officers in the police who favoured taking militants to court rather than killing them in encounters.

Guerrilla groups throughout this period may have had strongholds, but they have not been area based. Likewise also the political resistance, in the shape of human rights organisations and the Mann Akali Dal, have all functioned on a Punjab-wide basis. Revolt has been continuous though it has somewhat eased off since November 1992 as the interlocking police and army structures have trapped innumerable guerrillas. If at this stage there is no formal co-ordination through structures, the cultural co-ordination remains, for the permanent leadership is a set of principles contained in the Guru Granth Sahib. For the KCF (Zaffarwal), continuity of ideas and the pre-eminence of the authority of the people expressed through the Akal Takht has been, and is, primary. For the KCF (Zaffarwal), it also has been helpful to have part of their leadership in London, for, while unresponsive to local conditions and problems, they have been more detached and analytical about the long-term progress and future of the struggle. In the Punjab itself, those in police and army service help each other 'with the best of intentions' as one doctor put it. For example, when a soldier comes home on leave and talks about how he cannot get promoted or is given no medals for meritorious service, his brother in the police listens, and both are then certainly more sympathetic to another brother who is a militant. Essentially this type of situation has uncontrollable and unforeseeable consequences and more or less permanent repercussions on Punjab and India.

Areas of resistance: the Majha and the Malwa

One political leader remarked to me 'If only we had had the mountains or the sea, we would have had our freedom by now'. The guerrillas are without these escape routes. For their survival they depend on the support of the villagers. Hence, as more than one of them has remarked, 'the people are our jungle'.

All the main militant groups have been organised on a Punjab-wide basis though each has had strongholds, for example the Babbar Khalsa in District Patiala and the Khalistan Liberation Force (KLF) in Faridkot, Bathinda and Ludhiana. In the early years of the struggle the networks that guerrillas used were confined to one region of the Punjab – the Majha. At a time when the KCF did not have an organisation extending across the Punjab, it was difficult to know about the background of would-be participants from the Malwa areas. Sarabjit Singh claimed that militant activity was confined to District Amritsar in 1987 with a few pockets in District Gurdaspur and very stray incidents taking place in the Zira tehsil of District Ferozepur. The interviews show that kin and friendship networks were important as a method of recruitment. Kin networks were used for communication and they gave guerrillas from Majha a base from which to carry out operations in Malwa since many Majhails had relatives living in Malwai cities such as Ludhiana and Patiala. They provided back up services to the guerrilla movement – safe houses and names of sympathisers who would arrange their movement from house to house. One can say that, by virtue of Majhail networks extending into the Malwa, and large-scale army and police employment from all regions of the province, not just Majha alone, there was, from the beginning, no structure for enclosing the movement and restricting it to a particular region or district, or to a certain group of people.

The presence of so many historic *gurdwaras* in the Majha belt meant that the visible presence of Sikhism and its history had greater impact there than in the Malwa. Hence the response to any attack on the Sikhs was also greater. Various towns in the Majha had associations with the Gurus and their lives. Ranjit Singh's rule had never extended beyond the Sutlej into Malwa nor did many of the *misls* – the confederacies of equals into which the Sikhs divided themselves to fight the Afghans – exist beyond the Beas river. General Narinder Singh, from a village near Jhabal, comments on the people of the Majha that 'They were not slavish you see. They would not get involved in relations of dependence. They had a different temperament. They were more straightforward and their feelings of self-respect were more pronounced. And you know up until 1947 they wouldn't give any girl to the Malwa.'

Sarabjit Singh, also from the Majha, used the words 'Here, defiance is in the earth' to describe the nature of the people. Separately and individually these factors of historical and cultural inheritance and personality disposition would have had little effect in distinguishing the area from the Malwa, for guerrillas were operating on a Punjab-wide basis and police activities of the sort already described were also Punjab-wide. However, its proximity to the border, the neglect of its industrial development on account of that proximity and its above average unemployment hardened the people. Sarabjit Singh also stressed how the border helped the guerrilla movement in District Amritsar.

> The villages had a tradition of smuggling after 1947. For it was a very artificial border, each village merging into the other yet at the same time divided by an international frontier. The people are all farming neighbours. So they started helping each other out with small items such as betel nut, cloth, spices, cardamon, almonds and gold. The police turned a blind eye for small sums of money. Then opium came in a large scale from China via Pakistan. And in 1982 the government awoke to the situation that weapons were coming, albeit not very many and they weren't being used very much. Because of that the gravity of the situation was not realised. They seemed to have superior weaponry as from December 1987 and this remained the case until we re-armed the police in April 1988.

The smuggling networks were mainly Congress Party networks. Congress leaders in Amritsar District 'blessed so many gangs', as one human rights activist put it. They gave them protection in terms of safe houses, but by doing so they also gained protection. Not a single Congress leader has been killed in Punjab.

Largely because of how others regarded Majha – namely as the heartland of the Sikhs – it attracted to itself a very heavy police presence. It was well known, for example, that the present DGP knew he would have won the militant battle if he subdued Tarn Taran and Batala. His concern was with those two areas. Majha's involvement was due to the presence of the border but Sikh Jat assessments were that it was due to tradition. Otherwise the DGP (interview October 22nd 1992) thought that there was little difference between the Majha and the Malwa so far as revolt was concerned. As far back as 1987, he said, a small seditious group had been set up in Punjab Agricultural University (PAU) under Professor Rajinder Pal Singh Gill.[8] Militancy at PAU is perhaps a structural matter (according to one Akali leader) 'as the students are from the farming community and their teachers are from the same stock. They share experiences and learn from each other.'

More especially since December 1991 the difference between the two regions narrowed since the border was effectively sealed and weapons had to be smuggled in through Rajasthan and Gujarat. These routes took the guerrillas into the Malwa. Moreover, before they were eliminated, Sukhdev Babbar, Gurjant Singh Budhsinghwala and Rachpal Chhandran had brought a certain amount of activity into the region, as indeed had the election to Parliament of Simranjit Singh Mann. It was the presence of an open border in the early days that facilitated the struggle in the two Majhail districts – Amritsar and Gurdaspur – as well as District Ferozepur in the Malwa. Until 1991/92 escape was possible across this border and its proximity to Amritsar, Gurdaspur and Ferozepur facilitated the inflow of arms. The presence of the border was necessary in training as escape routes and supply lines had to be set up. All guerrillas, whatever their region – for example Manbir Singh Chaheru, the first head of the KCF, who came from Doaba (the area between Sutlej and Beas rivers) – trained in these three districts. As noted, many villagers, in any case, were involved in smuggling and knew the border intimately.

Malwa's history had produced a distinctive social environment whose effects reached into modern times. For example, the *misls*, as noted, had not competed over its territory, and hence the ancestors of present day Malwais had no experience of the Sikh institutions of the *gurmata* and the Sarbat Khalsa. There were relatively few historic *gurdwaras* over its wide stretches of territory. *Sants* (ascetics) exercised a great hold over the rural population. The area had been under the control of the five Sikh Maharajahs until 1947 and subsequently of its rich, capitalist farmers. Thus relationships of social and economic dependency of a type anathema to Sikhism were in evidence in this region especially its southern parts. The Green Revolution had benefited the larger farmers of this area who could invest in machinery and who, through their networks, obtained better seed, fertiliser and pesticide for their crops. This gave rise to a small farmers' union, the BKU, which represented the interests of farmers with land holdings below twenty acres. It was extremely effective on single issues of an economic nature. In the Malwa area, the forum of resistance and the type of organisation involved in protest was horizontal rather than vertical. Farmers expressed dissent through a political party or through a farmers' union rather than through a guerrilla band. All in their own way represented the interests of small farmers. As early as 1974, for example, the BKU had tried to stop the movement of wheat from the Punjab, though the effort did not receive adequate co-operation throughout the Punjab to be successful. In 1984 it was the BKU's decision to block the movement of wheat to New Delhi that allegedly precipitated immediate central government action in Punjab in the form of Operation Bluestar.

Perhaps the major reason, besides the absence of the border, why most of Malwa took so long to get involved in the armed struggle was because in the twenty-six years after the death of the Majhail Chief

Minister, Partap Singh Kairon, Malwa had predominated in all spheres of political life as well as in the body controlling the Sikh *gurdwaras*. Thus, when *gurdwaras* in Malwa were desecrated and young people from Malwai villages were killed during June 1984 and in the following three months, they turned to the Akali leaders and to their Sants. That leadership deserted them, disregarding their feelings of humiliation as Sikhs while also abdicating their responsibility to find a solution to the economic problems of the farmers. They had expected much of their political leadership and relied upon it. 'Malwa gives political resistance, Majha gives armed resistance,' Simranjit Singh Mann had commented in an interview to me. This did not remain so as unprovoked police action extended into the Malwai districts. As Lakhowal, President of the BKU, told me in an interview (September 1990), 'We consider these Punjab policemen as our sons because they are from the villages. They are now with the government and they are misguided in that. If the government carries on in the way it has been doing they will find the guns reversed in their own direction.'[9]

Treatment meted out to individual suspects

These suspects need not always be militants or militant sympathisers, as the first case in Chapter 1 shows. Whether they are innocent or whether they are involved in the struggle, as are the KCF guerrillas mentioned in the last section of the book, their suffering at the hands of the police is the same. Regarding the issue of torture which was routine in all police stations, one political leader, once a DSP CID said:

> *Ghottna* is a small thing for the police. They are a fearless organisation and can do anything. They are cutting the thighs of the boys.[10] Many have been rendered impotent and otherwise maimed. Others have been rendered useless throughout their life. Their injuries are such that they can't earn. Then, of course, many are missing. Previously brutality of such a nature had never been perpetrated. For Sikhs there is no law. There is no distinction between rule by a Governor sent from Delhi and rule by a Congress Chief Minister. For both draw no support from the Punjab. Their support comes from Delhi.

The poetess Sushil Kaur said, 'They are bent on finishing the quality of a young detainee's life.' An affidavit (certified 4 December 1992) of Manjit Singh, brother of the militant, Paramjit Singh Pamma, who was killed in June 1992, records that on 18 July 1987, the police punctured his brother's penis and passed electric currents through it, after which he became impotent.

Most damning of all has been the medical evidence. The following is a statement from a Hindu doctor working in the rural areas of Amritsar District.

> The police torture people very cruelly. Firstly they begin by savagely beating them. Secondly, they bend their hands and arms backwards and upwards towards the ceiling and tie them there (*kachcha fansi* or half baked hanging). Thirdly, they then administer electric shock. In Tarn Taran an electrically generated belt is used. Fourthly, they use wooden weapons on the body and crush the legs.[11] I see fifty to one hundred cases per year in such like condition within a five to ten kilometre radius. If a boy looks as though he is dying in the police station, they plan an encounter some kilometres or so away, the day before. It's very meticulously planned. Encounters are always 100% bogus.

One doubts that these were efficient methods of information retrieval. Indeed the said doctor blamed the police for deliberately picking up innocent persons and torturing them. 'This they do 75% of the time for financial reasons and only 25% for information.'[12] He describes a case which occurred on 12 September 1992, the case of an innocent boy running a roadside stall.

> He is a graduate but acting on some wrong information the police took him to the police station where he remained locked up for 20–25 days, the police beating him daily. After 20 days the people had no clue or information as to his whereabouts and it was only recently that the police claimed 25,000 rs for him and freed him on its receipt.

A second case in which he was involved was as follows.

> One night at about eleven o'clock four or five policemen knocked at my door. They were from a nearby village and they asked me to accompany them as a torture victim was about to die. There I saw two drunk policemen who were pulling apart the legs of this boy and crushing his private parts. He had been completely torn apart. I gave him 50–60 stitches and I requested that he be sent to a hospital in Amritsar. After three days they admitted him in the official hospital Patti and after one week he died. He was hardly 25.

He continued 'When the specific person they want is not present they take the women. The family then pay the DSP and SSP to get the women out.' He blamed both the boys' behaviour and informers in the villages for boys getting caught:

> Some of these boys are very beautiful. They are very young and they like watching videos and having relationships with girls and so they get caught. One day I visited one house where around twelve boys were present. They were enjoying themselves with dried fruit and cold drinks. The weapons in their possession were very sophisticated – AK-47, 74, 94 and automatic Mausers. They were mentally and physically alert, talked very sensitively and had a mixture of care and aggression towards the occupants of the house. They were careful about how they moved and where they stayed but neighbours informed on them. I visited their locations on alternate days and out of twelve or so boys that I met only one is now alive. They are extraordinary

men. I may meet 200 people per day but I can always make out when I see a *jhujharu* [fighter].

Ideological differences between the KCF (Zaffarwal) and the Babbar Khalsa

The mainstream guerrilla movement remained united until 1988. Subsequently the parent guerrilla group, the Khalistan Commando Force, henceforth to be referred to as the KCF (Zaffarwal), split into a number of small splinter groups. That process is detailed in the next chapter. The KCF (Zaffarwal) remained loyal to the policies of the Sarbat Khalsa and the first Panthic Committee. The small splinter groups came under the influence of the Babbar Khalsa and together they were grouped into what was called the *car jhujharu jathebande* (CJJ), as already noted in Chapter 2.

The KCF (Zaffarwal) and the CJJ, with the Babbar Khalsa as its principal component, had somewhat different ideological tendencies. There was also no agreement between them over methods or targets. Hence no unity was to be found on the issue of ideological mobilization. Therborn has noted (1980: 116) 'Ideological mobilization may be said to involve setting a common agenda for a mass of people: summing up the dominant aspects or aspects of the crisis, identifying the crucial target, the essence of evil and defining what is possible and how it should be achieved.' The KCF was clear that it fought the state. By contrast, 'The Babbar Khalsa and the Akhand Kirtani Jatha came into being to fight the Nirankaris, and never the state of India. They were against Sant Jarnail Singh Bhindranwale and at one stage they were asking for arms against him.' (Interview with the SSP Amritsar) He was not the first nor the last police officer to talk favourably of the Babbar Khalsa, though, significantly, the Director General of Police did not do so nor did his intelligence advisers.

Journalists, civil servants, politicians and policemen all reported that there was a close connection between the Akhand Kirtani Jatha and the Babbar Khalsa. The houses of the Akhand Kirtani Jatha were regarded as safe houses by members of the Babbar Khalsa. The Akhand Kirtani Jatha was primarily a religious organisation and has five thousand members in the Punjab and Delhi. According to intelligence reports its recruits came mainly from the lower middle classes except for a sprinkling of Jat military and IAS personnel. As its present leader, retired Squadron Leader Ram Singh (interview September 1992) explained to me, they were primarily a city-based organisation and they were weak in the rural areas in terms of membership because, he said, cultivators did not have much time on their hands to participate in their way of life.

Dr Jagjit Singh Chauhan,[13] a former minister in the Punjab government and now a member of the Panthic Committee, spoke of the Akhand Kirtani Jatha in the following terms:

> It was founded in the Malwa and contributed to the pacification of the area that the British embarked upon *vis-à-vis* the Sikhs. Its policy was to take people back to inward spirituality and thereby to demobilize them from any thought of social and political change. Its purpose has always been to take the Khalsa spirit [the spirit to fight social evils and restore or achieve justice] out of people. It is because the Akhand Kirtani Jatha oppose a Sikh state that they can be used. Historically they have functioned as an extension of the British colonial presence in that their role is to keep the people down. Their stress is on being active spiritually and passive socially and politically.

As one of their own followers put it to me: 'first Sant and then sipahi'.

The Babbar Khalsa have a long history of antagonism to those resistance groups spawned by the events of June–September 1984. Their leader, Sukhdev Singh Babbar, remained unarrested and was not attacked even once, until 9 August 1992, when he was killed, allegedly in a false encounter. He had attempted to kill Bhindranwale, and his group as such had been responsible for forcibly ejecting Bhindranwale from Guru Nanak Niwas on the night of 15 December 1983. A sectarian group, they were not at all in favour of the formation of Khalistan and were aligned to those who later had signed the Punjab Accord and earlier supported the introduction of a Sikh personal law proposed by a lawyer Gurnam Singh Tiir. This law would have disinherited daughters since the parents' property would devolve only on male heirs (see the *Sunday Weekly Calcutta*, 28 October 1983, for a discussion of this). They escaped from the Darbar Sahib complex before the serious fighting began on 3 June 1984. Accused of deserting Sant Bhindranwale by some, in fact they were never with him. They evacuated the Temple and fled to Pakistan on 2 June. They opposed the resolution for Khalistan put forward at the Sarbat Khalsa meeting. They did not surface again until 1986 nor re-emerge in any organized form until 1988 when the KCF was split by the actions of Rode and Gurjit Singh. Some of their old cadre consisted of Naxalites (extra-parliamentary communists) such as Wadawa Singh whose wife belongs to the Akhand Kirtani Jatha.

Adherents of the Akhand Kirtani Jatha were involved in ritualistic practices which cut them off from other members of the Sikh faith. Quoting Ram Singh, 'We do eat with others in the sense of alongside them but we don't take the food of those who haven't taken the *amrit* of the Akhand Kirtani Jatha. We also eat from utensils of iron because iron is a magnetic element and if our women in the villages took their food in that manner there would be no need for iron and B12 supplements during pregnancy.' They do not take food prepared in the *langar* (community kitchen) of Darbar Sahib. They cook their own meals and do not eat flesh foods or eggs. Adherents were also involved in a daily rhythm that was different to other Sikhs. 'As to the structure of our day we do exactly as the *gurbani* says. We rise at twelve at night when the day begins, we bathe, put on fresh clothing and say our prayers. We read our holy book until 3 o'clock then take a light refreshment. In the afternoon we sleep again and then we sleep at eight also.'

They concentrated on change in the individual's life rather than change in the organisation of society. Quoting, again, Ram Singh, 'We stand aloof from all these political happenings. We have no other aim than to sing our holy hymns and earn our living honestly. God's name is Wahe guru and the name is uttered with a particular frequency of our breathing. When we inhale "Wahe" is said and when we exhale "Guru" is said. People who are of the same persuasion gather together weekly and sing hymns.'

At a time when the Sikhs as a people were facing the wrath of the state and losing many of their young people, the Akhand Kirtani Jatha raised divisive issues. For example, they deemed certain parts of the Guru Granth Sahib such as the Rag Mala to be annexed since they were not written by any of the Gurus. They prohibited religious discourse on Scripture – a discourse that has been traditional in Sikhism. Scripture, they argued, must be taken at its face value; there can be no comment upon it. The word Akhand, Ram Singh, explained to me, means continuous, without interruption: 'There is constant *kirtan* [hymn singing]. There is no talk, no lectures, no debate. We don't need interpretation. We don't accept our own thoughts. Only the Guru's thoughts.' This absence of debate and dialogue in religious life had its parallel in the political intolerance exhibited by the Babbar Khalsa. The puritanical aspects of their code of behaviour, in which all forms of *nasa* or addiction (tea and coffee not just alcohol and drugs) were prohibited, as well as other consumer items such as gold jewellery, lipstick, jeans, eye make-up, has to be placed in the context of the state of rural Punjab society in the pre-1984 period. Quoting Shiva (1991: 185):

> The overriding culture of cash and profitability disrupted old socialities and fractured the moral norms that governed society. Circulation of new cash in a society whose old forms of life had been dislocated led to an epidemic of social diseases like alcoholism, smoking, drug addiction, the spread of pornographic films and literature and violence against women.

Quoting General Narinder Singh:

> The Babbar Khalsa are purifying the movement, Sikhs are the enemies of no one – but where anybody fights against this just struggle he becomes an

> enemy and here we mean government informers, the state apparatus and the erstwhile Akali leaders. At this stage, certainly, concentrating on reforms in peoples' lives is a diversion from the main political goal. Nevertheless it is a matter of fact that our youth are corrupted by narcotics and alcohol.

The Babbars projected themselves as good Sikhs in their private lives: supporting the Punjabi language, abstaining from intoxicants, wearing Punjabi dress and living according to a puritanical moral code. Murders of the KCF *jhujharuan* [fighters] were always couched in moralistic terms, as, for example, the murders of Sursinghwala and Samra referred to in the next chapter. Their constituency were those Sikhs whose reaction to the events of 1984 was to develop an inward looking spirituality. These were the middle classes taking refuge in personal development rather than participating in armed resistance, yet at the same time quietly admiring those who did engage in such resistance or who were thought so to engage. Whether or not a strong Naxalite influence was present in the Babbar Khalsa, as they sought to kill the evil within society through killing individuals whom they regarded as evil, is uncertain. They were certainly anxious to claim credit for the murder of Balwant Singh, the former finance minister, and Harminder Singh Sandhu, as well as the murder of the notorious SSP Gobind Ram, though undoubtedly they did not execute these murders.[14] Individual killings became a hallmark of their movement and it became élitist, advocating the concentration of the ordinary individual on his own spiritual development, leaving a small group of fighters prepared, as stated in Chapter 2, to take up the AK-47. Thus when a thirty-member action committee to fight against state terrorism was set up, the front organisation for the Babbar Khalsa, the Sohan Singh Panthic Committee, threatened its members to induce them to quit, otherwise they would be killed. Such statements invariably were issued from either Chandigarh or Patiala and not from the Mahja where they could have been tracked down easily. They increasingly resorted to force to implement their programme, which became progressively unpopular the more it was imposed. Their programme was as follows:

1. Punjabi was to be used in all government departments and all radio and television programmes were to be broadcast in Punjabi. Warnings were issued to all radio station directors that if they did not comply they could be killed. Some were.
2. That after 1 January 1991, 80% of the vacancies arising in the Punjab University Chandigarh were to be filled by recruiting Sikhs and 20% by recruiting *dalits*. No Hindu would be recruited for these vacancies in the next ten years.
3. That work in the banks be done in Punjabi, and that there be a 90%

quota of Sikh bank jobs. Cash deposits should not be transferred outside the state and preference should be given to Sikhs when granting loans.

4. Doctors were given instructions not to indulge in family planning operations and not to distort the reports of post mortems.
5. The Car Jhujharu Jathebande adopted a programme forbidding wastages in marriages – which were to be limited to eleven people – and dowry and forbade the consumption of *nasa*. Warnings were given to various faculty members at Punjabi University Patiala to give up their consumption of liquor.

The programmes over alcohol, opium and meat were not a great success nor was that concerning dress. Certain sections of the Sikh population lived their lives without alcohol and opium yet they did not welcome the barbaric force with which elements in the CJJ attempted to impose these rulings on the unaccepting. Ideas on dress such as long-sleeved *kameez* (shirt) and *salwar* (baggy trousers) rather than *churidar* (tight pyjamas), as well as wearing no make-up, were familiar enough to those living in the rural areas, where they were part and parcel of a different code, that of being respectable and not bringing dishonour into the family. Yet few wished them imposed at the point of the gun. And terror lay in the fact that they could be, quite arbitrarily and indiscriminately! The Babbars did not identify with Sikhism as a vehicle of liberation. They identified with it as a vehicle of repression and domination, threatening and killing those who did not obey their guidelines which in the space of two years affected all the professional classes – teachers, university professors, doctors, journalists, engineers and the financial sector.

Initially, they stopped illicit distillation, and, an IAS official commented, as a result, 'government liquor vendors started selling more than before and the revenue soared when terrorism was at its height ... Then eventually they allowed illicit distillation because they realised they could catch security personnel either attracted by this liquor or falling asleep intoxicated under its impact in the fields.'

In the implementation of all these policies they lost some of their popularity because they would kill people as examples. All of these policies had little to do with the achievement of Khalistan or, as the ordinary person saw it, they would not bring them a step nearer their own home where they would be safe. The bulk of ordinary people felt terror at what was happening, yet at the same time had some respect for their firepower. There was more than a little hypocrisy involved in who was attacked for disobeying the directives on marriages and dress, etc. For example, Dhian Singh Mand MP had a large marriage as also did the daughter of Devinder Singh Garcha (a former Congress MP) who was married into the Badal family.

The anti-dowry programme and the anti-drink programme had originally been KCF programmes and had had totally different aims. The aim of the anti-drink campaign had been to deny the government revenue on the grounds that that revenue given to the government funded the purchase of bullets which would kill one's children. The idea had not been to stop people drinking from their own illegal liquor stored beneath the *ruri*[15] but to dissuade them from buying at a store. Likewise the anti-dowry programme was to limit the size of weddings in order to help poor families with many daughters. Seen from a KCF point of view:

> On the face of it the Babbar Khalsa were stopping people from their bad ways, e.g. abuse of *nasa,* and it also looked good to push the Punjabi language forward. However, the effect of this was that it targeted those who'd been of positive help to the movement, such as truck drivers. For example, this rule of theirs of having Punjabi number plates alienated the truck drivers from the populations in other states through which they had to travel and it earmarked them too! The truck drivers themselves were puzzled as to why a so called militant organization could suggest such a thing when they were the ones so helpful to them by carrying their weapons. Likewise, the drunkards who could report on where the police *nakas* were and the opium addicts with their surges of energy carrying guns over long and difficult terrain. These were the people who practically felt the brunt of these policies (interview with Ajit Singh Khera, spokesman and Press Secretary, Council of Khalistan, London).

So, in other words, who were these policies really for? It was the position of the KCF (Zaffarwal) and of the first Panthic Committee that these reforms were an integral part of a counter insurgency programme. The emphasis on Punjabi, that is, on a cultural matter and on personal behaviour, was happening not only when the Sikh concept of the world was threatened but when the Sikh people themselves were face to face with the state's genocidal planning. It is calculated by Inderjit Singh Jaijee of the Movement against State Repression that one hundred thousand Sikh lives have been lost since 1984 (letter to the United Nations Secretary General, 20 March 1993). The absence of political discussion and critical debate over programmes suggested that they were afraid of mass participation and the culmination of this lack of democracy was their assassination of thirty-two candidates in the run-up to the aborted Punjab Assembly elections in June 1991.

The Zaffarwal KCF and the first Panthic Committee argued that the CJJ were diverting the movement away from a national liberation struggle and complicating it by raising social and cultural issues:

> The primary objective is independence and not whether someone reads the Rag Mala or not, if someone eats Jhatka or not, if there is a difference over whether the *patka* or the *kes* [long uncut hair] is the symbol. All of these things are an individual's wish. We shall not let these issues become national issues. During an independence struggle, code of practice issues cannot be raised. That can only happen at the Akal Takht when we have our sovereign state. (11 January 1991)

While the CJJ concentrated on imposing their will on those who refused to enforce use of the Punjabi language and attempted to stop the distribution of the Hind Samachar group of newspapers, which lost fifty hawkers and agents during the 1989–91 period, Zaffarwal emphasised that useless debates over social reforms should be discounted and that 'instead of settling disputes through the courts and police stations the villagers should settle their disputes through the Khalsa *pancayats* in the village *gurdwaras*. All village schools should have teachers. Nobody should cooperate with the BSF, the CRPF or pay their electricity and revenue bills. It was necessary to subvert men from the armed forces.' The KCF (Zaffarwal) focused their attention on economic targets rather than on killings of prominent personalities.

The ideological differences between the original KCF and the CJJ, of which the Babbar Khalsa was the most influential component part, are hence very clear. The Babbar Khalsa thought in terms of controlling and managing civil society. The KCF's aim was totally different. It was to reconstruct society according to the Sarbat Khalsa resolution. That resolution had set out progressive social policies that could form the basis for a reorganisation of states in the entire region. The KCF (Zaffarwal) were not interested in perpetuating the evil, as they saw it, of the old traditional structures, or of resurrecting a state for a state's sake that would reproduce those evils. The KCF (Zaffarwal) sees the establishment of a state called Khalistan as merely part of a general freedom movement for all of the subcontinent's nationalities. Hence the establishment of such a state would not be reflective of a ghetto syndrome – the only response possible to a mass of daily terror and abuse, some of it given in the heart of the home. For the most committed guerrillas and their supporters in the KCF, Khalistan was not seen as their cultural retreat nor was it a defensive measure. It was a challenge to implement a moralistic socialism whose basis lay in the Sikh values of worship, share and work rather then in those of international Marxism. Following on from this initial difference there could be no agreement between these two guerrilla groupings over targets. These two different sections of the movement did not identify the same points of antagonistic interest. They could not agree on their chief enemy because they did not have the same vision. Not having the same vision obviously was inviting disaster. Maybe, initially, the Babbar Khalsa appealed to the people in the rural areas because 'the peasant regards the reform of personal behaviour as being more important than transformation of social structures' (Roy, 1986: 29).[16]

Broadly, the Babbars are said to have been more educated and not to have engaged in looting. Yet this, if true, was only for a short period. As the mass base of all militant groupings broadened during the 1989–91 period, persons of all shades joined their ranks and their groupings became a mixture of the ideologically committed and the criminal. In this period most of the victims were Sikh villagers and their percentage of the total deaths rose from 54% to 73% in that period. The civil war had begun. The various differences over policy and tactics were exploited by the government and intelligence services. In an interview, Harinder Singh Kahlon gave his view that it was only personal differences that operated to divide the groups: 'There are no policy differences. They merely deeply distrust each other.'

Whether this was so or not, the past histories and allegiances of these two guerrilla groupings are very different and certainly, if the government were going to operate through a guerrilla group, it would be through one who had attempted earlier to sabotage Bhindranwale and the Sarbat Khalsa. Moreover, members of the *car jhujharu jathebande* had more things in common with the state than the KCF guerrillas. In the case of Dr Sohan Singh, for example, they had education, IAS position, a well-placed family and important friends. Daljit Singh Bittoo was the son of a professor and himself had a university degree. I make this point because of the connection that is made – in literature on a totally different guerrilla movement – between breaking down and becoming an informer and having things in common with those who control processes of repression.[17] Dr Sohan Singh, particularly, appeared well suited to a flexible role, having raised the issue of Khalistan in 1986 and then later denying that a resolution for Khalistan was passed. Additionally, the Naxalites under Wadawa Singh were not in favour of independence and sovereignty but only of self-determination and autonomy; and they would not agree to the conservation of the Punjab's river waters. Their perspective was apparent in a version of the 1986 Gurmata given to me by Dilbir Singh, who retained his leftward orientation. It mentions only the Anandpur Sahib resolution. Dilbir Singh states this was the original Sarbat Khalsa Gurmata. However, it is without signatures.

Harinder Singh Kahlon had been in jail when the CJJ were resurrected. He did express reservations, though, over their tactics and warned them, their advisors and supporters, 'don't measure bravery by killings, because the government can plant their own people among you and they can always kill more than you'. Of the many killings of prominent persons that occurred during this period as well as the train massacres (see pp. 121–3), it was the assessment of the KCF (Zaffarwal) that criminals did the actions, RAW[18] 'directed' them and the CJJ militants took the responsibility. During this period, rural society came to be controlled by a group of persons in the grip of a puritanical fanaticism that was anti-Sikh. They were prepared to impose their ideas. This created terror. Criminals who had infiltrated various militant groups in the rural areas created terror for profit. Still others used the terror created to unleash them from the repressions of traditional society; hence the number of rapes that occurred and which were given notoriety, primarily during and after 1989. Then, many were the instances where those who had sheltered in a house overnight, and been given food, returned the next day to wipe out the family. If the government had had a hand in setting up these groups, as the KCF (Zaffarwal) asserted, who then paraded themselves as a movement of genuine Khalistanis, then it was easy for them to get information. Afterwards they simply sent their vigilante groups to eliminate not only the boys and their families, but their supporters as well.

Chapter 2 presented a picture of the political sabotage of those groups who could be compromised and a neutralisation of those that could not. This chapter has suggested that the government projected its own groups.[19] These groups disabled the politically-minded and the intelligentsia and created disunity and diversion by stressing the need for personal reform and purity rather than sovereign status to protect one's rights. The policies of the leadership of the Babbar Khalsa International were such as to create a wedge between the guerrilla movement as a whole and the professional classes as well as the political movement. They antagonised journalists, doctors, professors, broadcasters, engineers and the liberal-minded. When the leaders of a cause betray it – for the CJJ made not one statement regarding independence – the disillusionment that ensues throughout a movement may express itself in many ways, one being in the form of wealth accumulation through extortion. Moveover it attacked the best cadre of other groups within rural society, and it attacked those sections of society which gave the movement, as originally conceived in 1986, its most practical help. Parallel to this, a massive influx of arms was coming into the province after 1988 through BSF-protected routes and a resultant swamping of groups by the politically uncommitted occurred. As noted, a high civilian death toll, principally Sikh, ensued. The Babbar Khalsa boys who moved into the villages were respected by many people. Nevertheless, one may say that intolerance intruded into the guerrilla movement with the formation of the CJJ. Illegality had entered prior to that. For in the countryside there were special police and intelligence units active in looting, extortion and massacre, to discredit the militants *en masse*. To this I shall return in Chapter 5.

Notes

1. Unrest began to grow, just as it had done at the end of the last century when there was a similar situation of low cash returns for crops. That unrest likewise had threatened political stability, a threat to which the then British rulers had responded positively (see Van Den Dungen, 1972 and Barrier, 1966).

2. Quoting one writer, Gurtej Singh (1989: 4) 'the primary cause of state terrorism today is that resurgent Brahmanism in the name of the permanent majority but for the benefit of a handful of people seeks to make perpetual arrangements for economically exploiting better endowed minorities.'

3. In the words of Gupta (1952: 135) the term *misl* meant a confederacy of equals under a chief of their own selection. Sikhs were grouped into such *misls* in the second half of the eighteenth century.

4. I much prefer Polly Hill's use of the specific categories of landlord, farmer, agricultural labourer and tenant, etc., as these state a specific relation to the productive process (1986: 8–15).

5. This definition is close to that of Lenin, who says 'the middle peasant is partly a property owner and partly a toiler. He does not exploit other toilers.'

6. Economic category explains so much and no more for 'one can always choose either resistance and death or obedience and life. Fear is the effect of ideological domination that brings about deference' (Therborn 1980: 97).

7. The same point in different language has been expressed by the writer G.K. Chadha: 'The growing level of education among the rural youth largely weaned the men away from agricultural work due to rising job expectations outside the rural areas. These expectations were largely belied for the simple reason that they were too high to be fulfilled.'

8. Professor Gill was Assistant Professor of Horticulture at the Punjab Agricultural University. He was from a well-to-do family in District Ludhiana. According to his wife Rajinder Kaur Bulara (interview October 1992), who became an MP after his killing on a large sympathy vote,

> he had always been religious minded and had been with Sant Bhindranwale, whom he liked, since 1978. In the process, he met many fine young militants at conferences, many of whom were engineers and doctors, and he kept in touch with them. On 1 November, his younger brother, who was a young captain in the army, was travelling to Ahmedabad. This was at the time when there were massacres all over northern India of the Sikhs in various cities following Mrs Gandhi's murder. He was murdered on the train. He intensified his political activity after that. After Labh Singh's bank robbery in Ludhiana [see p. 82] the police said he had been the planner. In the course of the next two years our nephew and our son were badly tortured. He himself was eventually killed in a false encounter in 1989.

9. One year later, following on this comment, it seemed that the guns *were* being trained in the direction of the police in a systematic fashion, with the explosion of a bomb detonated by remote control in Chandigarh wounding its SSP and three security personnel at the end of September 1991. A report published in *Tribune*, October 10, notes that an SP Ropar and three of his sons were

gunned down. Many attacks were reported on policemen's relatives. The threat became all too apparent when the then DIG police directed that his sole surviving son, a Punjab Civil Service Officer, be allowed to serve in Chandigarh and not posted to Punjab. One of his sons, who was a doctor, had been killed previously and '[s]everal of his relatives have been kidnapped time and time again by terrorists and were subsequently released in exchange for the release of their accomplices from police custody' (*Sunday*, 27 October 1991: p. 5). *India Today* (15 November 1992: p. 46) reported that on 2 October alone, 'the militants gunned down 26 relatives of policemen and in the same week killed 14 security men'. In total 100 relatives of police officers had been killed during 1991.

10. Not only the boys endured this treatment but civilians too. For example, Nirwair Singh, Manochahal's brother, was cut on the inside of his thighs and on his lower leg.

11. The second and fourth forms of torture pull the muscles rather than break the bones and leave people shaking for two to three months afterwards.

12. On his calculation an ordinary inspector was making 1 lakh rupees per month (100,000 rupees) and a DSP 2/3 lakhs.

13. Dr Chauhan was born in village Mangarh, District Hoshiarpur in 1928. He qualified as a doctor (MB BS) from Medical College, Amritsar in 1950 and in 1966 took a diploma in Public Health from the London School of Hygiene and Tropical Medicine. He was an elected member of the Punjab Assembly from March 1967 to November 1968 and was a Deputy Speaker in the United Front government. He was also a finance minister during the nine months of the Lachman Singh Gill Ministry. He was greatly affected by the martyrdom of Darshan Singh Pheruman on 28 October 1969 after a long fast, and when he became General Secretary of the Akali Dal in 1970, a resolution for a Sikh homeland was passed. In October of the same year he visited the UNO in New York and his passport was revoked in 1971. He went back to India on a travel document and the High Court reissued his passport. After again returning to London on 15 May 1980, where he remains, his passport was once again revoked by Mrs Gandhi's government.

14. There are many versions of this murder whose origin may go back to the days when the Accord was signed. The Accord had been masterminded by Sirdar Balwant Singh, who was the Punjab's ablest and shrewdest politician. Friends of Balwant Singh argue that he was undermined by the two landlords in the government, namely Surjit Singh Barnala, who was then Chief Minister, and Parkash Singh Badal, a former Chief Minister of Punjab, who is a very large landowner and has extensive property. Barnala and Badal have financial interests outside the state of Punjab, and because of those interests were doing little to have the Accord implemented. Due to Balwant Singh's identification with the compromise process in the shape of the Accord, he paid the price for it when it failed. Others say he was one of the persons who got young people politically involved in the first place and then withdrew his support from them. Still others say that the motive for his murder was monetary gain and that the particular day when the murder occurred he was carrying on his person a large sum of money. His son and the former IG Intelligence Gurbachan Jagat implicated Gurjant Singh Budhsinghwala's Khalistan Liberation Force in the murder. The difficulty with this explanation is that it does not go deep enough.

The problem arises when one tries to understand who the KLF are. Doubts have been cast over the composition of Budhsinghwala's force and it is alleged that that some of its units had been recruited by the intelligence services for single purpose actions. On 6 November 1994, an article in *Hitavada* acknowledged that Balwant Singh's security chief was also employed by the late Punjab governor, Surendra Nath.

15. Usually farmers stored illegal liquor in a drum which was put into the earth. A conically shaped head of mud cakes - *ruri* - is placed on top for five to seven days. When it is brought out, it is distilled immediately.

16. See the report by Monimoy Dasgupta (*The Telegraph*, Calcutta, 11 October 1992): 'The Babbar Khalsa has so far also been the most accepted terrorist outfit to the Sikh masses because its rank and file were believed to lead a spartan and puritan life. They were also said to be the most dedicated to the cause of Khalistan.' As I have shown, this is not historically correct. The Babbar Khalsa from 1983 onwards sought to actively undermine Khalistan. They were made out to be the cleanest group but in fact they were heavily infiltrated.

17. In this connection see particularly Feldman (1991: 132).

18. RAW, the Research and Analysis Wing of Indian Intelligence, set up by Indira Gandhi, owed its loyalty primarily to the Gandhi family. It had people in the IB but no permanent set of operatives recruiting its own freelance criminals as occasion demanded to execute political tasks.

19. Many Israeli staff officers similarly 'believed that the rise of fundamentalism in Gaza could be exploited to weaken the power of the PLO' (Schiff and Ya'ari, 1990: 223). It is not inconceivable that a similar role was planned for the Babbar Khalsa leadership and the *car jhujharu jathebande* as a whole, with or without its consent, since it was overall intelligence policy to make opposing gangs neutralise each other.

4

History and Organisation of the Khalistan Commando Force

There are three distinct periods in the life of the KCF. Firstly, the period between 1984 and 1986 is characterised by small groups in isolation carrying out unco-ordinated attacks against the occupying paramilitary forces. These groups were confined to districts Amritsar and Gurdaspur, though they intermittently operated outside those areas. This early stage in the guerrilla movement's history is referred to in the Zaffarwal interview.

Secondly, there is the period between January 1986 and May 1988. The Dam Dami Taksal had given a call for the convening of a Sarbat Khalsa on 26 January 1986. A resolution for Khalistan had been put to the convention held at the Akal Takht. It was debated and accepted. At the same meeting, the Sarbat Khalsa elected a Panthic Committee at the Akal Takht and formalised the KCF as its official military wing. Under its first two leaders, Manbir Singh Chaheru and Labh Singh, it became very popular and the number of operating groups mushroomed. Chaheru organised the attack on the police escort party at the Jalandhar courts on 25 April 1986 in which Labh Singh was freed from custody. The KCF, consisting then of 400 young guerrillas, was well-armed. In addition it was well funded through bank robberies: first at the Punjab National Bank in Ludhiana at Bharat Chowk in October 1986, at which 8 lakhs were taken, and then at the same bank on 12 February 1987, at which 5 crore and 70 lakhs were taken. After Chaheru's disappearance while in police custody in late 1986, Labh Singh attempted, from a popular base, to co-ordinate all groups within a centralised structure that was cohesive and hierarchical.

The first splinter in the KCF's unity was caused by personal differences. In 1987 Gurbachan Singh Manochahal, a member of the Panthic Committee, formed his own Bhindranwale Tiger Force for Khalistan (BTFK). His ego would not submit to joint decision-making and shared power. However, the second splinter proceeded with some external assistance and was of a more serious nature.

As the Zaffarwal interview records, the Taksal had not wanted a resolution for Khalistan put forward, nor had members of the Bhindranwale family. By not accepting the death of Sant Bhindranwale – allegedly so as not to offend his father – the Taksal prevented the political movement gaining momentum. They opposed the first Panthic Committee, as indeed did his family and the government. Not surprisingly the government subsequently took the help of the Bhindranwale family (specifically of Gurjit Singh and Jasbir Singh Rode) in launching operation Black Thunder in May 1988 to eliminate the influence of the Panthic Committee. Subsequently they relied very much on Gurjit Singh's cooperation to destroy the power base of the KCF and of its commander Labh Singh. In April 1988, a month prior to Black Thunder, the beginnings of a serious militant rift became evident. Gurjit Singh had begun to woo various guerrilla commanders away from Labh Singh as early as April 1988, persuading them that they could gain more through talking than fighting. Kanwarjit Singh, from Sultanwind, Amritsar, who had been a member of the Panthic Committee, headed a breakaway section of the KCF which eventually became a constituent part of the *car jhujharu jathebande* (CJJ). According to Harjabh Singh, his eldest brother, he thought 'he was bringing the KLF, the Babbars and the student federation together. He thought that what he was doing would contribute to unity. There were difficulties between himself and Manochahal.'

After the death of Labh Singh[1] in the summer of 1988, Kanwarjit Singh reassembled his group. He was caught alive in Jalandhar in May 1989 by a combined police and CRPF party, but took cyanide.[2] His body was not returned to his family. Harjabh Singh believed that the information which had led to the capture of his brother was given by fellow militants. The CJJ then took over his force of approximately twenty trained people. In the summer of the same year Avtar Singh Brahma, a much respected guerrilla, died in mysterious circumstances at Chak 41B Ganganagar. He had founded a breakaway group, the Khalistan Liberation Force (KLF). A Robin Hood type of character, he commanded respect until the end because he took revenge for the beatings of women and children that had occurred in his home village, Brahmpura. Also, he is reputed never to have attacked civilians. His force, comprising thirty to forty guerrillas, threw in its lot with the CJJ under the leadership of Charanjit S. Channi, who was to be killed only a year later.

Zaffarwal's remarks on this period are as follows.

> It was Jasbir Singh Rode's policy to eliminate all the important names in the guerrilla struggle. After Labh Singh's death the Babbars announced a new

> KCF and a new Panthic Committee. Brahma collected a few people together and they came to be known as the Khalistan Liberation Force (KLF). Such individualistic behaviour is doomed. Only those forces will continue to remain that have an institutional base. Organisations based on the individual perish when the individuals perish.[3]

During Labh Singh's lifetime, the KCF had been an expanding force. To obstruct its further growth and get rid of as many KCF guerrillas as possible, Gurjit Singh first got control of those in charge of the supply lines. These were very few in number. One of them was a paternal cousin of Labh Singh, Parmjit Singh Panjwar, then primarily a carrier of weapons rather than a fighter. Panjwar's usefulness to Gurjit Singh arose largely because he came from the same village as Labh Singh and was his relative. Labh Singh being such a fighting symbol for the youth of Punjab, Gurjit Singh felt that might give some legitimacy for whatever actions Panjwar engaged in, that is, as though Labh Singh himself had been behind these moves. Panjwar's initial following was due in part to Labh Singh's popularity. A large number of guerrillas in the KCF command structure were killed at this time – as many as two hundred. Only those who remained part of isolated cells escaped death. Those carrying the weapons were cut off from those picking them up. In other words the supply lines – the physical routes along which weapons are supplied and collected – were cut and all were killed. After these events the KCF was reduced to its pre-1986 position, functioning in isolated groups, with its organisation smashed and its more important leaders killed or bought over. Zaffarwal recounts:

> After Operation Black Thunder we lost contact with our groups, but after a time started reorganising. What saved us were the many individual groups loosely affiliated to us. They would carry out operations as they were the only ones with the supply lines intact. When these individuals came in, I'd supply them with weapons, link them together and they would inform the units cut off that arms were still being supplied.

Following Labh Singh's death, Zaffarwal, the only surviving member of the first Panthic Committee remaining with the KCF, attempted to reorganise it around the sole remaining active cells, those of Gurjant Singh Rajasthani, Balwinder Singh Shahpur, Harbhajan Singh Sursinghwala, Hardev Singh Kallia, Sital Singh Matthewal, Sukhdev Singh Jhamke, Pargat Singh Samra, Jarnail Singh Hoshiarpur and Sukhwinder Singh Gora. All were persons who had been in the field a long time; most, though not all, were small farmers. Theirs were the few cells with independent arms supply lines that had kept the movement alive when the main body of the KCF had been infiltrated and decimated. When the resistance picked up again, these groups were the first to make contact with Zaffarwal. However, when resistance was fully established, many were expelled for hitting soft targets or for extortion. Offers were immediately made to them by other groups. Inevitably there was a time gap between allegations of misconduct, its investigation and an expulsion. So, many had left the organisation already before a statement of expulsion was issued. Meantime they continued to refer to themselves as KCF (Zaffarwal).

Sursinghwala came from village Sursingh, a village that had seen over fifty of its young men martyred. His family had three acres of land, and Harbhajan Singh managed to get into the police force, falsely registering himself as a scheduled caste. When this was discovered he was thrown out. The loss of his job and the fact that he had contact with Bhindranwale led him into the militant movement after 1984. Sursinghwala married a girl whose family were involved in Babbar Khalsa and Panjwar networks and when they married there was a huge hue and cry and much pressure. He was killed by the CRP, but his killing was claimed by the CJJ, ostensibly because he had married a woman forcibly without his father's permission. Pargat Singh Samra, whose three brothers were involved in the struggle, was a graduate. He was killed by the Panjwar group. His killing too was claimed by the CJJ, on allegations of extortion. In fact he came from an extremely poor family. At the *bhog* in their village, his father displayed to all their demolished home.

Sursinghwala and Samra were from the Tarn Taran area, the heartland of the resistance and Manochahal's area of influence. No protection came from Manochahal. The KCF lost all their effective personnel in Amritsar District, though this was not directly due to Manochahal, although he wanted no rivals. Manochahal had been expelled from the Panthic Committee in 1987 because he thought the leadership of a single individual was more effective than a five-member committee. Even after he formed his own force – the Bhindranwale Tiger Force for Khalistan (BTFK) – Zaffarwal persuaded him to rejoin the collective leadership, agreeing that he keep his own personal force. However, by 1990, the same differences re-emerged and he was expelled again for not keeping to Panthic Committee policy guidelines for killing KCF members and a Panthic Committee member. His family, particularly his father, were involved in extortion. Two attempts were made on his father's life in Kakkar hospital, Amritsar, in the summer of 1992, before he was killed in police custody.

Nishan Singh, who was to reorganise the KCF with Zaffarwal, issued the statement of expulsion. As a Panthic Committee member, Manochahal had built up a considerable personal following, drawn from those who like to be close to and associated with those of influence. Hence, after his expulsion, the KCF lost the men that Manochahal had brought in while building his own personal power base.

During the period of KCF reorganisation in January–April 1990, the KCF lost to other groups several personnel who had been important previously. Leaders of these groups were unprepared to submit to policy guidelines and wished to retain their own independence. They lost Balwinder Singh Shahpur,[4] who controlled thirty men, Sital Singh Matthewal, who was eventually to die in an encounter near his village, and Hardev Singh Kallia. Both Shahpur and Matthewal were unprepared to be just one among many lieutenant-generals; they wished to remain individual leaders of their own private followings. One by one they went, Kallia for hitting soft targets and Shahpur for hoarding arms. Matthewal's defection was important, as he was a Panthic Committee member (1988–89), while Kallia was a leader of one of the oldest surviving cells. All were wooed by Manochahal with offers of arms. Rajasthani, in control of one cell, also made an alliance with Manochahal, though he did not join the BTFK. Manochahal's BTFK, the KCF (Rajasthani) and the Dashmesh regiment (Matthewal) allied in April 1990 to form a Panthic Committee for and on behalf of Manochahal.

The four *jathebande* referred to at the close of Chapters 2 and 3 are thus composed of those breakaway elements in the KCF and KLF who betrayed Labh Singh. Until the spring of 1991 they were aligned to the Sikh Students Federation affiliated to Daljit Singh Bittoo and to the guerrilla group that had fought Bhindranwale, namely the Babbar Khalsa. It was Gurjit Singh, who had already done deals with the government, who brought this opportunistic gathering of ex-KCF and KLF personnel together, in alliance with those trying to infiltrate and gain ascendancy in the guerrilla movement, namely the Babbar Khalsa, the purpose being to destroy it from within.

To sum up, this period must be seen as one when the state made extensive efforts to control and exert influence over guerrilla units, and succeeded except in the case of the core of the KCF (Zaffarwal). The KLF had importance as an organisation due to Brahma's high reputation, both as a fighter and as a person. He was universally respected as a gentleman. On his death the organisation was taken over by Charanjit Singh Channi, who died a similar pre-arrranged death as Brahma through betrayal. For the state, to control the KLF was important because of the good name of its founder. A young man, Gurjant Singh Budhsinghwala, became its head. Zaffarwal describes him as an '*am*' or ordinary local boy, but quite sincere. From this time onwards, despite the genuineness of Budhsinghwala, the KLF was used by anti-patriotic forces. An attempt was made to take over the KCF itself through Labh Singh's paternal cousin Parmjit Singh Panjwar. After smashing the KCF as a body by breaking the arms supply lines, he began to seduce and attack those with independent supply lines affiliated to it, since guerrilla units could only be maintained in existence through a constant supply of arms. Manochahal's BTFK collaborated with the state in this respect. The state could live with, as well as utilise, Manochahal's obsession to have the Tarn Taran area as his own personal fiefdom, until they no longer needed his services. He was not eliminated until 28 February 1993.

The period between the summer of 1988 and the spring of 1991 is one when the CJJ engaged in killings on an unprecedented scale. One KCF (Zaffarwal) guerrilla described to me how the CJJ 'were hunting us down in order to murder us', and he remarked that, with the killing of Sursinghwala, Samra, Nishan Singh Salarpur and Harminder Singh Sandhu, the struggle became internal to every village of the Majha region. Over this period the rift between the two main militant organisations widened on issues of policy and tactics and, from 1990, the KCF engaged in a fundamental reorganisation which would enable it to survive the defection of personnel and once again re-emerge for a number of years. As it regained strength, and its reorganisation made infiltration increasingly difficult, although only for a time, it endeavoured to defeat anarchist elements in the guerrilla movement while continuing to attack symbols of state power in the Punjab.

The KCF's reorganisation was planned by Zaffarwal in the early months of 1990 with Nishan Singh Salarpur, a member of the Panthic Committee who had spent some time with Zaffarwal. Nishan Singh was a very poor artisan from District Jullundur and, like Zaffarwal himself, was a family man in his thirties. Formerly he had been an associate of Manochahal. He was killed, on Manochahal's instructions, for his defection to Zaffarwal.[5] Zaffarwal's words regarding the new organisation are as follows:

> Each individual group leader is now responsible for creating his own supply lines and, as from January 1990, all our old groups have been recovered. Our new policy is to make all our groups independent, though they do have links and association and they do sit together, discuss and sort out rumours and misinformation until such time as clarification is reached. Each leader [of a cell] is given a free hand as to [local] operations and targets [within policy guidelines]. Specific instructions are given as to the rules of the struggle: never to issue letters demanding money; never to intimidate. Those who join the struggle must do so out of love or through persuasion.

Central to KCF reorganisation was the creation of a cellular structure. The various cells were independent of each other and they did not know of each other's existence, let alone of their plans or of their armed potential. What had defeated the KCF in 1988 was the close interrelation between the various small groups and the fact that the main supply lines were organised by so very few people, and hence hideouts became known if those people betrayed the organisation, which they did. A reorganised KCF now fought to win back its former position of strength. The overall head of the organisation was Zaffarwal, beneath whom there were thirty to forty lieutenant-generals. Below the lieutenant-generals were area commanders. There might be five area commanders under a lieutenant-general and between twenty and fifty men in an area command covering fifty villages. Area commands usually consisted of five cells. Cells were named after their most important individual, as were the groups of which they were a part. If groups were small they might consist of only one cell. There is usually a maximum number of ten in a cell. Each cell has two or three hard core members and seven workers. In some cases a cell outlives the death of the person who formed it but usually it divides on his death and is incorporated into other groups.

In theory, each level takes responsibility for, controls, and has information about the level below. It is a lieutenant-general's duty to build supply lines across the border and internally within India, and to organise resistance in the area under his command through the distribution of weapons. Lieutenant-generals are those who take the initiative in organising new supply lines, who have experience in organising networks, and who engage in successful exploits. The lieutenant-generals are area-based, and their number in a given area depends on the level of activity. For example, in Majha there are many lieutenant-generals, while in Uttar Pradesh there is only one. Lieutenant-generals know of each other, though each does not know the other's area commanders. Each has his own network of contacts and safe houses, unknown to the other. If a lieutenant-general from Majha wants to make contact with units in Ludhiana district in the Malwa region, he can do so only through the lieutenant-generals of the Malwa region who know the houses and who will transmit the message. This is so even though some of the lieutenant-generals in the Malwa originate from Majha. *Deras* (outhouses on farms) are used as postboxes. On the death of a lieutenant-general, area commanders struggle for his position.

Area commanders are responsible for the organisation of individual cells. Hideouts – both for personnel (i.e. safe houses) and, in some instances, for weapons and supply routes – were organised by each cell. Cells were encouraged to keep their own independent identity and not to merge it with any others. They were sustained through independent arms supplies. Each cell was encouraged to have its own individual supply lines internally within India. There was a tendency in policy, in the Majha region especially, to let cells develop their own routes externally as well. In fact it was only certain Majhail groups in the Tarn Taran and Batala areas who achieved this. In situations of arms scarcity, many cells and groups would endeavour to get their own arms independently. That presented problems, in that many groups did not realise they were receiving their arms courtesy of the Punjab police. Contacts were established and maintained through known safe houses. When guerrillas were going on actions they didn't carry their weapons along with them. These followed, their carriers leaving them in hideouts. They were then picked up *en route* to the action. Sometimes active fighters travelled alongside non-active ones. The latter had no access to safe houses. Only Zaffarwal was supposed to know the network of contacts and safe houses of each lieutenant-general.

As head of the KCF, Zaffarwal periodically calls the lieutenant-generals together. Jointly they work out policy and a programme regarding military and economic targets. The policy programme is primary. To this all are supposed to subscribe and in this all are involved. No one has the right to change the policy programme. No one has the right to issue statements which are contrary to joint decision. Zaffarwal also directs the distribution of weaponry. All lieutenant-generals may not be able to be present at these meetings, and if not, other lieutenant-generals will pick up their weapons on their behalf and are supposed to be responsible for distributing these to them. Otherwise individual lieutenant-generals also cross over to Pakistan on their own initiative to discuss their plans with Zaffarwal, describe local conditions in their area of operation and to take weapons back to Indian Punjab. Authority is not deputed to area commander level. Lieutenant-generals are supposed to be in control of their groups through remaining in control of arms supplies Policy is organised jointly by Zaffarwal and the lieutenant-generals. The technical problems of the moment and matters of detailed strategy are decided upon by the cell. Zaffarwal organised the internal supply lines within Pakistan as well as all the cross-border supply routes. However, as noted, certain groups belonging to districts Amritsar and Gurdaspur brought arms across the border independently. These were the groups under Gora (trained by Sukhdev Singh Jhamke), Gaggabhua (trained by Labh Singh) and Matthewal, who knew the border intimately. The organisation expanded (and contracted) on the basis of the weapons in its possession. In 1991 it expanded into Rupar and Sangrur where previously it had been non-operational. Nonetheless, the description of the KCF as an organisation given in previous pages was the ideal rather than the reality, with the exception of the Tarn Taran and Batala areas.

KCF policy tended to relate to those areas of life that practice and experience over the years had shown to be difficult or problematic for the individual guerrilla. The cornerstone of the policy was the acceptance of the Panthic Committee of 1986. Some guerrillas had had difficulty with this. For example Gora had taken *amrit* from the Taksal and he remained very influenced by its teachings. He was very offended when someone said Bhindranwale was dead. He believed him to be alive, 'because Baba Thakur Singh told him so and he's a *brahm gyani*' (sage). The second important element of policy was that Zaffarwal alone should decide with whom to forge links. Thirdly, it was a key element of policy that arms should be distributed and not hoarded. The making and breaking of groups depended on the supply of weapons. Shahpur and Kallia had tended to use their arms to acquire personal followings and not distribute their weapons throughout their area of command. They were expelled from the KCF. Fourthly, it was policy neither to kill the innocent, nor to kidnap or steal for personal aggrandizement nor to become involved in personal vendettas. Regarding the second of those points, one member of the Panthic Committee had laid down a rule whose aim was to prevent extortion – namely don't ask individuals for anything but approach the village *sarpanc* and request him to organise a donation of five rupees per acre. However, it was the last point that was perhaps the hardest to practise for the individual guerrilla. It is inevitable that a farmer who gives shelter and food will ask for help if he is involved in a feud with a neighbour. Young guerrillas are trapped into giving such assistance if they succumb to the stress laid on the value of reciprocity in the traditional and still existing social system. An informant told me that those who were joining the movement in Malwa were engaged in intimidation on a large scale in pursuit of family vendettas.

It is KCF policy to disown the cells involved in any such activity because they discredit the movement. However, those disowned merely make common cause with those opposed to the KCF or begin to operate in a freelance manner. There were cases of rampant extortion in Ludhiana. The culprit – a milkman – was eventually tracked down and expelled. The KCF had no control over the leaders of individual cells whose actions very frequently did not conform to guerrilla policy. Generally, the further away from the border a guerrilla cell was, the less authority the KCF as an organisation had over it. Cells mushroomed after 1989 with a massive influx of arms from Pakistan. There were no authoritative figures who could control the formation of cells and the use of the KCF's name for actions which were not in accordance with its policy. The KCF asserted the primacy of its *dhancha* (organisational structure) over the individualist tendencies of its members. In consequence it suffered losses of its personnel among those of its cadre who regarded the guerrilla movement as an enterprise in which they had to display personal success over others. This was perhaps not surprising in a society in which the adventurer always had an important place and which had accorded value to the entrepreneur also.

Defections from the KCF continued right up until its defeat. These defections left the international leadership of the organisation unaffected, though they affected overall social stability in the rural areas of the Punjab. Guerrillas desert for different reasons. They may be bought over by arms. In April 1991, Gurjit Singh (killed in early November 1991) approached Jassa Singh Santuwal, a KCF guerrilla interviewed on pp. 179–80, with the promise of more arms if he defected. Santuwal refused, which may have had something to do with his death in July 1991. 'Everyone knows he died after meeting Gurjit Singh' commented one informant. Ambition, egoism and the search for purely individual fame and glory caused guerrillas either to be disowned or to desert and cause the break up of groups. Thus a one time member of the KCF, Balwinder Shahpur, who had become very popular, left the organisation. Various attempts had been made to woo him and, thinking that he could survive on his own because he had enough arms supplies to maintain a personal following, he deserted. Things did not work out as he planned, and he allowed himself to be used by the intelligence services. In August 1991 Rajasthani was killed. Sital Singh Matthewal was killed in mid-September of the same year. In both cases the police were led to their exact whereabouts. Others having association with Manochahal had been captured with their weapons. Manochahal, who had been one of the original members of the first Panthic Committee, was the prime example among the guerrillas of the controlling drive of individual ambition and egoism. In order to secure control of the Tarn Taran area like some warlord of old, he began to undermine all individual leaders with popularity, guerrillas such as, for example, Satnam Singh Chhina and Sukhwinder Singh Sangha. He killed those who deserted him, such as the former KCF members, Matthewal and Rajasthani, in so far as he gave information to the paramilitary forces as to their whereabouts. However, sometimes other circumstances came into the picture. For example, in the case of Chhina, who had gone out of the Punjab for a rest in mid-March 1991 and who was captured by the police immediately on Manochahal's information, he and his wife were recruited by the intelligence services as the latter had important work for them to do. Chhina took over the BTFK after Chhandran's killing, decimating all of Chhandran's fighters.

Guerrillas tend to join those groups which perform the most successful actions if those groups will accept them. However, as the KCF's fortunes revived in the early spring of 1990,the commanders of the various groups who had aided its survival in 1988 saw their bargaining power increase and they left the KCF, wooed (to their death, so to speak) by Manochahal's arms.

Allegiances worshipped 'the rising sun' and were a major cause of the disintegration of guerrilla units and their realignment. Problems with the acceptance of authority, resulting in a group pursuing its own independent line, were common to all guerrilla organisations and led to inefficient overall functioning. Some cases were more blatant than others, for example that of Sukhwinder Singh Sangha. Sangha was a very popular area commander with some fifty to sixty guerrillas under his control. He had been part of the BTFK at one stage, though as a leader with an individual force. He left it to become a freelance operative. As such he had to make his own arrangements regarding contacts, weapons and supply routes. In the latter half of 1990 he had attempted to join the KCF under Zaffarwal as its star rose once again. For a time Zaffarwal helped him with arms and supplies on condition that he adhere to KCF policy. Sangha argued that since he was in the field, he knew better what policies to pursue. He was very popular in his area and with his men. He was insisting on eliminating all the informers in his area, whereas Zaffarwal thought this to be a waste of time and that he should concentrate on economic targets. He told Zaffarwal he was not going to get his boys killed 'pursuing a policy' and he refused to merge his group into the KCF on Zaffarwal's terms. Its members were then sent back from Pakistan without arms. To survive he engaged in a number of robberies. He also began flirting with the CJJ, successfully selling his allegiance to them in order to get arms. However, by November 1990, the CJJ had added another group to their alliance – Manochahal's BTFK – and after a while they eliminated Sangha and took over his following. What were now the *panj jhujharu jathebande* (literally, five militant groups) were grouped against the KCF as from November 1990. The PJJ always targeted KCF fighters, especially if they refused to defect.

Culturally moulded personality factors were involved in group formation and dissolution. When boys became powerful, they also became popular. They loved their popularity and fame. Their popularity led to a certain carelessness and they were killed in action, while those remaining in their group were taken over. Popularity also led to ambition, as boys got wooed by other groups. Once their name became associated with successful exploits, other groups tended to court them. Boys responded to this acclamation by defecting. They knew no political leader could build a base without them. For example, Rajinder Singh Mehta, who was president of a section of the Sikh Students' Federation, tried to attract Gora in his capacity as deputy chief of the Majha region. Gora had risen to his position through his daredevil actions, his shrewdness and his planning. These were of value to the KCF. They were also of value to other groups.

In cases where cells disintegrated due to individual guerrilla commanders changing their allegiance, the KCF would lose their respective cells without damage to its organisation. However, the fallout was on rural society. For if a cell or group is without wider support and without arms, its members can live only by extortion. In cases where a cell has disintegrated in this manner its members might find employment as hit-men in family feuds. There was visible reliance on the protection of large landlords, in return for aid to them, in the case of Parmjit Singh Panjwar who headed the breakaway section of the KCF. Alliances of such a nature meant that the rural areas suffered violence from some guerrillas that was little different in nature to police violence, that is, it was arbitrary.

As an acclaimed guerrilla one was marked out for special treatment: death or an offer one could not refuse. For example, pressure was put on Dr Barjinder Singh Panjwar, who was President of the Sikh Students Federation after the death of Gurnam Singh Buttar, to join the CJJ. Initimidated, he defected. The CJJ then eliminated him. This was a familiar pattern.

In terms of personnel, the cadre of the KCF were just like those of other guerrilla organisations and, as has been shown, there was considerable mobility between guerrilla organisations. However, the KCF, unlike the other guerrilla bodies, did disown and expel from their organisation those who behaved badly. Moreover, as stated in Chapter 3, differences regarding policy and tactics between the two main guerrilla organisations were stark. Regarding the Sikh struggle as a war against the Indian state, the KCF attacked CRP and BSF pickets, police stations and a variety of economic targets, for example government transport vehicles and electricity generating stations, Food Corporation of India *godowns*, wheat storage depots, petrol tanks, etc. Many actions were not reported. The Babbar Khalsa, and the CJJ as a whole, chose influential targets and ordinary Hindus, that is, they attacked persons. The differences emerged very clearly in the last week of November 1990 when a KCF guerrilla by the name of Uppal was killed. The KCF responded to his death by attacking paramilitary targets. However, when CJJ guerrillas were killed, they responded by killing innocent persons indiscriminately. Individual killings and attacks on Hindus have not been the work of the KCF. Killings of prominent persons – large landowners and industrialists – may reflect the Naxalite influence within the CJJ. However, this was not always the case. The hated SSP Gobind Ram was murdered by persons within the Punjab Armed Police. In the case of the former Finance Minister, Balwant Singh, who had become dispensable to those he served, or Harminder Singh Sandhu, who was the subject of a successful smear, some form of official collaboration is suspected, that is, criminals performing the deed on behalf of RAW, with the CJJ claiming the responsibility. For example, Panjwar claimed responsibility for the KCF boys he murdered, creating confusion, disillusionment and demoralization among the Sikh public on a large scale. He now claims these were 'false responsibilities'.

The KCF interest was in reviving old Sikh institutions which expressed the will of the people, institutions such as the Sarbat Khalsa and the *gurmata.* Due to the difference between them and the Babbar Khalsa over both tactics and policy and due to widespread infiltration by government intelligence into other groups, all members of the KCF were instructed not to recruit from other militant organisations. It was thought, also, that taking guerrillas from other groups would create unnecessary personal conflicts. As of 1991, the KCF were being very careful about whom they recruited. They were taking only new recruits and extensive checking was done to verify details of a recruit's background. Even after that process of checking was completed, recruits were not given active work immediately. They were also persuaded during their training to become *amritdhari,* trained to do their Ardas morning and evening for the success of the Sikh struggle, and to say five prayers from the *Japji* each morning.[6]

KCF members were urged not to retaliate when their members were killed. The KCF was, in fact, losing many boys until April 1991, when the leaders of the five *jathebande* were called over to Pakistan to account for the destructive way in which they were using their weapons. They crossed to Pakistan untroubled by either intelligence service; Indian intelligence informed the BSF that 'these are our spies' (informant cannot be named) and opened up a crossing point for them at the Attari rail bridge. An informant recalls how he himself saw Sohan Singh walk across the bridge at Attari. On arrival in Pakistan they told Pakistani intelligence that they had bribed someone in the BSF. It was not entirely a lie. They utilised the services of a smuggler from village Khassowal on the borders of districts Amritsar and Gurdaspur who had contacts in the BSF.

The various parts of the CJJ alliance had fallen apart when elections were announced for June 1991. They were very keen to contest elections. An informant who met them in April 1991 reported Bittoo's view that 'we should set up our own candidates and not hand over the reins of the struggle to Sirmranjit Singh Mann. We should become a political party.' However, not being such a political party, they could not contest elections and killed the candidates of other political parties. Thereby they collaborated with government agencies in providing cause for the government in Delhi to cancel elections. Since some of those who joined the CJJ had done so solely because they thought they were fighting the state, and because they were in the ascendancy among the militant groups, their level of support was henceforth to drop away. The Punjab police eliminated many of their own agents among them[7] and was to eliminate more in the years that followed. For example, in November 1993 it eliminated Satnam Singh Chhina. Sohan Singh was taken into custody in 1994. Those accompanying him across the Nepal border were killed. He was placed in a forest rest house and subsequently in hospital.

The KCF networks were built using traditional bases of association. The Mafia-type spread of links operating on the basis of friendship, kinship, indebtedness for past favours and expectation of future ones, may not affect the possibility of realising Khalistan but may affect the possibility of realising it in the shape of a people's democracy as is envisaged in the 1986 document of independence. Both the believers in a separate state and those fighting against them regard society's traditional links as a resource to be used. However, those advising the KCF and belonging to the international wing of the Panthic Committee were by no means committed to the perpetuation of these traditional ties.

It will be clear, from the interviews, that the young guerrillas are sincere and committed. However, as one observer pointed out, not unfairly, 'the guerrillas can be so easily undermined by the suave and articulate élite. There is a danger that the mango tree they have planted, others will eat.' The International Wing of the Panthic Committee is aware of the clash between the organisation's aims and policy programme and the rural culture which forms the guerrillas. It is unsympathetic to the local rivalries, family feuds and personal loyalties and enmities that are the backbone of that culture. However, its leadership sees the guerrillas as being formed by the experience of struggle and they are not bothered about defections or deaths, 'out of this fire we'll get good bricks', they say, a reference to the peasant saying that 'a house made of *kachcha* [a mixture of clay and other materials, not pure cement] bricks will not stand. It will be washed away.'

Desertions occur not just because of lack of arms or greediness for more arms, but because members cannot keep strict policy guidelines and hence are threatened with expulsion. In the summer of 1991, a prominent family of transporters in District Ludhiana reported that it was being harassed and intimidated by a cell affiliated to the Zaffarwal KCF. This particular cell had connections to persons with whom they had had a personal feud over the last thirty years. During those thirty years the family of transporters had, through skilful use of its political connections and links in the police and administration, gained the upper hand. Members of the other family were threatened in such a manner that they could not personally farm their land – in excess of 600 acres. Both sides always had armed protection. It is into such a situation that the KCF enters with its rule 'do not intimidate, extort or kill!' It is in the same position as the Criminal Courts have been since Independence, that is, unable to impose its particular concept of justice over and against the vitality of customary law and the feud. The only way it will do so is to monopolise force.

Facts such as have been presented may give rise to doubts as to whether the struggle is, for some of its participants, in any way concerned with the identity and sovereignty of the Sikh people. Yet, on that question the guerrillas interviewed leave no doubt. Nor do some of my own interviews in 1990, 1992 and 1993, with journalists, civil rights workers and politicians, and innumerable ordinary villagers. The first claim of the movement as a whole is of a spiritual order, the wish to be free of a distant centre, now regarded as foreign, who support their immediate oppressors, the police. There is moral unrest. Problems emerge because participants have a mixture of motives for joining a political movement. Normally a family would use such a struggle as the present one to redress longstanding grievances. Difficulties arise because some participants attempt to realise their aims – personal and national – by methods of organisation that relate to the concerns and interests of the family. The KCF would like to establish the primacy of its *dhancha* (organisational structure) over individual and family interests. However, its ideological concerns provide, as yet, no direct answer to peoples' day-to-day problems and needs and there is, as yet, no supporting infrastructure for their idealism at the time of writing. Moreover the KCF has an ambiguous attitude to culture. They have supported certain aspects of culture – such as the philosophy of martyrdom – at certain stages of their existence, specifically when they were losing recruits, yet still capable of winning the war, thus exploiting the willingness of the young and the committed to die for their people and for freedom. Many young guerrillas became *shahids* (martyrs) within the first three years of their recruitment. Thus their accumulated learning and experience could not be transmitted to the next generation of fighters. The guerrillas claimed that the act of *shahidi* (martyrdom) would bring about Khalistan. Certainly it meant that the struggle never lost momentum. Martyrdom provided the cause with unlimited manpower. However, if Khalistan, when it comes into being, is run by those who have made no sacrifices to bring it into being, this will be entirely due to the philosophy of *shahidi* which has cost the Sikh people so many of their young sons. A government cannot be formed from these young fighters as they are now. However, if fighters survive their experiences by many years, managing to mature despite the presence of over 100,000 security personnel, it will be a different matter. Small in number, they tie down large numbers of men and materials. Food Corporation of India *godowns*, the water supply, the canal system, rail and electricity supply systems are manned by the paramilitary or the armed forces. A massive amount of cash is spent on keeping the border closed and floodlit. They have succeeded in weakening the state.

At the time of writing the amount of military manpower in the villages was so high that it would have been pointless and suicidal to resume guerrilla attacks. Yet it is going to be difficult to establish a political base because that has been destroyed through the belief and practice of *shahidi* and presently there seem to be no structures that can incorporate, channel, direct and train the young who are genuinely interested in the fate of their people. The KCF made a major mistake before the 1992 elections of trying to associate conventional politicians with the guerrilla struggle. This same mistake had been made by a considerably more experienced fighter, Che Guevara. However, the fact that it had been made so long ago, in 1967, and not learned from, is sufficient testament to the as yet undeveloped nature of this struggle.

The KCF (Zaffarwal) sees itself as having survived the government's counter-organisation which organised its own supply routes, publicised the more violent actions of its leadership, gave prominence to their statements and saw that arms were readily available. Insidiously eating away at the morale of its fighters, too, has been the Dam Dami Taksal claiming that Sant Bhindranwale is not dead. Then, also, prominent personalities of a religious bent having influence over rural people have argued that what happened to the Sikhs in 1984 was because they were not spiritually pure. Such views sapped the spirit and will to fight. As Kapur Singh stated over twenty years ago, 'We are now throwing up a class of pseudo intellectuals who are engaged in preaching day and night that Sikhism is a church of worship only.' Their views were a threat to the idealism of 1986, a threat as great as the gangs of police and guerrillas who together joined in a project of reciprocal benefit to terrorize the rural areas.

The KCF suffered from an infiltration which will remain hard to combat in a non-stratified society. However, infiltration would have been more difficult had discipline and sanctions among the guerrillas been tighter and had their level of ideological commitment not been so rudimentary. As General Narinder Singh commented, 'There was no effort to test the chap ideologically and then, of course, when there was this large inflow of arms, it made it easy to infiltrate by the opportunistic whoever they were. Naturally the government encouraged both the inflow of arms and the opportunism.'

Yet the infiltration could have been two-way. Perhaps with time, training and awareness, the penetration will become more reciprocal in nature. Most recruits received no training in surveillance tactics, for example. The KCF was in fact very carelessly organised. For example, the cost of running such a guerrilla organisation had not been worked out in advance (and hence extortion was inevitable) and there had been established no preparatory network of linkages which were certain to remain more or less intact through adverse circumstances. In some cases, quarrels in civilian life unnecessarily spilled over into the organisation. Self-reflection on one's own nature and on the structure of one's society was completely absent as was any analysis or prediction of the enemy's strategy.

My own evaluation is that the decentralisation introduced into the KCF organisation in 1990 became its biggest problem. Its purpose and intent had been to prevent further losses among its fighters. It was a measure primarily concerned with the safety of its personnel. However, the cell system which was introduced experienced problems, partly because of how it was understood culturally: and instead of being a measure contributing to the overall efficient functioning of the organisation, it gave each group the freedom to be its own master. As each individual guerrilla leader gained local fame and popularity and became a legend in his lifetime, he converted his popularity into a private, local power base, that is, into an anti-national gain. As each put himself out on a limb for his own personal fame, he was indeed at the centre of interest, attracting the attention of his rivals and of the security forces. Each was easily picked off.

The KCF's decentralised structure was interpreted by its fighters as being for their own individual benefit. Many left the organisation once their own local area base was secure. There were some local area commanders who were heroes and who remained part of the organisation while others, who set up their own organisations, at least did it no harm. The manner in which arms were supplied merely accentuated the organisation's tendency to fragment. Hence, in this particular culture, the operation of the decentralised cell system meant uneven achievements for the movement as a whole. Groups were sustained through their independent access to arms, and, particularly in the border areas, some cells developed their own cross-border routes. Others did not, and in situations of arms scarcity it was easy for them to fall into pre-arranged traps. For example, boys who had carried out a few actions and become popular would often not realise that their route to Pakistan had been facilitated courtesy of the Punjab police and the BSF. They then had to cooperate with these bodies. It was death either way.

KCF policy of disowning those who had committed various social wrongs also enhanced the negative effect of the decentralised pattern. It would have been better to eliminate those who deserted and who proceeded to rob and kill in the organisation's name. Their activities in this respect discredited the name of the KCF. Moreoever, as the number of groups proliferated, rural instability increased. The more it did so, the more the KCF ceased to function as an association supplying protection.

By the winter of 1992, civilian morale had collapsed completely, and the KCF suffered high losses. The final cleaning-up job by the state, in the villages of Amritsar District in February 1993 appeared brutal, though the level and intensity of the violence had always been high. On almost every page of this book, reference has been made to civilian suffering. Incidents such as at the one which I witnessed at Chogawan (tehsil Baba Bakala, District Amritsar) on 18 February 1993 were commonplace. A full truckload of commandos dressed in gear destined to frighten – that is, totally in black from their turbans to their running shoes – descended on the village. The prisoners filled a large civilian truck in front. In minor ways too, the state kept up its provocation of rural populations. For example, simple acts such as the giving of food and shelter to strangers, which are fundamental to the practice of religion in the rural areas, had their meaning distorted. There were limits to the amount of pressure that a civilian population could stand, especially when it came from two sources, official police and their undercover agents and gangs.

The KCF has now laid down certain rules which its members have to abide by in the event that the struggle resumes with greater intensity. The *nitipatrika* outlines what are in effect rules of engagement:

a. No innocent person should be killed.
b. You shall not consider raising your hand against children, old people, women and the sick under any circumstance.
c. Your enemy who has lost his weapons and is injured should be spared. He should be treated as a prisoner of war and his rights respected.
d. You are forbidden to obtain what you require through stealing or fraudulent means.
e. You must not be partisan in village disputes.
f. You must not attack a fellow Sikh. If he is suspected of being an informer he must be given an opportunity to present his case.
g. There can be no controversy over the *Rehet Maryada* [the Rules of Approved Conduct] at this point in time. This is a delaying tactic.
h. The political process should be promoted on the basis of the Sarbat Khalsa resolution.
i. Conditions for dialogue with police and members of the security forces should be created to try and persuade them to support the independence movement.
j. It should be explained with friendliness and affection to local Hindus and non-Sikhs that in Khalistan there will be no discrimination against them.

It may be correct in the interim to emphasize the rules of engagement rather than policy. Firstly it matters little what an organisation's policy is if it cannot enforce it; bases for private armies among the KCF still exist. Secondly, as the data in the following chapter shows, the position of the guerrillas seemed to advance or fall back according to the personality and moral character of the local area commanders, who became either villains or heroes. At grassroots level in the villages, ordinary civilians faced a reality of mixed groups. Some guerrillas gave their primary loyalty to a set of ideas rather than to an individual, and were willing and capable of subordinating certain cultural practices to the overall needs of the movement. Others epitomised society's values, and acted in accordance with them rather than with the organisational requirements of the guerrilla group. Still others were insincere to all but themselves, or undisciplined. When they were thrown out of the KCF they simply joined another group and traded all that they knew to the state. Each group was an unfortunate mix of patriots, myopic traditionalists, individualists and criminals. It was such mixed groups that ordinary civilians had to face on a day-to-day basis rather than the ideological differences between the KCF and the CJJ. Hence the relevance of the rules of engagement.

Main figures mentioned in text

Khalistan Commando Force (Zaffarwal)

Manbir Singh Chaheru
Labh Singh
Wassan Singh Zaffarwal
Sukhwinder Singh Gora
Jarnail Singh Hoshiarpur
Jassa Singh Santuwal
Rachpal Singh Bhola
Sukhdev Singh Jhamke
Affiliation: First Panthic Committee

Individual leaders affiliated to the KCF (Zaffarwal) until 1990

Gurbachan Singh Manochahal
Sital Singh Matthewal
Balwinder Singh Shahpur
Gurjant Singh Rajasthani
Hardev Singh Kallia
Satnam Singh Chhina

Constituent parts of the Car Jhujharu Jathebande (CJJ)

KLF (Budhsinghwala)
KCF (Panjwar)
All India Sikh Students Federation (Bittoo)
The Babbar Khalsa
Affiliation: Second Panthic Committee (Sohan Singh)

Notes

1. The historic *bhog* notices recorded in the *Ajit* are placed in Appendix Two. I interviewed Labh Singh's wife on her husband's murder. She told me that Labh Singh and his cousin, Parmjit Singh Panjwar, had travelled together to the house of one Nirmal Singh at the Thanda bypass.

> He had informed me where he was going and I was not worried as he was known to Nirmal Singh as he often kept money in his house. When he reached there Nirmal Singh suggested that, since his house was searched often, he should sleep in Gurdit Singh's house at Khuda Hospiarpur. Gurdit Singh was also known to my husband as he often left money there as well. Gurjit Singh, the then AISSF leader, knew all the people around my husband as they all had been together in the gunrunning. Panjwar did not remain with them and Gurdit Singh had evidently spread a rumour throughout his village that he was going to Bombay and the USA. Nirmal Singh took my husband to his village. There something was put into his milk that put him into a deep sleep. His body was taken by the BSF and dumped at Darapur. The owners of the petrol pump report that in the early hours of the morning a car was seen approaching and that a single shot rang out sometime between two and four in the morning. The body was identified as being that of my husband by SSP Izhar Alam and Swaran Singh SSP. The next morning at 10.00 the SSP Hoshiarpur informed myself and my father-in-law. A smell came from the body. Many people started collecting at the petrol pump from the surrounding villages to see the body and fifty thousand came to the *bhog* there before it reached Panjwar where a *bhog* was also held ... Gurjit Singh had been jealous of his popularity. My husband was a deeply religious and determined man who always kept his word. For two years before Sant Bhindranwale's death he had been meeting him frequently.

2. Cyanide is carried in the fold of one's shirt collar, usually on the left side. In some respect all such actions could be covered by the term political suicide as described by Dunkerley – 'the taking of one's own life to avoid treatment by the enemy that may well fall short of death but threatens indignity, pain and the coerced revelation of cultural and political secrets' (Dunkerley, 1992: 4).

3. There is some indication, though no proof, that Kanwarjit Singh and Brahma broke away from the alliance being made with the Babbars before they were killed, because they realised the latter were getting a popularity they did not deserve in the light of their past actions.

4. Shahpur eventually committed suicide by swallowing cyanide after being surrounded by police in a locality near the Darbar Sahib on 2 October 1992.

5. The killing was done by Sital Singh Matthewal and there was perhaps an element of personal interest in it in so far as Nishan Singh had been responsible for sacking Matthewal from the Panthic Committee for violating its policy.

6. The emphases that were given in training would depend on the security situation. For example, in 1991 boys were advised to cut their hair because of the conditions of war. As a Panthic Committee spokesman argued, 'if you cannot cut your hair for the Guru's work, how can you give your head?' – i.e., sacrifice

your life. So far as I know, no training was given in methods of surveillance.

7. An example is Balwinder Singh Jethana, who was killed in the summer of 1991. He had made an attempt on the life of the SSP Chandigarh Sumedh Saini. The day after the attack, Saini went to his house and killed his entire family. Jethana himself was killed eventually. On his dead body an IB (Intelligence Bureau) card was found.

5

Police, Guerrillas and Local Populations

> People have turned against a movement they thought had given expression to an aspiration.
>
> (The Director-General of Police, government of Punjab, K.P.S. Gill, 29 September 1992)

In his book *Islam and Resistance in Afghanistan*, Roy (1986: 154 and 203) remarks 'The Afghan resistance takes great care over the civilian population ... However, the challenge for the *mujahidin* is whether they can establish more flexible links between their military organisation and the civilian population so that civilian morale does not suffer.' In the rural Punjab, neither the various guerrilla groups nor the police has had the capability to safeguard the innocent. Its civilian population has had no respite from suffering. It has not been possible to shield it for two reasons. First, each guerrilla organisation did not have total exclusive control over a defined piece of territory and all were competing for control of the Punjab. Civilian casualties resulted from contests between the different guerrilla personalities and their respective followers. This was especially the case in District Amritsar which was the home to several militant personalities, notably Gurbachan Singh Manochahal and Parmjit Singh Panjwar. Districts Gurdaspur, Amritsar and part of Ferozepur were KCF strongholds, yet the KCF had to fight other guerrilla organisations in these areas to attain and maintain supremacy. Second, the struggle between the state and the guerrillas is a struggle over the loyalties of the civilian population. Here, the state enrolled criminals in its service in order to alienate the rural population from the guerrillas as a whole. To discredit and defame the guerrilla struggle, they would announce responsibility for criminal actions, such as murder, rape, extortion and looting, in the name of a guerrilla group. Many reports of such activities surfaced during 1989, that is, after the guerrilla movement had been split. They are prominently reported in the press.[1]

The official police had units attached to them recruited from those dismissed for their involvement in criminal activity. One of these units was particularly infamous, the Alam Special Forces, so called after the then SSP Amritsar, Izhar Alam. All district police chiefs had such special units at their command. *Frontline* reported (14–27 May 1988: 107) that 'In Punjab it is an accepted view that at least some of the death squads have been unleashed by the government'[2] and an *EPW* news report of 16 April 1988 had asked 'Are all killings in Punjab the handiwork of the Khalistani extremists? ... Strategic killings by ... officially planned *agent provocateurs* may help the government to precipitate further authoritarian control by assuming more military powers.'

In September 1988, the then Director General of Police Julio Ribeiro had acknowledged that there was an official policy of counter-terrorism in which police-backed vigilantes were encouraged to use unorthodox methods to identify and eliminate terrorists. In October 1989, in an interview with *India Today*, he remarked 'Covert operations are a part of police work ... We need undercover groups to find out terrorists' movements.' However, in an earlier interview in the *Tribune* (31 July 1989: 13) he had admitted that he 'felt that the police officers in charge had no control over those operating in this manner and they had got out of hand ... Members of these underground squads were indulging in looting and extortion of money.'

Official police agencies were also extremely heavy-handed against the civilian population, as was admitted by Chaman Lal, IG Border, on his resignation. He remarked that during his tenure he had been asked 'to let loose a reign of terror in the villages where terrorists gunned down seven train passengers'. All police and paramilitary activity aimed at creating a wedge between the guerrillas and the civilian population. It was the undercover police inside the militant organisations, or forming groups on their own, who were particularly successful in that respect. As one guerrilla remarked, 'Government agents in the garb of freedom fighters have been the main problem for us [in gaining people's confidence]. Many of these killings have taken place to give others the image that we are murderous and violent.'

Certainly the resistance movement in Ribeiro's day was permeated by those who, in the Punjab, are known as 'anti-social elements', and they engaged in activities that had little to do with achieving Khalistan. Hence when a body of people presented themselves as living by a more puritanical code (I refer here to the Babbar Khalsa) the rural population immediately accepted them and put their faith in them, until they too were undermined by the same anti-social elements and discredited in a similar manner. Ribeiro's separate police squads were an early attempt at counter insurgency and worked imperfectly as they were organised by the Punjab police. Many of their operations were revealed by the Punjab police. Thereafter the BSF and the CRPF protected the government's counter-insurgency plans.

The police view of the militants and of society

One of the reasons why the police took the insurgency so seriously was because of their view of the Pakistani involvement in aiding it. Police intelligence in Punjab were adamant that Pakistan was advising, giving weapons, and training the Sikh youth. Informants tell me that Pakistan gave weapons freely and indiscriminately after 1987. The KCF (Zaffarwal) were without arms for 1988 and 1989 due to the destruction of its arms supply lines, but arms were coming in from Pakistan and going to the CJJ. They created an increasingly chaotic situation and there appeared to be no plan beyond that. Any training that the KCF (Zaffarwal) groups received was given by Sikh members of the armed forces. Matthewal's unit contained a number of army personnel who had mutinied or resigned in 1984. All his boys, as Gaggabhua's and Gora's too, had been given a measure of military training. The police must have known these facts. Nevertheless, they projected the young of Punjab as terrorists, used by Pakistan in its war against the Indian state. The SSP Amritsar, Hardeep Singh Dhillon, in an interview in September 1992, explained how he thought Pakistan was one of the sources of the militant problem in the Punjab.

> India had won freedom for Bangladesh and Pakistan was thenceforth a divided nation. Especially under Zia-ul-Haq, the aim became to repay India in the same coin. Likewise it wanted to pay India back for Kashmir. For in 1947 the Kashmiris had wanted an independent entity and they were promised their wishes will be honoured. You can see article 370 of our constitution in this respect. The main opposition to Pakistan comes from the Punjab which will face the brunt of any attack. So Zia's intention was to utilise the Punjabis. They have managed indeed to achieve considerable internal turmoil and the Punjab police has not been able to curb terrorism but only to manage it. In so doing, it loses a large number of officers and men yearly ... During Operation Woodrose, many rural youth crossed the border. They were hence available to Pakistan and were launched back into India by the Inter Services Intelligence (ISI). The ISI pumped a huge number of AK-47s into the Punjab. Initially, Pakistan gave those weapons. Now it sells them. We are holding onto the Punjab because we are holding onto some prominent families ... Punjabis had suffered greatly at the hands of the Pakistanis during 1947. And the failure of our policies lies in the fact that the people who got our Gurus killed could turn the followers of these very same Gurus in their favour.

However, as the former Indian Ambassador to Norway, Harinder Singh Khalsa, said, 'There is no point in blaming Pakistan. Pakistan did not attack the Golden Temple' (*India Today*, 15 August 1991). Neither is it Pakistan's police attacking one's family members.

There are 553 km of land and riverine tract between Indian and Pakistani Punjab. As from February 1993, all of this has been fenced and provided with floodlights, with observation posts every 500 yards. Quoting Sarabjit Singh, the former DC Amritsar:

> In April 1988 we had a meeting at senior level in which Amritsar was trifurcated into three police districts and a decision was taken to rearm the police with self-loading rifles equipped with night vision devices. It was at that meeting that we decided that if terror has to be checked, then the flow of arms has to be stopped and, since Pakistan was at the back of this flow of arms, there had to be border fencing. Additionally, we took the help of the army to guard the border in places where infiltration was still easy. They formed a second line of defence to check the smuggling of arms and that paid dividends. Pakistani involvement had been there from the very beginning in 1984. There were incidents where either a cow's head or cow's tail was put before a Hindu temple and then tobacco was thrown into the Golden Temple. It was thought that this would be enough instigation for both communities to fight. In 1947, when the country had been partitioned, the immediate cause was the communal riots which the state could not control. This was a model before Pakistan. They were trying their best to incite communal tension. Whenever they saw the communal situation improving, they would start using bomb blasts, as in 1987.

Regarding Pakistani training of militants he said the following:

> Certainly they needed a think tank, or a man who could plan their strategies for them as to what they should do in the changing situation. For, after all, every move that they made, we were reacting to it. After some time we had been able to obtain them and so their tactics had to come under review. And in this policy, they were helped from abroad. Regarding training, I myself, with my binoculars, have seen boys from our Kamalpur post at Dera Baba Nanak. At the *gurdwara* across the border [this is, in fact,a military camp], the boys would be there. Definitely, there has been Pakistani training. There is no doubt about it. The police have caught many letters written from here to Pakistan.

During the years 1988–90, police intelligence portrayed the guerrilla movement as being one of religious fanatics, in order to depoliticize it. This coincided with a period when they exerted some political control over it through the leadership of the CJJ. Then, subsequently, as their military counter-insurgency operations bore fruit, they portrayed it as by and large a criminal movement to ensure the demoralisation of the rural population. They knew very well that this was a political movement for independence. Hence the very great effort that was put into attaching those labels to it that would bring most opprobrium from a world audience, namely labels of religious fundamentalism and terrorism. In fact the activities police intelligence attributed to the guerrillas were no more than standard tactics for such organisations: diversification of targets; attempts on all vital installations and means of communication with explosives; acts of arson; and subverting the loyalties of the security forces.

The intelligence services appeared to see all members of rural society as a potential threat. This emerges very clearly in their descriptions of the militant movement as having connections in all quarters. Their reports mention the movement's foreign connections, principally Pakistan, whom they allege is offering motivation, advice, training, weapons and money to recruits. They describe the movement's criminal connections, a reference to smugglers who undertake border reconnaissance. The reports stress the commercial links of the movement. Transport companies provide cover, shelter, employment and mobility. Among the movement's religious connections it mentions the Dam Dami Taksal but, significantly, not the Akhand Kirtani Jatha. Above all, human rights activists aid the terrorists because they foment dissent. An SP Intelligence Officer in Chandigarh, directly responsible to KPS Gill, constantly stressed in conversation the hold human rights activists had over the guerrillas. According to him, intellectuals were the brains behind the Khalistan movement, a view no farmer nor militant would subscribe to.

After the Congress Party came to power in February 1992 *bhog* ceremonies,[3] which human rights workers had attended frequently, were banned, except for family members. This privatisation of the *bhog* ceremony was part and parcel of a policy that banned all recollections of recent acts of resistance and struggle. The movement was to be cut off from its religious and cultural roots as well as its immediate historical past.

The *bhogs* of those who were prominent were repeated yearly. An example is given below:

> *Barsi* [Annual Commemoration]
>
> In the present struggle Bhai Sukhdev Singh Ji Jhamke has gone to the feet of the Guru [that is, has become one with the Creator]. Readings from Scripture will be held in Bharatpur near Udanwal, Gurdaspur. The whole Sikh people are invited.
>
> Signed, servants of the people Bhai Sukhwinder Singh Gora and Wassan Singh Zaffarwal.

According to the intelligence services, '*bhog* ceremonies were used for preaching sedition and they had an adverse effect on impressionable youth. Members of the families of terrorists were honoured at these functions ... These numerous *bhog* ceremonies led to a glorification of terrorism and provided the motivation of the youth to join the ranks of terrorist outfits.' Certainly, political speeches were made at *bhogs*, and by banning *bhogs* police intelligence aimed to inhibit the development of relationships of solidarity between professionals, civil rights workers and the people.

Police intelligence also asserted that terrorists had political connections, saying that they stayed with prominent politicians and that these intervened on their behalf. They also asserted that they had intellectual connections. 'Some intellectuals are their ideologues. Others are their brokers, producing documents allegedly purporting to be their views. And they have official connections, as is shown by the subversion of police ranks.'

From police statements one can see that all forms of participative power were targeted as militant fronts. Of those involved in the movement 80% were Jats. The Jat family structure was such that its members could be in a range of occupations, since all could not live off the land. For that reason alone, rural society, particularly its Jat Sikh component, was seen as potential enemy territory and this was particularly so after the February 1992 elections when so few rural people voted at all. However, no sector of society felt itself free of threat.

From 1991 when Gill took over briefly as Director of the CRPF, there was greater co-ordination visible between the CRPF and the Punjab police. An SP operations was attached to each police district. Frequently he was a Hindu from outside the Punjab, though not always. Those in charge of the *thanas* or police stations were already the rougher elements among the police. Detachments of paramilitaries were attached to each police station and they formed the back-up staff in the interrogation centres. The Movement Against State Repression asserts that it was these detachments who were responsible for the many disappearances of Punjab's youth (interview with Inderjit Singh Jaijee, June 1993). Others put the matter more strongly, but do not wish to be named: 'The Punjab police are a front and have played an insignificant role in controlling the militants. When the intelligence services want to eliminate someone, they merely pass on the information to the Punjab police. KPS Gill takes the glory for actions that are not his.'

After returning to his old police job, and well into his tenure as DGP, Gill asserted that a police officer's performance would be judged solely on the basis of his success in neutralising the militants. This encouraged police officials to kill. The real butchers were, in fact, from the ranks of the police force: Swaran Singh, originally a constable, who was in turn SSP Faridkot, Kapurthala, and Jagraon; Ajit Singh Sandhu, an inspector, SSP Tarn Taran and presently SSP Ropar; Sita Ram, an inspector, now an SSP. Other police officials of low rank were Narinderpal Singh, now SSP Kapurthala, Izhar Alam, once a constable, then SSP Amritsar. There were many Hindus, some from outside the Punjab, who officered the force, for example S Chattopadyay, SSP Ludhiana (previously Faridkot), and many Hindu officers in a predominantly Sikh force, for example Suresh Arora in Patiala, Sanjiv Gupta at Rupar and A.K. Sharma, formerly SSP Ludhiana.

Law and order is normally an individual state matter but in the Punjab law and order issues are controlled by Delhi. Elimination lists were drawn up not by the DGP but by the Director General Intelligence who took his orders from the Intelligence Bureau (IB). Law and order became further controlled by New Delhi with the large army presence that was despatched to the province in December 1991. At that time thirty-eight divisions[5] were deployed in the state. The Punjab police formed commando battalions, some of whom were trained by the army. Searches intensified as, too, did raids on active hideouts. The increased army involvement gave the police time to use spotter operations. Spotters are those who, in police terms, are reformed militants (in other words, turncoats) or they are those whose relatives have been killed and who are recruited as vigilantes. They work under the watch of the police in all public places and are used to identify youth committed to the Sikh cause. After December 1991 vehicular checks on the roads increased and were indeed innumerable, though they were most common and frequent in the border areas. Due to the army's presence there could now be surprise sealing of suspected areas, often of a group of villages within a 10–20 km radius. Thus, once guerrillas were free of the police, supposing they managed that, they had to face a second encirclement. In this way, many were mown down, an example being Sukhwinder Singh Gora whose interview is recorded. The army actively helped the police pick up youth, though it took none of the discredit for the disappearances that occurred subsequently; these took place in police or paramilitary custody. The first time they implemented the 'encirclement policy', as villagers called it, was at Dehriwalla near Tarsikka, and from then onwards the co-ordination of police and military forces in combination lessened the militant grip within six months. Perhaps the police and military were also aided by a certain tendency within a rural population that had suffered so greatly to passively side with the forces whom they foresaw as gaining the upper hand. I return to this issue later

Indian policy was not preoccupied with the underlying causes of conflict in the Punjab but with the elimination of guerrilla groups through counter-insurgency tactics. As has been shown in Chapter 3, these guerrilla groups had conflicting enthusiasms. These divisions gave the police the opportunity to catch and kill, and to drive a wedge between them and the civilian population. The security forces were working through Sikhs to attack Sikhs. Additionally, there were many guerrillas who had cut themselves off from their parent guerrilla grouping to establish their own individual power bases. If they were without adequate arms and protection, they were exposed to security service threats, and to shield themselves would work for the security service temporarily. Thus, for example, Balwinder Singh Shahpur captured the brother of the KCF guerrilla Jarnail Singh Hoshiarpur at the insistence of the police and at their behest put pressure on him and on his family to secure the return of Jarnail Singh from Pakistan. When his family refused to succumb to police intimidation Shahpur was given the task of killing Hoshiarpur's brother. The government was provided with a way into local rural communities by those guerrillas who were partisan in family feuds or, as in the case above, when those who have been part of a guerrilla organisation leave it because they feel they are not being given enough prominence. They are then contacted by the police and find the weapons and importance offered to them a temptation. Guerrillas of this hue operate in close collaboration with the police.

Guerrillas and the rural population: general comments

The various police agencies, official and unofficial, were partly responsible for the progressively high cost in terms of civilian lives. However, the dynamics of group formation and dissolution among guerrilla organisations also contributed to high civilian casualties. Civilian casualties occurred at times when groups or cells were without the support of one of the major guerrilla organisations. In order to survive, members of the cell became freelance criminals. Killings took place in the interlude between the breakup of a group and the realignment of its members with other groups, and the situation stabilised once a particular group was in control of an area, for it could then offer protection to the inhabitants of that area. These reorganisations between and within groups occurred because of the egoistic character traits of their members, because of desires to be on the winning side or they were the result of government attempts at subversion. Although the decentralised cell organisation among the guerrillas minimised risk of infiltration, it increased risks of civilian casualties in cases where a cell deviated from official KCF policy, or threw its loyalty into the market place.

Paramilitary units were unable to defeat the guerrillas without attacking them in many places: in homes, in the fields, or on the streets. Thus the way this war is fought, by both sides, is causing much violence to civilians, many of whom are not active with either the guerrillas or the police. Both guerrillas and police operate on the assumption that there are no innocent bystanders. Due to their decentralised pattern of organisation and the many and varied types of police unit operating, it is difficult for the public to unravel who is killing who and for what reason.

From press reports and from interviews it would appear that arbitrary killings have their origin in three categories of person: first, the private forces of the district police chiefs and of the intelligence services; second, local criminals who receive periodic and temporary police protection in return for doing some dirty work for a family who have a vendetta, or for the police themselves; third, those guerrillas compromised by their own individual egoism and hence not subject to the discipline of an organisation.

A former general secretary of the Akali Dal, now an old man, though once very active in organising Sikhs during partition as well as evacuating them safely from Pakistan, tried to identify for me the contributors to the present-day violence which was claiming the lives of so many young people in the rural areas. These are his words:

> Firstly some deaths are caused by smugglers in connivance with the police. Secondly, there are those who suffered during Operation Woodrose. Many young Sikhs moved over to Pakistan at that time. The population now feeds them willingly. Then when they are discovered, the police take them away, torture and kill them in false encounters. Thirdly, there are a large number of people, daily growing, honest yet desperate, who see people taken away from their houses but who see their disappearance subsequently reported as a police encounter. They are convinced there is no justice and they then begin to support the guerrilla movement. Fourthly there are the real motivated people, small in number, whether misled or not, wise or not, but definitely there and highly committed.

His words provide some independent confirmation of statements made in interviews by the guerrillas, with whom he has no direct contact. Regarding Khalistan, he quoted the Persian saying 'Zaban i halk nikhara Khuda' (Whatever the public calls for is God's call). What does the public call for? In an interview with Kanwar Sandhu, the correspondent for *India Today* on 20 September 1990, he had commented 'There is a strong sympathy element throughout the rural society for the guerrillas. Their ranks are swelling and they will soon wield political power. The writ of these chaps does run.'

There were some overt past manifestations of this. For example, Labh Singh was held in high enough esteem for educational institutions in the border area to close and for there to be two *bhogs*, one at the spot where he was killed and the other in his home village. In the winter of 1989 there were prayer meetings all over the Punjab to honour Satwant

Singh and Kehar Singh, hanged for the murder of Mrs Gandhi, as also *bandhs* (total shutdown of commercial life and a halt to all rail and road transport) and a closure of all educational institutions in protest at their hanging. The older generation of Sikh writers such as Sant Singh Sekhon expressed considered, if saddened, sympathy for the young guerrillas of the Khalistani movement. Referring to them, Sekhon said (interview September 1990) 'They are my sons and my daughters. How can I disown them? Their tactics may not be right. But nobody places their life in danger for fun. There is some powerful idea that propels them and they therefore must be respected. They are equally well supported here in Malwa. Sympathies for them are strong in this region.' (He was speaking of the Jagraon area of District Ludhiana.)

Aside from any evidence given by the guerrillas themselves, the level of support for them in 1990 can be gauged by the fact that they lived within the population. The Zaffarwal interview records that the local population fed the guerrillas, hid their weapons and let them take shelter on their fields and homes. They were and are totally dependent on the people. As Clutterbuck (1980: 26) notes: 'If ... the guerrilla has to live clandestinely among the local population ... then a higher proportion of the people need to be involved in his support if he is to survive. There must be an adequate number of safe houses in which he can be sure of taking refuge in an emergency.'

However, the level of support was to change from the end of 1991, as police and paramilitaries took on the help of the army. By the spring of 1992 there was more or less an even balance, and by the summer of the same year many important guerrilla figure heads of the CJJ had been eliminated. By January 1993 those who supported them – by giving food and shelter – or even by their thoughts, were being gunned down or simply disappeared.

Guerrilla success increasingly depended on linkages established within the army, administration, transport and the police itself. Mercenary elements in the BSF occasionally and in places, and as a result of prearranged plans, desert their positions at night in return for a few AK-47s. For a large cash payment of 200,000–300,000 rs a crossing, they will allow one guerrilla cell to cross the border.[6] Attempts to play on the susceptibilities of officers with known corrupt tendencies and to develop internal supply lines increased as border crossings became dangerous.

In the text of the interviews one guerrilla remarks 'the people are our jungle'. Not all the people. Sikh members of the IAS for example, often of rural origin, were paralysed by fear. Some of them felt distaste for those fighting, while being in sympathy with the goals of their struggle, Other IAS personnel exhibited obvious envy of those young people, simply because they themselves were not strong enough to withstand a hard life underground. Besides, as one IAS officer who had been close to Bhindranwale remarked, 'The boys are not educated so they will have no impact.' This betrayed a poor understanding of liberation movements, where organisation, rather than education was the key to tactical success. There was a gulf between the IAS and the guerrillas, despite the fact that both usually came from families in the countryside who had been brought up to respect Sikh moral values. The IAS and the intelligentsia had been displaced from the centre of Punjab political life by the young guerrillas, and were hence experiencing the alienation of the politically oriented deprived of their power and their influence. Needless to say, they also disliked those other usurpers of power, the police. A meeting of administrative secretaries of the Punjab government belonging to the IAS made a statement to the effect that '[t]he police were perpetuating violence in the state and that ... civil servants holding enquiries into complaints of police excesses were afraid of submitting their reports, apprehending danger to their lives' (*Tribune*, 3 August 1991). They complained that normal law was being circumvented and that no inquests were being held into police encounters. It was a polite protest and it seems no one in the police paid any attention.

Whether the gulf that existed between the IAS and the guerrillas also existed between the guerrillas and the army is, as one informant put it, 'open to question'. It has to be kept in mind always that throughout the rural Punjab, because of the smallholder economy, the guerrilla, the policeman and the military man may be part of the same family. Moreover, the military had been, traditionally, the guardians of Sikh tradition, and they were conscious of that. The border districts, especially districts Amritsar and Gurdaspur, always had a high percentage of their people in the army, the police and smuggling, because of smallholdings. And as one journalist laughingly put it 'They are now serving the Panth [Sikh nation] as well' (that is, by joining the freedom fighters).

Those serving in the army and police do tip off both their kin and affinal relatives about approaching danger. Friendship connections and other personal links can be relied upon by the guerrillas. All of these connections are used to collect basic information about police deployments and suitable safe houses. The existence of kin, affinal and friendship networks with no precise geographical location is advantageously used by those engaged in the freedom struggle. However, the very same links that the guerrilla uses are also used by the forces of counter-insurgency. Moreover, because the service tradition among the Sikhs is particularly strong, guerrillas cannot rely automatically on the neutrality of, or on a positive response from, those army personnel coming home on leave. Many have conflicts of loyalties between their regiment and their people. Thus enemies as well as friends may be found within the one village. The feeling of apprehension is voiced in the line of a poem 'our enemy is everywhere in Hindustan, even in its leaves'.

Guerrillas and the rural population: counter-insurgency and its effects

The Tarn Taran area

It was police treatment of civilians that had driven the population to support the guerrillas and that had made the ground so fertile for guerrilla operations. They had the terrain prepared for them, for the alienation of people from government was complete in the 1984–86 period. Equally it was police operations that would detach those very same guerrillas from their friendly bases in the local population. The number of groups within the KCF subsequent to 1988 proliferated and their rise was fostered and exploited to gain information on the supporting population and to drive a wedge between them and that population. In the process, the confidence of ordinary people in both police and guerrillas was destroyed. The confusion of militant and criminal was one of the successes of the police and intelligence forces. Such confusion was particularly noticeable in the Tarn Taran area on two visits in 1992 and 1993. In the Tarn Taran area the police showed a marked tolerance for what may be called the gangster element; it was as though the latter were being used to partially keep the area down. Some groups were also intelligence creations and others were simply loose alliances to manage security and profit. The population got caught between local power struggles between militant groups and between police and militants, while also having to protect itself from criminals. A large part of the problem for ordinary villagers was that they had no means to identify a genuine militant. At one stage a family would be visited by persons masquerading as militants with their loosely tied turbans and their AKs. At another stage, the same family would be confronted by the same persons dressed as police who accused them of feeding and sheltering militants overnight and then either killed them outright or took from them a large sum of money. Innumerable families could report events of such nature. Police intelligence was bent on detaching the population from the militants, through such terror or through defamation. Also, it was recruiting record numbers of young people to join the intelligence services from the border villages (intelligence source, February 1993).

When it came to creating divisions in militant ranks, one of the very first members of the first Panthic Committee from the Tarn Taran area, Gurbachan Singh Manochahal, came in useful. Manochahal had the same level of education as most militants, that is, he was a matric.

pass. He had been a surveyor in the army's artillery division. He became a *granthi* after he left the army and joined Bhindranwale for a couple of years. After that, he lived at his home in the village of Naushera Pannuan and often, after *bhogs*, he would give his thoughts to the people in rhymed form. He became locally influential, and, when he came to know there were letters allegedly written by Guru Gobind Singh lying scattered in some of the *gurdwaras* he built a new *gurdwara* to house them. In the words of one schoolteacher from his village:

> After 1988 leading personalities in the movement started to clash and formed their separate groups and they therefore had to collect their own money and weapons. The other groups didn't like him much as he always wanted to be on top and the Pakistanis had no faith in him. Since he was in need of weapons he had to collect from the people. Many others were collecting money in his name. Most of the people in his group were smugglers and his weapons came through them. When one is powerful, people tend to cling to one. And the police were quite keen to see him continue with this way of operating because it was one they understood.

This indeed consisted of nothing more than snatching wealth and power in traditional style, collecting a following on a personal basis and thereby damaging the militant cause. Balbir Singh Sandhu, a General Secretary of the Council of Khalistan, a body which existed in the pre-1984 days to further the cause of independence, said in conversation that when Manochahal had left Pakistan in December 1989 after collecting 18 lakh rs. from outside, he had told him 'I'm going to take this money and buy property in the Tarn Taran area. Nobody can become a political leader without money and status.'

However, his activities puzzled and silenced the people. He was responsible for innumerable kidnappings and a fair amount of extortion. Such behaviour was quite consistent with police policy of bringing discredit and ill fame onto those associated with the struggle and, indeed, it freed them to deal with those genuine militants and finally, to tame them. Observers report that he had two weaknesses. He could not leave his wife for long and he was always to be found in his in-laws' house. Secondly, he had a huge ego and could spend hours at a time listening to tapes singing his own praises (*jagowali* tapes, as they are called), in which the recitations are sung without instrument. His in-laws' village was guarded by the CRP, and Manochahal merely took this to be an indication of his own importance. As reported by those who knew him well, it appeared that he was true to himself rather than the Sikh cause. All he wished for was to become a local leader. His mentality was local. Since he was not a threat, and useful in creating the terror in the area that the state needed to be ascribed to a militant, he was surrounded by a certain amount of protection. Unlike

Sukhwinder Gora, who was also in his home area for many years, or Gurjant Singh Budhsinghwala who rarely left his home area, he was not popular. Yet he remained there, since, until the militant movement was smashed, his divisive personal qualities suited state purposes.

The Tarn Taran area in which he functioned was close to the border with Pakistan. There were few chances for employment off the land, save in the army and police. Traditionally there had been a lot of smuggling in the area. The countryside was swarming with police. There were vehicular checks at all road crossing points, whether main roads or link roads, and at every canal junction. Both the police and the military were present in far greater numbers than elsewhere in Punjab. There was also a higher preponderance of police and army commandos among them. In their day-to-day experience, ordinary villagers found themselves harassed by both police and militants. The population felt preyed upon. One small farmer said that the police demanded vegetables from him. If he refused, they said they would register him as a militant. Every third day or so, he said, they would come demanding vegetables, and then in the night militants would ask for milk and food. 'I'd gladly give them food' he said 'because in our religion it says share. But I resent having a gun pointed at me when they ask for food. And if our religion says share. They must know that too.' He was implying, as indeed did many other farmers, that the boys were willing to take, and to pass on the trouble of their presence, but were not there to defend the people when the police came the next morning.

Most villagers I talked to in Rataul, Behla, Sangha, Sarhali, Chowla, Usman, Jamarai, Naushera Pannuan, Sursingh, and Sabrawan lived in a state of total fear of all armed groups. Most of all, families were bothered about their sons being implicated in false cases. For example, one night militants came to the house of a schoolteacher in Naushera Pannuan, asking for a meal. Police informers came to know and the police arrived the next day.

> I gave them assurances that I was not linked to the militants in any way. They then asked me how many children I had. When they found out I had a son of 23, they said, produce him in the police station. We didn't do so for fear of the torture they might inflict on him. This is the reason why people usually give money to the police, to save their families. We gave no money and they have not arrested him though they have a case pending against him to strike fear in us. We have thirty acres and they assess how much we can pay by looking at the size of our house and our land holding.

A farmer owning one hundred acres describes his experiences of life in the area:

> My three sons were standing outside our house which is on the Tarn Taran Fatehabad road. The SSP Tarn Taran happened to be passing. He thought the boys looked very suspicious and he flashed a wireless message. My sons were then roughed up and thrown into jeeps. Luckily I knew the local SHO and he intervened on behalf of my sons. I asked him, didn't we even have a right to stand in front of our own house? My house was searched but I got my sons out of jail. Subsequently, my youngest son of eight years of age was kidnapped by the Manochahal group. By paying a heavy ransom I secured his release. I suppose he was kidnapped because of my affluence. Having property in this area one is scared of both the police and militants alike. For although the ideas of the guerrilla movement remain, the movement itself is in bad hands, while the police are both judge and executioner.

The picture throughout the Tarn Taran and Patti countryside was that the wealthier families were leaving their property and abandoning good holdings for life in the cities. There were many kidnappings of retired military personnel. This was not just for weapons. They were targets because they were presumed to be militant sympathisers. It was also useful to create a degree of alienation between this category of respectable citizen and the militants to ensure that no sympathetic quarter would be given. One army Major stated to me 'Whatever is happening in the Tarn Taran area, is happening because of the Punjab police. First, Ajit Singh Sandhu [the SSP] comes from the area and has local knowledge of it – enough to break the back of the militant groups. Additionally, because of his initial low rank, he wants to make good quick just as some militants and criminals are doing.'

During 1992 police made people fed up with the militants, all the better to control them. Thus there was in the end no sanctuary for them. Many were created by the police or by the chaos that the police had been happy to see flourish. So since they did not belong to the people, it was the people who informed on their whereabouts. When they were eventually killed, there was no protest from the people. On my visit in September 1992, there was overall relief that the activities of extortionists were being curbed and that one could walk in one's orchards or one's fields without fear of abduction. By January 1993 fear of the police had increased further, although people were happy and could carry on with their everyday lives. Yet a silent, sullen hatred, visible in so many eyes, could wait many a long day for revenge. The dinners that were offered to policemen implied no feeling of friendliness towards them, simply a need for survival.

At Behla andărataul, village populations were made to pay collectively for their harbouring of militants. In outright blatant fashion, massive police and military force was used against these villages which became, in effect, free fire zones. At Rataul, in early May 1992, militants had kidnapped six boys and brought them to a house in the village where, allegedly, a bunker had been constructed. They had lost their nerve and, fearing an attack, they had released the boys, who then told the police about the militant presence in the village. Twice the entire village population was subjected to a house-to-house search. The police found no militants; but on the third occasion they were surprised by eight militants who opened fire and killed two policemen. A 72-hour encounter began, in which eight militants were killed and the entire population beaten up. The police were going to use petrol to burn the houses involved to the ground, but the army personnel on duty prevented this. There was much damage to the two affected houses. In one of the houses all the clothes had been burned, the *sandook* or large chest had been riddled by bullets and the interior walls of the house were peppered by six-inch deep bullet marks. There was no compensation. Rather, as the lady of one of the houses concerned put it, if they found 10 rs. they took it. She was traumatised by these happenings. Inhabitants told me that the police collected young boys and put them in front while they did house-to-house searches. For three days they kept people away from their homes – that is, evacuated them – and for three days they were free to take whatever gold and valuables they found. One old man said to me 'We can stand this destruction', pointing to their ruined homes, 'We accept the damage. But this humiliation at the hands of the police is unforgettable and unforgivable.' The latter statement was a reference to the entire population of the village having been beaten.

However, it was Behla that was most famous of all for collective punishments. A live encounter took place in this village on the nights of 10 and 11 June 1992 and, because it lasted so long, army assistance was required. The background to the incident is the friction between two brothers Gurminder Singh Behla and Manjinder Singh Behla over landed property of just over one hundred acres, twenty-five acres of which was in orchards. Manjinder also had stables containing prize stallions. The property had been owned jointly in their mother's name. She refused to divide it between her sons. In practice it had been run by the younger brother Gurminder, while Manjinder, the better educated of the two, occupied political posts, having been a former member of the Legislative Assembly and an ex-Minister. Over a period of four to five years from 1984, Gurminder began deceiving Manjinder over payments from the land produce. To prevent Manjinder entering his own property, he contacted a militant of the BTFK, a group affiliated to Manochahal, by the name of Surjit Singh Behla, who was an ex-army man of small farmer background. The militants shot dead a prize stallion belonging to Manjinder and sent him threatening letters regarding his life. This suited Gurminder. However, slowly they gained control over Gurminder by giving him protection and buying his land at throwaway prices. In course of time they constructed a sealed bunker behind the kitchen where they could hide and evade arrest.

The immediate events leading up to the encounter start off with a workman giving a statement to the police, under interrogation, that he had made a bunker at Behla. This was followed by a police raid. They did not expect to find militants there at the time, but were surprised by Surjit Behla. The militants shot two police on the spot and the remaining police officials got trapped on top of the house. As is reported in the *Tribune* of 12 June, '[a] helicopter was used to rescue the trapped security personnel including the SSP Tarn Taran and two deputy commandants of the CRPF.' This was the beginning of a 36-hour long encounter in which two of the militants fought with security personnel including one battalion of the army. In this battle police picked up ten people and used them as human shields (that is, hostages), one of whom was a close relative of Surjit Singh Behla. Two of these human shields just happened to be working at a tube well in the neighbouring fields. Others included six relatives from the house of Surjit Behla's uncle six miles away. They were badly injured. The whole house was reduced to rubble. Gurminder was forced to sell his share of the land which had been purchased by the militants. Police took it over and refused to let anyone till it. However, as of January 1993, the property is being restored to him. Manjinder is buying new horses. Both brothers now live separately in Amritsar. For the villagers of Behla, the ending was not so happy. The dead persons and their relatives were branded as militants. Even the famous wrestler Dara Singh, now an old man, was taken to Tarn Taran police station. He reported that the bodies of the dead had not been cremated according to Sikh rites and their ashes were never returned to their families.

In the above case, the militants involvement in a family dispute had brought down the wrath of the state upon the villagers of Behla. Land disputes within the family and between neighbours were a major cause of state violence in villages. For example, the landlord mentioned in case three of Chapter 1 held as much land on his own as had the three brothers on a neighbouring farm. It was they who were suspected of spreading a rumour that he was harbouring Manochahal, and for this reason his farm had been surrounded by the CRPF. The villagers were domesticating the guerrilla struggle and making it serve their own immediate ends within the village structure. The public as a whole were using the young guerrillas in their own internal conflicts whether within the family, or the village. Likewise the police were using these rivalries and feuds for their own purposes to create fear and distrust and divert the mainstream struggle. Both militants and police were predominantly Jat Sikhs.

The Behla case shows the way in which the militant movement's goals can be warped not only by the self-limitation of individual guerrillas and their opportunism, but also by the lack of overall discipline. It seemed, also, that it was the local, contingent and situational factors that were affecting the viability of the militant struggle. At any one time, the attitude of local populations to the guerrillas shows considerable variation. On a Punjab-wide basis, the pattern of support for the insurgency differed from district to district. Even within the one area, the Tarn Taran area, impressions of the guerrillas who came from other than Manochahal's group were positive. The boys who came from Gurdaspur – that is the KCF (Zaffarwal) – were said 'to speak properly and to be educated' according to one army officer who had met them while being held captive by Manochahal. He said 'Even though I was technically a prisoner, they were polite to me, asking how long I'd been in the army. One of them was a doctor and the other had been in the National Security Guard [NSG] and had left because of the torture he had witnessed.'

Impressions of the Babbar Khalsa were also good because they always paid for their food. In the Tarn Taran area, therefore, it appeared that the state was using Manochahal against these other groups. The state's exploitation of rivalries, looting and fear for one's life neutralised the population. In this atmosphere such harassment as was perpetrated by genuine militants occurred at a point of desperation when police and informers were everywhere. It was a reaction to not knowing who was who in the houses into which they went. This was especially pronounced in the case of new recruits. Nonetheless, when a group of militants entered the house of a family in the middle of the night, its inhabitants were not to know whether the type of behaviour they exhibited was the result of their unease, fear and inexperience or was such as to present a real and tangible threat to their lives: the prelude to an attack. It was a terrifying time.

Districts Bathinda and Faridkot

'We love them. They are exactly like their name – *kharkhus* – brave persons willing and committed to fight for a just cause' (small farmer, District Bathinda). This was a fairly unambiguous comment reflective of the general feeling towards militants in this region as encountered in October 1992. Bathinda and Faridkot were the areas of operation of Gurjant Singh Budhsinghwala of the Khalistan Liberation Force (KLF), who was killed on 29 July 1992. Since my visit in October 1992, the area has suffered greatly from killings of its young men by paramilitaries.

Budhsinghwala's family owned sixteen acres of land in District Faridkot. It was good land because of the subsoil water. They were traditional supporters of the Akali Party and particularly of the ex-

Chief Minister of the Punjab, Parkash Singh Badal, who came from the area. His father had campaigned for the Akali Dal (Badal) candidate, Shaminder Singh, who was killed in the campaign for the aborted June elections. Budhsinghwala was a religious person and unmarried at the age of twenty-seven when he was killed. Speaking of his son, his father said:

> Gurjant went his own way because he was a dedicated, devoted Sikh. However, prior to 1984, an incident had taken place at Bibi Kahan Kaur *gurdwara* in Moga in which eight Sikhs were killed by the BSF and the CRPF. One of our elderly relatives had been helping with their *bhogs*, and thereafter the police picked him up and tortured him. Gurjant went underground at that time. I was arrested and sent to Ferozepur jail [he showed me the burn marks on his legs, the legacy of his stay there]. I was acquitted during Barnala's period in office. But after the Barnala government lost power, terror was let loose. All our family were beaten publicly and my brother was killed in custody while Gobind Ram was DSP here. For three years we couldn't come to our land or our house and none were allowed to rent the land either. We stayed with relations and the whole village took it in turn to give us our meals. The police had removed the hand pump and all our kitchen utensils and the tube well.
>
> Gurjant had only 1½ years' education but he had learned further while in jail. At Akali conferences he had come to know Kulwant Singh Khukhrana B.A. and they had become like brothers while underground. Later Manohar Singh Tira advised him. He had always been influenced by religious persons throughout his life and he was not the type to murder people indiscriminately. He thought that Hindus who speak Punjabi should be allowed to stay in Punjab. Only he wondered why those who participated in the massacres of 1984 were not punished. This is why the divide is deepening, he thought. He thought they are responsible for that deepening divide.

Budhsinghwala had been popular enough in his area to be able to remain there almost always. He had refrained from killing people in the rural areas or engaging in looting and extortion. Outside the area, his organisation, the KLF, were blamed for the train massacres at Kila Raipur and Baddowal on 15 June 1991, in which seventy-four Hindus were killed, and at Sohian on 27 December in which sixty people were killed. He was also blamed for the murder of Indian engineers at Indian Acrylics, a factory at Bhawanigarh, District Sangrur on 10 March 1992. However, it was difficult to see these complicated initiatives being planned just at the right moment, with exact co-ordination as to para-military and police deployments, by some one who had only 1½ years' education, whose family were apparently decent and involved in democratic politics, and who had, above all, a religious disposition of a non-fanatical nature. Moreover, in each of these incidents the perpetrators spent a long time at the scene of the crime, suggesting that they had security cover. For usually at the sound of gunfire mobile units of police and paramilitary reinforcements arrive in large numbers within minutes. Additionally, at Kila Raipur and Badowal, the actions took place in the middle of the day. Furthermore, ten people would usually not be involved in an operation, as at Sohian, if it were a guerrilla operation. At Sohian, the fact that those killed were killed at close range meant that the killing must have taken time. Time and men are what guerrilla units do not have to waste.

I did not manage to meet any eye witnesses of the train massacres but did meet one of the managers of Indian Acrylics at the time of the massacre. He is the son of a DSP and his account is as follows:

> Indian Acrylics was a 250 crore project technologically supplied by Dupont. We were going to manufacture Orlon. It was at the stage of commissioning. All we managers were still sitting in the plant at 7.30 in the evening of the 10th March as we used to work late. At 7.30 a call came from the personnel manager at the residential complex that there were some miscreants about. When we got there we saw three, two of whom had AK-47s. Our chief executive, a Sikh, tried to reason with them, saying that we would abide by their conditions and that we were only employees. They took out eighteen non-Punjabis and put them in three rows of six according to height. Four men did the killing. Out of eighteen, two were saved. They spent forty-five minutes inside the complex. This incident was witnessed by their wives and children.
>
> I have heard that this incident could have been one of industrial rivalry. Also on the day that it occurred Beant Singh [the Chief Minister of Punjab] and other ministers were in the company of the Managing Director of the plant in Chandigarh. He hosted a dinner on that very same night. I also heard that it might be a political stunt to devalue the Congress Party. After the elections, this was the first major incident. However, the letter that I was forced to read out simply said that the Punjab and Delhi governments were not giving jobs to Punjabis and that it was objectionable that the plant was going to use imported raw materials. They wanted to tell the Punjab and Delhi governments that they would not sell the land of Punjab. The letter was signed by Panjwar and Budhsinghwala.

This was an unlikely combination, even though the two men were part of an alliance, the CJJ. The only other connexion between them appears to be that they stayed in the houses of two landlords who were connected by ties of marriage. Whatever were the facts of the case, as one political worker reported:

> Whenever a police officer who had been a butcher was killed, people were happy. However, if selected innocent people were killed for political ends, as at Sohian and Indian Acrylics, people were not happy. But the media and the newspapers would blow up these stories for international consumption, and to some extent militants would think it to be a good action and would

> be reluctant to condemn it even though not involved in it. But those militants who were based with the people were told by the people that they were upset over these happenings.

The consensus view, from a wide range of people to whom I talked, was that the strategy of these massacres and killings was planned elsewhere.[7] It was also a general view that they were carried out with a view to discrediting a group that appeared to have roots among the population. The massacres were carried out within Budhsinghwala's supposed area of control or near to it and attributed to him. He may have suffered as a consequence. As one local lawyer expressed the matter 'What happened to Budhsinghwala was a product of the alienation of militants from the public.' Yet I doubt this. It may have had nothing to do with the public but more to do with the police and intelligence services. For as Kanwar Sandhu (October 1992) pointed out in an interview 'When it came to the bit, Gill was able to control militant activity within three months. When the police wanted to control it, they did.' All the main militant leaders, with the exception of one, were taken in the July–September period of 1992.

No evidence was given to me to suggest that the roaming squads of hitmen that suddenly would descend on trains had anything to do with Budhsinghwala. I doubt if there was any public alienation from him in his home area over the murders of Hindus because, as the next few pages show, peoples' minds were preoccupied in struggling with their own problems. His father's description of his son's *bhog* certainly shows no such alienation.

> Our son was martyred on the 29th July. Nobody could come to his *bhog* from his own or nearby villages. There were two thousand police all around. We held the *bhog* here in the house and noticed that the Sikh officers behaved in a very respectful manner. However, there was a loudspeaker on the roof and one Sikh DSP advised us to disconnect it because of the Hindu SP in charge of operations. The behaviour of the Sikh officers contrasted with that man's, who was standing opposite our house smoking.

Happenings to families in the area

There was barely any visible presence of the CRP or the BSF who were so noticeable policing the GT roads in districts Ludhiana, Jalandhar and Amritsar. In October 1992 there were none in sight over vast stretches of road in Sangrur, Bathinda and Faridkot. Yet despite the lack of any overt presence, families were experiencing the same terror as those in other districts. The Movement Against State Repression listed the names of a total number of 164 persons killed by police encounter in one district alone, District Bathinda, during the period

1 January 1991 to 29 February 1992 (Annexure 6 of documents sent to the United Nations Secretary-General by Inderjit Singh Jaijee of the Movement Against State Repression on 20 March 1993, entitled 'State killings in Punjab').

Quoting one father, 'The police pick up the young, especially if they have long, flowing beards.' He had lost his three sons. Many young people were missing from the villages, disappearing after an ordinary errand such as taking their tractor to the city to get mended, or picked up as they returned from a relative's house or going to their fields. Most of the missing persons had been abducted by plain-clothes police. When children had gone underground, their elderly relatives were picked up. One mother was picked up in place of her son by police on 2 September 1991. Since then, no one has heard anything about her even though her son was killed on 30 January 1992. What happened to people was very arbitrary and sudden. For example, one old man had his house demolished and his cotton crop destroyed. He lived in an isolated place at his tube well. This had formerly been an indicator of prosperity but, under the new conditions of armed struggle, such habitations attracted police and militants alike. Since the destruction of his property he has been living in the *gurdwara*. All of this happened because 1½ years ago, he had sheltered an area commander at his house under duress for two to three days.

Militants in this area did not commit the same wrongs against the people as they did in the Tarn Taran area. Hence, once families were able to lift their feelings out of their own particular loss, they would tell one that 'People who are doing wrong are going scot-free. We're just ordinary working people but we feel that precisely because of that we need our own sovereign home' (small farmer). 'We want our own sovereignty now. We've lost too much: our honour, our respect, our dignity. We've been greatly humiliated. And we cannot afford to lose more of our children. So we need our own country' (farmer with larger than average size holding, formerly in service).

In the villages I visited, people would gather, sometimes twenty to thirty at a time, anxious to have their own particular case recorded. It was most moving. Although these cases – almost always of paramilitary or police irregularity – are a replica of what happens in other parts of Punjab, I will present two of them, to whom justice has not been done.

1. Joginder Kaur, mother of Gurmit Singh, aged 19, from Faridkot.

'My son wanted to escape abroad as he had been involved in the movement as a youngster and had been imprisoned for a while. He had escaped, only to be caught at Bombay airport. Our local Muktsar police went to Bombay and produced an order before a judicial magistrate that he be returned to Punjab. The defence counsel petitioned the court that there was grave danger to his life if he were sent back to Punjab and that he feared liquidation at the hands of the police. The court produced an order [5/7/89] that he be kept in safe custody. But I feared for my son's life and sent telegrams to the Chief Justice, Punjab, the SSP Faridkot and the DC Faridkot. These telegrams said "My son Gurmit Singh of Machaki Kalan has been brought from Bombay by local police. Fear false encounter. Save his life."

'The court's order was not complied with. We claimed his dead body but they would not agree, either to handing over his body, or to a post mortem. In a telegram to the DSP Muktsar, I said that I wanted a post mortem done elsewhere as the local doctors were under the influence of the police. I asked them not to cremate my son before that was done. That was not agreed to. I was told he had been killed by snake bite. I was allowed to approach the body but not to touch it. I noticed there were depressions in his head and blood in his eyes and that an arm had been broken. There were black and blue abrasions around his neck. He was my only son.'

2. Man Singh, retired police constable, police station Sadiq, District Faridkot. This family had a thirty-acre land holding. The following story is related by his wife.

'On the night of 23rd July, 1990, two gypsies [a type of jeep] and one van stopped at a turn in the road one kilometre or so away from our house. Eight to nine persons came to the house on foot. Five came in and four surrounded the house. Two caught hold of my son and asked him to call his father. He shouted to him that government commandos had come. Their faces were masked. They greeted Man Singh but he did not reply "Come out to the courtyard, talk to us," they said. Meanwhile two persons took hold of my son and they shot my husband in front of his very eyes. Then, as he tried to escape, they killed him. He was only sixteen at the time and had just passed his matriculation exam. I recognised one man in this group, a head constable, because of my husband having served with the police. So I informed the SHO and the DSP Mamdot. Their response was to kill my elder son while he was watering his fields. They left the dead body lying there. Another of my sons was underground at the time. Whether or not all that happened was a punishment to the family, I don't know. He has since been involved in a fake murder case and tortured. Afterwards, police threatened us, forcing us to blame what had happened to us on the militants. We could not come to our house for 1½ years. We took shelter at Chowk Mehta. My remaining son has been arrested many times, the last time for harbouring militants, though the courts acquitted him in August 1992.

Frequently it would not be an individual's intention to get caught up in things, but one could not prevent militants arriving at one's door, no more than one could predict Operation Woodrose in 1984. For example, at the time of Operation Woodrose, Randhir Singh of village Rampura, police station Phul, District Bathinda was running a dairy farm on a commercial basis. He had fertile land and it was a successful business. However, he was a baptised Sikh and so, during that operation, he was picked up and imprisoned on a false charge. This happened time and time again. So eventually he lost his dairy farm, as no one but himself had the expertise to run it.

Experiences of villagers with the security forces in the the Dehlon–Samrala–Macchiwara area of District Ludhiana were no different to those described for Tarn Taran and Bathinda/Faridkot. However, the degree of support for the militant movement in late 1992 was higher. As one ex-serviceman stated 'There is a Sikh movement in all of the two hundred villages of the Samrala–Macchiwara area. Neither have the people gone against the militants nor have the militants harmed the people. There have been no extortions in our villages. And more police repression is not alienating us from the militants, rather it is helping us to close our ranks with them.'

The Samrala–Macchiwara area of districts Ludhiana and Ropar had been the area of operation of Rachpal Chhandran, who was an immensely popular area commander. Belonging to a small farmer's family, his father and brother had been killed and Chhandran himself was brutally tortured while in police custody in June 1992, the police pulling out his eyes. The crowds of people wishing to attend his *bhog* ceremony stretched for miles.

On the basis of the evidence so far presented it is not sufficient merely to say that militancy presented diverse patterns from area to area. Its pattern also varied within the one area, depending on the activities of the local area commander – not only whether he refrained from killing innocent people in his area, but also whether he protected them. Within the one militant group, both extortionists and principled people were working. For example, Chhandran had a very different character to that of Manochahal and evoked different responses from the people, though both were part of the BTFK. Villagers were responsive to the character and nature of the local area commanders and their view of the struggle for independence was one determined by those in charge of their areas and how they behaved with them and their families.

The issue of extortion and the general condition of society

The issue of extortion has been referred to frequently in the preceding pages. From a historical point of view, Sarabjit Singh's account is useful as he had taken over as DC Amritsar in 1987:

> It was after 1988 that extortions began in earnest. Before, with the terrorists concentrated in the Temple, they merely telephoned a rich person in the city to come with guns, or if not, then to provide the money to pay for them. Only a very few extremely rich people were touched. They could come up with this money and the terrorists were very polite to them. An implied threat was there, but no explicit threat was given that you'll be eliminated. Since they stayed in the Temple they could not make private use of the money. Once out of the Temple, many who were criminals or who had criminal leanings, and who never had any political ideology, thought that they could become rich by joining the terrorist ranks. Extortions and kidnappings started occurring irrespective of a man's ability to pay. And when the Babbars stopped illicit distillation, many of the criminals involved in that started kidnapping for money instead. The early extortions conducted from a central base within the Golden Temple were for weapons and money and they were used for the movement. Then Pakistan picked up the movement and gave a lot of guns free. You could enlarge your group only if you had weapons with you. And weapons were coming in the trolley load. The base increased, the leadership lost control and political idealism went out the window. The weapons kept on flowing and it was clear by the end of 1989 that no political ideology was guiding the movement. Economic interests were guiding it, sustaining it in fact, especially the unemployment and the economic advantage that participation could bring. Some terrorists purchased land. This gave incentives to other youths to join and because of this and the weapons, their ranks swelled. The police have been the gainers in all of this. The boys themselves came to the police if they had broken with their group, offering to trade information for weapons.

The paramilitary police in particular were a direct contributor to the state of lawlessness that would eventually engulf Punjab. They were part of the atmosphere in which extortion became acceptable and which made it impossible for farmers to function within the limits of the law. For example, it was not possible for an indebted farmer's family to secure the release of a family member when the police demanded a large bribe. If they were not to sell off their land and their entire property, as in some cases they did, it was virtually impossible to find this money legally. The old man mentioned on p. 124, whose house was demolished simply because a militant had stayed in it overnight, as it was in an out of the way place, and whose crop had been destroyed, could not stay in a *gurdwara* forever. If he had sons, no doubt one of them would join a militant group and acquire the money to rebuild their house.

As has been noted, extortion was political policy, especially in areas such as Tarn Taran. However, the movement was exploited in very many different ways. As one doctor expressed it 'everyone was into the business of making the movement work for them'. A former IG of police recounted how 'even ordinary decent people are extorting. For example, the stepbrother of Giani Kartar Singh [a respected politician, now dead] was extorting money on the letter pads of the KCF. He was receiving sums of money duly deposited in his bank.'

Less than ordinary people were also using the situation to take what they could, as an article by the journalist Ravi Sidhu, in *The Hindu* about a well-known Akali politician shows ('Terror Rules Chandigarh', 3 December 1991). Usually those who were the victims of this sort of activity received no protection from higher authority. Close to 62 Majitha Road, Amritsar, there runs a small lane. The inhabitants of number 62 are long-standing friends of the DIG Police Jalandhar Range, Gur Iqbal Singh Bhullar. Their son was constantly losing motor bikes on that lane. Eventually the family found the person responsible: he was none other than the son of a local DSP. They reported it to Bhullar who advised them to do nothing. He himself did nothing. 'You see,' said Gurdarshan Singh Grewal, 'there is a problem with who is joining the police.' He then proceeded to relate the experience of an industrialist from Ludhiana. 'Not only was he rich, he was very well connected with both the police and army administration. And one day while sitting in his office he noticed four Sikhs, unknown to him, but armed, approaching. They were asking for the owner. He telephoned senior members of the police and the army. When the police arrived they recognised them as their men. "They are not militants," they told the industrialist, "we've sent them for your security".'

The owner of Escort Agencies outside Amritsar felt very nervous about the policemen assigned to him for his safety. He told me 'One never knows who their brothers are in the villages and what sorts of connection they have.' Precisely because of that he also employed two of his own security guards to watch the police. Escort Agencies handled the tractors through which 50% of the food grains from two districts arrived on the market. He also had a high yield sunflower crop, on the produce of which militants were extracting a percentage. He had been the subject of a kidnapping attempt and he said 'If they were to demand a one time payment that would be one thing. But people ask for payment regularly and not only that, several groups ask.'

Nijjar Farms, also on the main GT road outside of Amritsar, which grew the largest number of varieties of tomato in the Indian subcontinent, as well as having the largest plant for tomato processing, paid no money in bribes, though it had been demanded frequently. Their house was like a fortress. They had a bulletproof car and two professional gunmen.

The contours of the situation in which extortion became rampant, as well as other forms of behaviour not accepted by traditional society, had developed cumulatively over a period. Shiva has mentioned the degenerate consumption that was part and parcel of the way of life introduced by the Green Revolution, laying strong stress on the alcoholism and drug addiction that had fostered family breakdown. To this I would add that in the pre-1984 period, the political world was setting its own goals in the shape of the Anandpur Sahib resolution; goals that were realizable. There had been a peaceful mass movement for political change. Yet this democratic approach achieved nothing. So disillusionment had set in already before the events of 1984. Then, following these events in both Amritsar and Delhi, the spirit of resistance, fostered in many, gave way to despair and hopelessness in some. A few were recovered by the Babbar Khalsa and the Akhand Kirtani Jatha, with their message of inner hope rather than societal rejuvenation. Idealists who had previously only had death before them or who could not cope with events as they unfolded, turned to 'normal' channels, trying to settle down with a family and a job. Yet when they could not find a job, what route was to be taken? As one IAS officer commented 'Even those who had passed their matriculation could see no future so far as employment was concerned, and in the Punjab, people are out for a government job. That is their first preference.'

The disillusionment produced much gratuitous violence, a violence unconnected to the political movement and not associated with the political struggle in that it did not purport to further its aims. However, it was produced by the political situation, particularly by the absence of a climate of hope. The violence had political impact – the militants could not control it, while the police used it as an excuse to attack local habitations physically, and for propaganda purposes. In this climate it would have been relatively easy for an intelligence agency to pick up a number of civilians for random atrocities on civilians of the type described on pp. 120–3 of this chapter. All values were overturned by the state itself, as it attacked traditional groups who had respect in society: the landlord who carried out his responsibilities, the ex-serviceman who had served the country, etc. A certain social breakdown was in evidence. How otherwise could mothers be dragged off to police stations and beaten in place of their sons; the old tortured by the young; daughters of eminent persons gunned down; respected persons killed in a hail of bullets; the talented and able murdered on the open road. And the lives of ordinary farming families were ruined by plundering bands. There was an orgy of murder after 1988. To small farmer families it mattered little whether these bands belonged to the militants or the police. It was not surprising that it was the view of people in Amritsar and in much of the surrounding countryside in 1992 that such activities as went on in the name of militancy had, in fact, no ideological basis, and that the militant groups were Mafia-like networks. Yet that was what counter-organization meant to achieve. Counter-organization is a term used to describe a method by which the government can build up its control of the population and frustrate the enemy's efforts at doing so (Kitson, 1971: 79). In the Punjab, this counter-organisation was confined almost exclusively to the field of special operations, using gangs, turncoats, informers, captured guerrillas and the building of new gangs. However, as has been indicated there is some suspicion that the leaders of the CJJ were an integral part of the government's counter-insurgency network, some of them without knowing how or why.

Counter-organisation

The roots of counter-insurgency go back to Ribeiro's role as police chief when, as noted, he inducted such elements into the militant movement as would malign its cause. In the name of militancy, these groups created terrror, endeavouring to break the ties between militants and people. When the police gives protection to certain activities such as kidnapping and looting, rape and murder, signals are given that this behaviour is tolerated so long as you are powerfully patronised. This was an unfortunate lure for many young boys. That it was a lure at all was because of the division in the movement in 1988 and the creation of a new Panthic Committee with different aims. Subsequently, the CJJ's concern became, not social justice and the collective well-being of the Sikhs, but an alleged personal purity. This led the Sikhs in a different direction to that outlined in the programme of the Sarbat Khalsa resolution of 1986. It is not surprising that there was some confusion in militant ranks, particularly among the ideologically committed and their supporters. Descriptions of counter-insurgency gangs begin appearing in the newspapers during 1988 and continue so long as the CJJ has hegemony. It was during the same period that arms were coming into the Punjab on a large scale and militant groups were proliferating. According to Zaffarwal, the arms going into India through BSF-protected routes were being monitored and controlled by the Sohan Singh Panthic Committee. Regarding the counter-organisation described by Kitson, its more overt nature in the Punjab was as follows:

> The police had letter pads of all militant organisations. Additionally they had set up what were purely their own organisations [the Khalistan Armed Force under Shamsher Singh and the Khalistan Liberation Army of Bhai

> Kanwar Singh]. They would issue statements on the behalf of the militants. They had set up their own area commanders throughout the Punjab. They would have their own Lieutenant-Generals, give them prominence in the newspapers, saying he's killed so many. Thereby they would keep on increasing the reward on his life that they can claim. Whenever these people are killed, there is never any informer. Police take the reward money.[8] Frequently, when these groups or organizations have been formed their alleged leaders are already in custody. They would nominate one of them as Lieutenant-General, say he has been killed after a while, and then claim the reward money. Then they will announce the name of another in their custody and in his name many murders and lootings will be carried out. After a while he'll be killed too. Latterly they have simply threatened the relatives of the boys, taken them hostage, then approached the boy, built him up, made him popular and left him in place for a while to collect information, paying him 5,000 rs per month, but holding his relatives in custody as security.

The above is a condensed version of a recorded conversation between a journalist and a political worker. Arguably the CJJ leaders and some of their cadre were part of this counter-organization. Doubts were raised in many quarters about the connection of the CJJ leaders with the intelligence services. They had survived a long time and they were all captured around the same time. Sukhdev Singh Babbar was killed in an encounter deemed by some to be a false encounter in August 1992 (see the article by Simranjit Singh Mann, 'Fake encounters of the Brutal Kind', *The Telegraph* 10 October 1992). Budhsinghwala was killed in July 1992. According to local reports, Manochahal had been in custody since September 1992. A genuine ideologue of the Babbar Khalsa, Gurdip Singh Sibia, was called over to India from Pakistan in July 1992 by the Babbar Khalsa leadership. He found himself becoming the fall guy for the killing of Sukhdev Babbar. Sibia did not go to India of his own accord. He knew the dangers and he also knew he could not stand up to torture. These events raised suspicions that the Babbar leadership had some connections in intelligence circles. Perhaps as the dust settles it will be possible to further assess their role in the guerrilla movement and their identity.

A new state is not created by its mere declaration, and since the Sarbat Khalsa resolution of January 1986, the only guerrilla group remaining loyal to the programme outlined in that resolution has been the KCF (Zaffarwal). It has been able so to remain because it has had no contact with RAW. Immense psychological pressure has been placed on Zaffarwal and on Jarnail Singh Hoshiarpur to return to India.

I have related earlier how the CJJ's mode of operation, as well as its policies and personnel, certainly made them useful in undermining the movement. Firstly, they had divided the movement, setting up a new Panthic Committee with contradictory goals to the 1986 declaration of independence. These internal contradictions were easily utilised by the government in Delhi. Secondly, the marginalisation of political debate and dialogue by the CJJ served the interests of a government that was bent on suppressing the movement by force. The CJJ proceeded to identify the movement as fundamentalist and terrorist. It took responsibility for killing the youth federation leader, Harminder Singh Sandhu, and those in the KCF cadre who were committed and sincere. It justified these murders in terms of treachery to the Sikh cause, immorality, as in the case of Sursinghwala, and extortion, as in the case of Samra. Having established that those they had killed were traitors or immoral persons, not too much outrage was felt. As the French Resistance leader Claude Bourdet recounted regarding a murder in a very different place – that of Said Hammami, the PLO representative in London – in 1978 'There are many ways of provoking a killing. Other than doing it. Other than ordering it' (quoted in Seale, 1993: 163).

The leadership of the CJJ were allowed freedom of movement. Sohan Singh and Daljit Singh Bittoo travelled across the border all the time. Most of the CJJ leadership had passports. Sukhdev Babbar lived a completely normal life. They did not attack the security forces and did little to support the struggle, though they did impose rules for living on the Sikh people. Here their non-collectivist orientation and their stress on inward personal purity, at a time when the rural public was suffering brutal attacks on their lives and property by any group of bad characters who had guns, was tantamount to sending the message, turn your eyes away from these social happenings, it's only your immortal soul which counts. This, in turn, reinforced the fragmentation and atomization in a society that was already adequately individualistic. Most of their operations harmed the Sikhs and appeared to benefit the government. For example, whether the massacres attributed to Budhsinghwala were undertaken by him or not, or whether they were directed from other quarters, did not matter; their effect was to provoke cleaning-up operations in the areas where they occurred, in which innumerable young people were picked up at random, as well as giving the Sikhs the international reputation of being assassins. The rural population felt abandoned. It had been abandoned. The elimination of so many candidates in the June 1991 elections had the desired effect of sickening the public and by the time of the Manchanda killing (Manchanda was the Director of All India Radio Station, Patiala, murdered in May 1992) the public was mesmerised no longer by the alleged firepower of the CJJ. This indeed was to mark the beginning of the elimination of the leadership and cadres of the CJJ by the state. Terror in the name of an alleged militancy was removed. Direct, unmediated, police and paramilitary terror remained. These eliminations did not take place before the CJJ had served their usefulness in the February 1992 elections. All the militant organisations, but especially the KLF of Budhsinghwala and the KCF (Zaffarwal), had been in favour of participating in the elections. First the CJJ approached Badal to announce a boycott, which he did. Bittoo then telephoned Simranjit Singh Mann, speaking to him for one hour, requesting him not to participate. Panjwar subsequently made a threat against Mann's family members, according to a reporter from *The Hindu*. Some view the boycott as preparing the way for a Congress government, for the electorate did stay away from the polls due to threats issued by the CJJ.

According to Bard O'Neill (1990: 126), 'a key point to be addressed when evaluating a counter-insurgency programme is how well the government knows its enemy.'

Certainly under Gill's direction, the police exploited to perfection the divisiveness within rural society and among militant groups. The DGP on 22 October 1992 seemed to be in particularly happy mood, until all the encounter deaths and the indiscipline of his *thanedars* were mentioned. Happy that he had got rid of the Babbars, and more happy that Pakistan's intelligence network had been fooled, he said 'whoever controls their intelligence services, if I were Nawaz Sharif [the then Prime Minister of Pakistan], I'd sack him.'

Notes

1. *Indian Express*, 8 September 1989, 'The Cat is out of the Bag'; *Indian Express*, 14 September 1989, 'Police "Cats" Licence to Kill'; *Indian Express*, 15 July 1989, 'Terrorist Gangs Gun for each other'; *The Hindustan Times*, 11 August 1989, 'A Tale of Two Punjabs'; *The Sunday Tribune*, 16 April 1989 'Victims of Terrorists' Lusts'; *Indian Express*, 16 April 1990, 'Rape fear drives families out'; *Hindustan Times*, 24 April 1990 'Police Cats Confound Kidnap Confusion'.
2. This was a comment on a story reported by a freelance journalist that RAW was using imported AK-47s and RPG-7 anti-tank rocket-propelled grenades in incidents in the Punjab in order to justify the introduction of the 59th amendment to the constitution, by which government can impose an emergency on the state and suspend the right to life.
3. The *bhog* was a religious ceremony and occasion. However, in a situation in which there was little public political participation, *bhogs* were similar to paramilitary funerals in Northern Ireland, namely 'the ceremonial response to violent death' (Feldman, 1991: 106).
4. A report in the *Indian Express* of February 1993, and recorded as Annexure Two of a document sent by the Movement Against State Repression on 20 January 1993 to the United Nations Secretary General.
5. The army strength one year later was only ⅓ of that, and paramilitary numbers had dropped from 460 companies to 200 companies.
6. *India Today* 31 December also reports that elements of the BSF have been compromised by the rich profits from the gun smuggling trade and have failed to check the influx of weapons.

7. Everyone had their own theory and sources of information regarding these massacres. The journalist Kanwar Sandhu mentioned to me, with regard to Sohian, that the interrogation of one Supinder Singh had revealed that one of his accomplices was a grandson of the Chief Minister. A staunch supporter and member of the Babbar Khalsa thought that the boys, who had come from families who had suffered could perform such deeds easily. A third theory was that the government 'managed these incidents through their infiltrators'. The International Wing of the Panthic Committee condemned these incidents and issued the following statement dated 27 December 1991: 'For many years the Indian Intelligence Services have carried out the massacre of innocent people in buses and trains and have laid blame on the doorstep of the Khalistanis. These intelligence services have obtained the help of breakaway and bought over Sikh groups to aid and abet them in their killing of innocent people. The train massacres at Ludhiana yesterday is yet another such attempt to discredit our struggle and to create conditions in which the killing of countless Sikhs could continue unabated in the Punjab to hoodwink international public opinion in the name of countering terrorism.'

8. On 28 August 1993 the Punjab Civil Service demanded a 'Judicial Commission into the Rise and Decline of Militancy during President's rule *vis-à-vis* the role of the Police'. It stated 'inflated figures [of killings] were given in order to justify the extraordinarily high awards given for the killing of terrorists'.

TWO

Children of Waheguru

6
Introduction

These interviews – eleven in number – of which nine are presented in Chapter 7, were conducted during December 1989 and April 1991. They are the authentic voices of those who joined the Khalistan Commando Force, mainly young men from the ages of eighteen to twenty-six. I chose to give this section the title Children of Waheguru because those interviewed, with the exception of Zaffarwal, were so young and had been subjected to torture in the course of the interrogation process, during which they frequently invoked the name of Almighty God (Waheguru). They considered it was by His grace, blessing and authority that they would be free. This was not meant in a specifically religious way. Its meaning was political, namely that no government could bestow freedom. Only the Creator had that power and right. As with Kriger's account (1992: 7) of peasants in revolt in Zimbabwe, the interviews inform us 'of how much they suffered not only from the abuses of government forces but also from ... coercion [from other guerrilla groups]'. Thus Guha's query (1983: 15): 'How then are we to get in touch with the consciousness of insurgency when our access to it is barred by the discourse of counter insurgency.' is circumvented in such instances.

I have not met, personally, the guerrillas whose interviews are on the following pages. Their interviews are recorded on tape. Their voices show unexpected calm, and betray no rancour; no flavour of bitterness is apparent. The interviews were conducted by Ajit Singh Khera who is Press Secretary and Spokesman for the Council of Khalistan. I provided him with a set of questions which he was to go through with each guerrilla he managed to meet. These questions concentrated on obtaining specific information as to the class, age, region, village and education of those involved. I was also interested to hear in detail about the specific personal experiences which drove them into guerrilla activity, whether these were family experiences in their village or at university. I wanted to know to what extent kin and friends had exerted influence upon them and who and what had inspired them to join the armed struggle. They were encouraged to speak at length and without prompting on these issues. Previous political affiliation, job, strength of religious orientation were noted as well as what they said about Hindus. I tried to reach the determining personal experience which made them identify with fellow Sikhs rather than with India. I also wanted to know what sort of future they had in mind for the Sikhs and what were their links, if any, to other sectors of Sikh society not engaged in open resistance.

Eight interviews, six of which are presented, were conducted in December 1989, and a further three in April 1991. These last three interviews contain some information on the KCF as an organisation, and may appear shorter since some of the material given has been transferred to a general chapter on the KCF. In them the interviewer also introduced some of his own queries. For example, he took the chance to get the reaction of the KCF guerrillas to the cultural reforms that an opposing guerrilla organisation was imposing on the rural areas. All those interviewed, with the exception of Zaffarwal and Hoshiarpur, have been killed in the years between 1990 and 1992. Jassa Singh Santuwal, interviewed in April 1991, was killed in July of the same year. Sukhwinder Singh Gora, the Deputy Commander of the KCF, was killed in January 1992.

It has been particularly difficult for me to assess this material. It was an obvious disadvantage not being able to look into their eyes and observe the expressions on their faces, to see how they interacted with each other or to catch the general aura which they communicated. It was a handicap not knowing what information had been missed. As an example, it just happened to be mentioned by the interviewer in casual conversation that both Anup Singh and Jasvinder Singh were shaking uncontrollably while they were speaking as a result of the effects of the torture upon them. These two boys were interviewed on New Year's Day 1990 and they were killed as they crossed the border two days later. One other important point that just happened to be mentioned in discussion was that Hindu doctors very frequently treat the boys when they are ill and that some of the guerrillas (in this particular sample, Beant Singh, pp. 174–7) stay in Hindu houses. In all the cases, the *ad hoc*, almost accidental nature of their entry into armed activity stands out.

None of the interviewees were poor. None of them belong to rich families, either. Their parents are small farmers, though some own over twenty acres, or are comfortable artisans. Their family milieu is typical of the Punjabi smallholding pattern where the inherited farm is subsidised by the service employment of some members of the family.[1] They are from both the rural and the urban areas of the Punjab. What they have in common is their youth. Some can be found within the modern institutions of society, for example the colleges and universities.

Quite a number of them have had a Sikh upbringing. If not, they have certainly evinced interest in Sikhism since 1984 and many became *amritdhari*. Though they became baptised Sikhs, this does not betoken strong religious feeling. The return to their traditions has been brought about by happenings in civil life during the past eight years – particularly the experience of terror. Only one of those interviewed had a deep-rooted religious belief which he chose to let govern his actions. In others, any religious feeling has been tempered by the demands of secular life. Indeed, one cannot understand their struggle without looking at the actions of the state in the villages of the Punjab. The interviews show the manner in which the state intrudes into their lives. These interviews are therefore much more than a series of 'immediate experiences'. The reality of state power is the common thread running through subjective individual experience.

The guerrillas of the Khalistan Commando Force are the children of the events accompanying the army combing operation in the villages of the Punjab during the months of June to September 1984. Known as Operation Woodrose and already referred to in detail in Chapter 2, it targeted those who had made a commitment to the Sikh cause, as also those with suspect, though not necessarily proven, sympathies for the fate of their people at that time. As noted, Sikh youth in the age group 15–25 were taken away from their homes in large numbers. Some disappeared while others remained in police and army custody for a significant period. Those who survived made contact with each other through friends and through kin. Kin networks were important as a method of recruitment. Jarnail Singh Hoshiarpur explains how he became involved naturally due to the death of close relatives with political involvements. All except the youngest among them had prior organisational experience before their arrest and, in one case, had belonged to an institution of state, namely the army.

Survivors of Operation Woodrose were aided in forming some sort of rudimentary organisation by those among them with trade union experience, with experience in the All India Sikh Students' Federation or who were members of the religious seminary of Dam Dami Taksal. Initial recruits were of an age group captivated by the personality and message of Sant Bhindranwale, though this captivation was insufficient to propel them into the armed struggle or its organisation. Then there were those with trade union experience who saw the military oppression against the Sikhs as a mere extension of existing economic oppression. However, all guerrillas mention that it was the behaviour of the security forces towards them and their families that finally drew them into the struggle. All mention that it was a matter of honour to resist. Operation Bluestar and Woodrose were an attack on the Sikh sense of honour. Particularly the attacks on *amritdharis,* simply because they were *amritdharis*, caused outrage. It was only they who were arrested, intimidated and killed. Likewise, entering the house, removing the women and taking daughters and sisters to police stations offended the Jat sense of honour. The outrage to the Panth and the outrage to innumerable families merged. The dishonour families have experienced motivates them to fight to remove the existing system. Quoting Jasvinder Singh (p. 170) 'What sort of Punjab is it where boys younger than me have their legs broken or are shot? We shall have to have a return to justice so that our sisters and daughters may be safe.'

None has taken the decision to resist light-heartedly. An accumulation of negative experience had first to occur before the person concerned became active. One guerrilla describes how his first experience of horror was the sight of bloodstains in the Darbar Sahib when he went for prayers. That experience subsequently merged with knowledge of the torture of friends and became even more personal with his own torture and threat to female members of the family. An accumulation of abuse resulted in the decision to resist actively. Certain themes recur in each interview. Issues of injustice and inequality emerge in all of them. Such injustice may relate to the pressing economic need for a good market price for agricultural produce and fair employment according to merit. These classic small farmers' concerns appear in the Zaffarwal interview.

The need for an egalitarian way of life, or, in Sikh terms, a just society, is expressed in religious terms by the then deputy commander of the KCF: 'A Sikh cannot be oppressed. That is imprinted upon his heart. The life of a Sikh is like water flowing in a stream. Each time you utilise it, it will replenish itself. But when you try to stop this flow, the water will become stagnant and its level will rise.' The latter words are a reference to one of the Sikh principles of living – *Wand chako* (share). Through sharing one establishes the just society. The results of not sharing are that pressures build up in society. The trade unionism of Zaffarwal and the inspiration of *bani* or Sikh scripture governing the life of his deputy Sukhwinder Singh gave the movement considerable creative force.

The issue of injustice covers torture in jails and police harassment. Here too, the experiences of these young guerrillas are in no way extraordinary, but similar to what has been reported for the ordinary citizens of Punjab. Most of the torture of which they speak took place before they had indulged in any armed action. All who became guerrillas have gone underground because of police harassment. If they are lucky enough to survive the police torture, they are released on payment of a substantial amount of money. Release after interrogation on payment of a considerable sum and then re-arrest and the same treatment were common. The various laws mentioned in Chapter 1 give the police free rein within interrogation centres. They are matched by the terror of police practice in the villages where, as one woman from Gurdaspur put it, 'we are troubled by the police throughout the day and by criminals working for them at night. We cannot live our lives.'

The persisting optimism of the participants in this struggle, and, associated with this optimism, an attitude to torture which diminishes its significance has been of interest to me. Words are used for torture which reflect neither its intensity nor its cruelty, and which certainly do not acknowledge its demeaning and dehumanising aspect. When one guerrilla was given *ghottna* he used to say 'they're winding me up. They're just needling me.' Another guerrilla, after particularly savage and demeaning torture, uses the word *tahuni* to describe it. This is a word to describe the mild thrashing one might give to a child for naughty behaviour. The appropriate word reflecting the severity of his torture would be *tashaddar*. In all the interviews, terms are used which conceal the actual nature of the torture used, terms such as 'beat me almost to death' (*kutt marna*). Indeed I have actual descriptions of the torture process only because the interviewer made specific requests for them. Even so, no one has been graphic.

The optimism has three sources. Firstly, it is based on an actual situation in which the guerrillas of the KCF to a large extent were successful, for so many years, in gaining the support of the people. Moreover, until 1992 such support was growing with respect to area, and it was coming from a wider base. Sukhwinder Singh Gora's interview, particularly, mentions the extensive cooperation of the rural population as does Baljit Singh's interview.

The leader of the KCF comments on the cooperation of ordinary villagers in the following manner: 'Wherever we went, people gave us beds to sleep on while they themselves slept on the floor. We never missed home or family. We felt that those who gave us shelter and food were our families. When our clothes were torn or too dirty they would give us their own.' He adds, 'Our policy for our own people in the movement is very clear: if you don't have food, stay hungry, but don't hurt anyone or force anyone to give you food. If you need, plead, and you will get their support.' With commitment to the movement, family ties are relinquished. One commented 'Since I became committed to the movement in 1985 no longer have I been interested in the household. I took a pledge that whenever the Sikh nation needs my head I shall give it.' Another says to his wife, 'I've become a Singh of the Guru and my life is now dedicated to the Panth. I'm not yours any more and you are not mine.'

A second source of optimism is the fact that usually families have supported the decisions to go underground and to actively resist. Zaffarwal quotes his wife as saying 'Please be sure you don't confess to the police and bring harm to others should you be caught. Don't look back towards the house – look forwards toward the nation.' Some families have found this difficult but, after seeing the results of interrogation on the bodies of their sons, they have seen no alternative to the route they have taken.

A third source of optimism is their faith. One guerrilla comments, 'We have a sense of well-being since we joined the struggle. Now that we have dedicated our lives we are without fear. We pray morning and evening and remember our *shahids* who have joined the Guru. I feel better than when I was living my earlier life. For independence we have to make sacrifices and certainly we have difficulties and problems. However, I am happy and without worries close to my heart. I am marching towards my goal.'

There exist many legal reports by prestigious individuals and organisations, from many countries, documenting the extent of the terror in the Punjab rural areas. Some of these are mentioned in Chapter 1. There exist many photographs. There is also a substantial amount of poetry and song on the condition of the people. The proof of atrocities is ample, the writing eloquent. Yet the condition of the people worsens. In the words of the poet Faiz Ahmed Faiz (as translated by Kiernan, 1973: 113) 'For your rooted trouble, what is my rhyming worth?' Yet this pessimistic note would not reflect how the guerrillas feel. Quoting one of them, 'As to our present life, what can I say about that? When we have weapons we are free and independent! All the forces that have been despatched to put us down, have surrendered, in the end. All we need now is some international lobbying for our struggle, for we ourselves never get demoralised. We've made a pledge and that's why we're fighting for the nation and will sacrifice our head for the nation. So what is there to worry about?'

Note

1. See the article by Sucha Singh Gill (*EPW*, 1988: 2167–73). Specific examples from among leading guerrillas are: Sital Singh Matthewal who was a bank employee, Gurbachan Singh Manochahal who was a surveyor in the army's artillery division, and Labh Singh and Manbir Singh Chaheru who were in police service.

7

Profiles of Khalistan Commando Force Guerrillas: 'Sparrows into Hawks'

Wassan Singh Zaffarwal

Former trade unionist. Leader of the Khalistan Commando Force (KCF). Panthic Committee Member. Close to the second commander of the KCF, Labh Singh, who sent him to Pakistan. Ancestral village Zaffarwal, near Dhariwal, District Gurdaspur. Background: small farmer, born 1957. Two brothers and sisters younger to him, and one elder brother. All are married.

Early home and political background

My father went to jail during the Punjabi Suba struggle.[1] When he came out, he started working for the Akali Dal at local level. Many political people dropped in to the house. From an early age I knew from them that the Punjabi language was being destroyed. During the Punjabi Suba struggle many people from our village were arrested. I knew them personally; I remember their names. My home education was firmly Sikh: *nam japo* [pray]; *kirt karo* [work]; *wand chako* [share with others]. Both my religious and political education came at home. We had a routine in our household – supper, a glass of milk and a discussion on Sikh history. My father always had magazines and books on the Sikhs. I joined the Khalsa School in Dhariwal at the age of twelve or thirteeen and they, unlike the state schools, gave me an education in Sikh culture and history. My elder brother attended to the farm while Father was in jail during the Punjabi Suba struggle and we had to employ a few people to help us. We do have a tube well, though we're not large farmers; we're simply doing okay and no more than that, thanks to the grace of God. I had little opportunity to enjoy myself, because work at school and at home kept me busy. Also, my mother wished all the family to be good Sikhs and wished that she should hear no complaint from others about our behaviour. I always wanted to be able to read the Guru Granth [the Sikh scripture] and I studied part-time with the help of the local *granthi* [scripture reader] and would do *akhand paths* [continuous reading of the Sikh scriptures] in the villages. From my childhood I had wanted to join the army. And as a schoolboy I had been a member of the National Cadet Corps and gone to their training camps for three years and passed some exams. I thought I'll be a soldier and bring honour to my family and village. I wasn't *amritdhari* then. I wanted to join the army but my family had no connections and no recommendations from anyone. After many interviews I didn't get a job with them. Then on one of these visits the PA to the recruiting officer said to me, 'You've been here so many times, don't you know you've got to pay money to get a job?' Since I met all the job requirements I refused to pay any bribe. The only way to have paid that bribe was to mortgage my share of the land and I felt this was not right. So I was forced to take other work. I could see there were no benefits from farming. Our cost of inputs was always so high. We were always taking loans and incurring debts. When I was nineteen I got my job in the cloth mill [at Dhariwal] due to my father's contacts. The pay was good; it was better than a teacher's pay. However, there was discrimination against Sikhs from those Hindus in the management who came from Punjab. Most of the Sikh employees were recruited by the non-Punjabi Hindu Welfare Officer. Punjabi Hindus discriminated badly at all levels of employment, allocating bad, dirty jobs to Sikh recruits. I was working in the milling section at an unskilled job. After I'd been there for a month I was called by the manager and accused of working while under age. I produced a certificate showing that I was nineteen. As soon as that Hindu left, I got my promotion. I became an *amritdhari* because of that man's constant taunting. Whenever anyone wanted his holiday he had to press his legs [i.e. please him]. Had it not been for this Hindu pushing me around I might never have taken *amrit* [he laughs]. It was my personal statement to him that precisely because of his discrimination we [the Sikhs] shall go forwards not backwards.

I started to build a little movement in the mill. I saw the union was weak. I started persuading people to fight discrimination in areas concerning rights and promotions. Twenty-five of us also started having discussions about Sikhism. We persuaded some of those who were drinking their wages away to ease off and finally to give up the habit. Many also stopped cutting their beards. At that time the unions were not very strong and unions were associated with political parties. The largest was that associated with the BJP.[2] I started to work with it and also got some experience of the Arya Samaj.[3] I also contacted the Naxalites at mill level. Basically their movement had failed due to lack of people's support. They said there was no God. I had joined them for three years in the '70s but their talk of revolution was without any basis. They talked only of Lenin. Their inspiration came from him, but they never talked anything about Sikhism. We want our independence on the basis of what Guru Gobind Singh told us, not Lenin. At one union meeting some communists started ridiculing the wearing of the *kirpan*. I got up and spoke to defend the *amritdharis* and that drew me into working full time for the Akali Dal. There was already talk at that time about the Anandpur Sahib resolution.

Progressively in the mill, things got bad. There was no treatment if one got injured; there were no schools for our children. The worker is producing and the officer is sitting in his chair! The worker's son is not at school; the officer's child is at boarding school! He has accommodation; we, the workers, have none! So I sought to work within the Akali Dal to bring about some changes to this situation in the light of Sikh principles.

However, the Akali Dal paid little attention to the working man and his needs. It also made no attempt to implement the Anandpur Resolution. The issue of Chandigarh, and the issue of the exclusion of Punjabi-speaking pieces of territory from the newly formed Punjabi-speaking state in 1966, were never tackled. If the demands for Chandigarh for example, and for the Punjabi-speaking pieces of land had been met, the movement for Khalistan might never have begun. It is only when the *morcha* [mass demonstration] started in '82 that talk of Khalistan started among younger people, while the older people in the Akali Dal were still only thinking of the Anandpur Sahib resolution. However, they could not articulate much about it.

I became a union official in 1983 for the Akali Dal union within the mill, but in fact I could do little as I was involved in the Sikh movement. In 1983 I was arrested and put in Ludhiana jail. The villagers in prison were talking to each other, saying, 'what is this struggle for, they should talk about *Khalsa raj*' [Sikh rule]. They were courting arrest for *Khalsa raj*, not for the Anandpur Sahib resolution! One hundred and fifty thousand had courted arrest. So why waste time with the Anandpur Sahib resolution! The Akalis were trying only to get state power. These villagers were not concerned with Chandigarh. Give it to Haryana [the state adjoining Punjab] they were saying. Their demands were national and economic! They wanted recognition that Sikhs were a nation. We want Sikh universities and a Sikh educational system. We are not interested in becoming MLAs [members of the Legislative Assembly] and having a good life. During my tours around the villages I had met Sant [i.e. Sant Bhindranwale]. Sant also talked about national issues. Sant kept the struggle going. He became disenchanted with the Akalis as they had no vision other than seeking immediate government office.

After the Sant's death the Federation [the All India Sikh Student Federation] came into prominence.

I went very little to Darbar Sahib [the Golden Temple] during the years when he was especially active ['82–'84]. However, I did go to see Sant personally on one occasion when the mill management would not fulfil a court order about working conditions. He sent a letter to the mill management that they must meet the conditions laid down by the court. Due to this he [Sant] gained a lot of popularity among the workers at the mill. Sant sorted out the economic problems of many individuals.

Delhi controls the teaching syllabus and materials in state schools. There is no literature on the Sikhs included. Even holidays and festivals were not based on local and national traditions in these schools. On the martyrdom days of the Sikh *gurus* [teachers], there was never a holiday. The students used to force these holidays out of the headmaster. All the literature we read was in Hindi. The intention of the educational policy was to slowly stop people being aware of Sikhism. In my primary school we were never taught anything about our heroes and of what they did or of how Sikhs fought to free their *gurdwaras* [congregational centres]. In this sort of alternative education *dhadhis* [eulogists] have a big role to play. For example, at festivals in the village when the *dhadhis* used to sing and they referred to sacrifices for *des* [country]. *Des* was the nation of the 10th Guru, not Hindustan. This was important, for the Hindus were distorting our history. For in fact the 5th Guru was martyred due to the Hindus. The *sahibzadas* [sons of Guru Gobind Singh] were betrayed by the Hindus. A distorted version of our history has been presented to us. Our troubles were always with the Hindus, not the Muslims.

Before I joined the Khalsa school in Dhariwal neither I nor my Sikh class-fellows had ever had an opportunity to study our history. Whatever we were taught in primary school was based on Brahmin ideology. For example, when reference is made to the independence of 1947, all the books mention Gandhi and everything is written about him and Nehru but nowhere is the contribution of the Sikhs to independence mentioned. At least, during the British period, they were a people from outside. They didn't interfere in our culture or force any traditions that were not our own upon us. But this government is imposing brahmanism.[4] I used to be quite disturbed at school at what they used to say and often spoke about it to my father. They used to say that when the country was freed it was due to Gandhi's and Nehru's efforts. I would discuss this with him and he would tell me that during the independence struggle in Malerkotla, the Sikhs would be tied to the front of the cannon and blown up. And one hundred and twenty of them went *haz hazke* [cheerfully] to the gallows in the Andaman Islands. When I went back to school. I would challenge the teacher on all these points. The teacher replied that Nehru went to prison. I replied, in turn, that there were more than 100,000 went to jail in the Punjab, yet they never talked about Sikhism or Sikh culture. Occasionally, now, when they do mention Guru Nanak [the first Sikh Guru] they refer only to his spiritual meditation, despite the fact that Guru Nanak did say fight against oppression and cruelty. When Babur [the first Moghul emperor] brought his army to the Punjab, Guru Nanak raised his voice against domination. What a contrast this was to the *fakirs* [Hindu ascetics] and the *pirs* [Muslim holy men] who prophesied that when Babar descends on the Punjab they would blind him with their magical powers. Guru Nanak watched their drama. He taught us that by magical thinking you cannot oppose injustice. After watching and learning from these events Guru Nanak began to travel and he came back to the Punjab with a model by which our life should be lived.

Not only was there much cultural discrimination in the Punjab. It was becoming increasingly difficult, also, to get jobs. To obtain employment in the army, the main qualification seemed to be a bribe. In fact, what was needed was a test of one's ability. Even in the mill where I worked, whenever it came to promotions to non-manual jobs, the non-Punjabi Hindus in the management would favour the Punjabi Hindus, even when the Sikhs were better qualified. We had many Sikh labourers with us who had BA qualifications and many of the Hindu supervisors were not even matric. pass. In my own department there was one who could not sign his own name. I also noticed in the mill that Sikh workers were given the most degrading of available jobs. In '82–'83 during Congress rule, the Congress union in the mill started agitating for workers' rights. All the other unions joined in except the communists, and an agitation began. It started with one Sewa Singh offering to fast to death until our demands were met. A strike then began. During that strike I was to learn that in Hindustan there is no such thing as people's rule. There are only the permanent interests of the rich and wealthy, no matter which government comes into power. I realised that what was needed was not a small struggle in the mill but a larger one outside. Within the mill it was the menial workers who were among the most exploited, for example, they had no eating or cleaning facilities. I thought one must widen the struggle to a Punjab- and India-wide level. Each individual has his rights and each people has the right to grow. So I visited other workers in Batala. They had no rights, no voice at all, and only those unions were allowed to flourish who collaborated with the management. I found that a lot of trade union leaders were killed by management using local criminal gangs. I used to feel bad about this. The smallholder is in the same position. The sole and final voice is that of the capitalist. If you look at each smallholder you will see that he is toiling and, at the end of the day, he doesn't know what the price of his produce will be. He knows the sacrifice and effort put into his farm; he knows his production costs. But he cannot fix the price for his produce. The government fixes the price. Wheat is purchased by government at a fixed price. We have no market for it; we cannot take it outside the Punjab. When we grow our rice we have to take it to the sheller. The owners of the sheller sell it at inflated prices outside the Punjab. Whenever the farmer wants to buy any inputs he has to buy them at market price. We produce a lot of potatoes in the Punjab; why can't we sell them abroad? Producers should have more say and they should have the freedom to sell their produce inside and outside of India. Look, too, at a worker who travels fifteen miles to work on his bicycle and ends up with a few rupees per day. He is not in a position to tell the owner that this will not feed his family. All that a worker is concerned about is how he will feed his family at night. Yet some don't get their wages for several months. No doubt there is a lot of talk about increases in production. What people fail to see is that each year the farmer gets more indebted. Increasingly lands are being mortgaged. All the natural resources are being taken away from the Punjab – our water is being drained away, our electricity taken away, and our men, too, are used to fight other people's wars. [This is a reference to the invasion by India of Sri Lanka. Many Sikh soldiers died during the Indian occupation.]

Political experience after 1984

In the immediate post-Bluestar period, i.e. June–September, I travelled from village to village. Many young boys were being killed. All the stories from village families were the same: mothers and sisters raped, then taken outside the village boundaries and stripped naked, the houses searched. The worst thing was that the menfolk were taken out of the homes and then the army would go into the homes on the pretext of searching when our daughters and sisters were at home. [An indirect reference to rape.] This was the worst thing of all. We didn't know what they were doing. We could accept our own humiliations, but not the humiliation of our women. I clearly saw that we'd have to mobilise for armed struggle. At first, though, I thought, let's be peaceful and don't return bullet for bullet. At this stage I dedicated more of my time to simply meeting people and gaining information. I'd work at the mill for eight hours and then spend the rest of the time meeting people, spending different nights in different villages and leaving for work from there the next day. What was positive was that wherever I went people wanted to do something. They did not want to sit back. Wherever we went, villagers would give us money and beg us to go forward, not backwards. My family didn't stop me in my activities. I had their full support. When people saw us sticking together they thought we're not finished yet. The worst thing was that we couldn't bring to the attention of the world what had happened to us. There was no place for us to go; we had no refuge. Prior to June 1984 we used to talk about the Anandpur Sahib resolution because it contained the right to self-determination within India. After 1984 we needed our own independent home. The government that could kill hundreds, send thousands to prison, rape our women and generally humiliate our people, there could never be a compromise with them! We now needed an independent home for the Sikhs. There were many incidents when the army went into villages that Sikhs fought back with their *kirpans*. Many chose to die in this way. Many young men slept on the rooftops and when the army trucks came, would flee.

It came to police notice that I was travelling from village to village and one morning, while going to work, they arrested me. It was 13 August 1984. They wouldn't tell me why they'd arrested me. My father mobilised a lot of people and rang the local SHO [head of a police station]. Even the mill management rang up and said I had never been involved in any criminal activity and they came to speak to the SHO. Eventually, they did a deal, paying 2,500 rupees for my release. But before that I had been interrogated. I did my *Ardas* [the Sikh congregational prayer] and kept on praying. I could hear them constantly repeating, admit to your crimes. I kept on saying my prayers. They subjected me to *ghottna* and with that your knees get crushed and you can't walk properly afterwards. The next morning sixty to seventy people from various village *pancayats* [councils] came to the police station. They had to give 2,500 rupees for my release. And you know in our households we don't have that much. I borrowed some from my friends in the mill and further expenses [he means other bribes] cost me 5,000–6,000 rupees.

Instead of having such things inflicted on one, it is better to die. Two members of the Legislative Assembly had approached the SHO. He did not respond. The people from the mill management came. He did not respond. They all gave guarantees of my conduct to no effect. He was able to hold out because we are ruled from Delhi, not from the Punjab. We have no democratic government. Four or five Sikhs were being tortured while I was there. They had been brought in order to intimidate them; to frighten them and extract money. They were almost half dead from the torture. I realised when I saw this that never, now, could peaceful agitation be the answer. If I live, I want to live with honour and if I die, I want to die with glory.[5] This was the time I took the decision to resist. I said my *Ardas* and asked *Waheguru* [Almighty God] to give us the strength to arm ourselves to give us ample weapons.

We are going on the path of our *gurbani* [scripture]: 'When all peaceful means have failed it is right to resist.'[6] All avenues were blocked to us and we were forced to take this path. I'm convinced now that no one listens to you unarmed. Many Sikhs have been slaughtered in Punjab just as there have been Muslims slaughtered in Moradabad and Bihar. Other nationalities have suffered brutalities. And the world is silent. We feel armed struggle is the only way for us. And we shall continue until we achieve our freedom.

I kept up my associations after gaining release from prison. But after two to three weeks they started looking for me again. They came to the house. We had no more money to give them. Neither was I prepared to suffer torture. At that point I decided I had to flee from home. As long as I'm going to live, I'll live as a free man and therefore as an armed man. Our first group consisted of a core of only three people. And soon one of them was arrested. During torture they cut off his hands. Later they removed his eyes and then they cut off his feet. Finally when they could extract nothing they killed him in a fake encounter. After a time we armed many in Gurdaspur and then moved into other districts. Wherever we went, people gave us beds to sleep on while they themselves slept on the floor. We never missed home or family. We felt that those who gave us shelter and food were our families. When our clothes were torn or too dirty, they would give us their own. We went to Hoshiarpur and created links in the colleges. By the middle of 1985 we had covered all of Punjab apart from districts Bhatinda and Ferozepur. When I went to Malwa side (Ludhiana especially) we met professors and advocates and educated people who gave us a lot of ideas and advice as well as strategies for struggle. By that time, it was becoming more of a national movement and people from all sorts of background were coming into it. In fact we had a special affection for all those who were non-Jats. We were trying to create an organisation which people would join, not because of any individual personality, but because of issues. All our intellectual friends used to advise us: never support a personality! Align yourself with your freedom, with Khalistan, not with personalities. That is our policy and it is also the policy of the political wing of the KCF. In all our statements we appeal to the Sikh nation to support the principles of the struggle rather than individuals, because individuals come and go. Indeed if people had not aligned themselves with the struggle, it would have been over by now. As far as I am personally concerned, from the very beginning, in all our activities, we were never very far away from the principles of Sikhism. My father once gave me this advice that 'Now you have chosen this path, don't do anything wrong.' I still remember his words, and whatever I do, I do for the *chardikala* [buoyant spirit] of the *qaum* [nation]. Mother's advice was also to keep on struggling for the cause and not to worry about the family. My two brothers also, in due course, were arrested and jailed under the National Security Act. My wife told me that should I ever be arrested, 'Please be sure you don't confess to the police and bring harm to others. You must bear the consequences yourself.' Such comments from my family gave me tremendous support. My wife's message was 'Don't look back to the house. Look forwards towards the nation.'

In the early days wherever we went we were given much support voluntarily. We have robbed banks and distributed money to the needy and we have eliminated looters when we have found out about them. Our policy for our own people in the movement is very clear – if you don't have any food, stay hungry, but don't hurt anyone or force anyone to give you food. If you need, plead, and you'll get their support. Slowly we created cells to distribute weapons. We also created some groups whose sole purpose was to care for the *shahidi* [martyrs'] widows. These self-help networks are still operating. Other networks were formed to include students and intellectuals. Time kept passing and the struggle widened with each day. The boys involved were encouraged by the warmth and cooperation they received in the villages which was beyond their expectations.

In 1985 we forged links with Manbir Singh's unit.[7] For a long time we gave no name to our group. We only said we were aligned with the Taksal. In 1985 the Taksal gave a call for a Sarbat Khalsa [a General Assembly of the Sikh nation] on 26 January 1986. It further declared that decisions of national importance as to how to further the struggle for independence would be taken on that day, at that meeting. As that day came nearer the Akali government was thinking of ways and means to stop it. Among the *jhujharuan* [fighters] there was a tremendous urge to hold this convention and it was difficult to stop. When the time finally came, the Taksal started the *Akhand Path* at Shri Akal Takht Sahib. In order to torpedo this meeting the Akali Dal, led by Barnala's younger son, Gagandeep Singh, sent bus loads of people – about 1500 in all – to the Akal Takht. These people were mainly from Malwa. They were armed, and some were under the influence of alcohol and opium. They came to Darbar Sahib and started shooting and a number of Sikhs were injured. Sensibly, those Sikhs meeting there were not provoked. The troublemakers left Darbar Sahib, planning to return the following day. The police were supporting them. Some were criminals and others were misguided. An Akhand Path lasts three days followed by *bhog* [last rites]. After this the convention was to be held and thousands of Sikhs had started gathering. Privately, Bhindranwale's father, Baba Joginder Singh[8] was holding meetings complaining that he had no say. We told him that if relatives were important why hadn't Baba Nanak passed his torch to his son? When he saw our weapons, he left

Darbar Sahib. And I questioned those remaining what did they think they were doing fighting over their personal glory and control at such a time. We then sat down to discuss the resolution to be passed in the meeting the following day. Bhindranwale's wife was also there. There was also a discussion as to whose names were to be proposed the next day. We didn't want to be members, but people insisted. Our group was the largest at that time. After this, Joginder Singh convened another meeting in Room 29. He wanted his son, Harcharan Rode, to have a high position in the Akal Takht. He was turning everything around his own personality. The rest of the Singhs were not in sympathy with his views. The following day, a resolution was proposed that the Sikhs must now exercise their right to self-determination, and call for a sovereign Sikh state, Khalistan. It was accepted and it became a *gurmata* [therefore with more legitimacy than the Anandpur Sahib resolution]. People were there in their hundreds and thousands. All Sikh organisations were represented. The international press was there. To implement this resolution a five-member committee – the Panthic Committee – was elected. It was given the task of organising the struggle for the political objective of Khalistan. This was the first time in 150 years that the institution of the Sarbat Khalsa had been resurrected under the authority of Shri Akal Takht Sahib (whereas the SGPC cannot meet unless the Deputy Commissioner, Amritsar, is present). This was a turning point in Sikh history. The most exciting thing was that the Sikh people decided to be independent and to continue the struggle until freedom was achieved. At the time we did not realize the significance of these decisions. We realised much later on that they were crucial. It is important to stress that the Panthic Committee was given a mandate for the establishment of Khalistan and if any individual does not continue to work towards that aim then he will be removed [a reference to Jasbir Singh Rode].

We started encountering difficulties in the functioning of the Panthic Committee from Baba Joginder Singh. I told him that the Panthic Committee is going to continue the struggle through an armed wing. So why don't you struggle in a political manner. He couldn't understand my point. The Federation under Harinder Singh Kahlon's leadership went to the villages to explain to the people what had happened at the Sarbat Khalsa. It played a vital and positive role. The Federation, as the political wing, began to flower and we eventually organised the Khalistan Commando Force as the armed wing of the Panthic Committee. A lot of youngsters were of the view that the Indian government was giving a wrong view of them, presenting them as criminals and thieves and they thought it was important that a statement of objectives was issued. So, on April 29 1986 we held a press conference. We announced to the world our intention to become free and that we wished to state we were not talking, as was Sant Jarnail Singh, of self-determination within India but rather of an independent sovereign state called Khalistan. Whoever associates with us will have to follow this programme and policy. All the sacrifices the boys are making are only for the establishment of Khalistan. Barnala then sent in the police. In 1987, to strengthen the movement further, we announced the formation of an International Wing, The Council of Khalistan The government arrested those nominated by the Panthic Committee to be head *granthis* at Darbar Sahib and Anandpur Sahib [the Panthic Committee members were all underground]. Once arrested they started having meetings with Rode and were taken to Delhi. When released along with Rode, they gave it in writing that they would have nothing to do with Khalistan and that they would bring the youth back within the fold of the constitution. They came out of jail in February 1988. From whichever platform they spoke, they spoke against Khalistan, and they conspired to hold a Sarbat Khalsa at Dam Dama Sahib. This is against tradition, because a Sarbat Khalsa can only be held under the authority of the Akal Takht. It is only then that it constitutes a Sarbat Khalsa. At Dam Dama, Rode started saying 'Let's form our government now, have our ministers and our own people in the police and move to the next phase of the struggle'. Some of the boys were told we'll get passports for you. The idea was to get some of them off to overseas countries, to get others involved in elections and to eliminate those who do not agree. And then the struggle will be finished. When all these plans did not materialise and they were not able to persuade the youth to give up the struggle, then instructions were given to eliminate those inside Darbar Sahib. And that was the beginning of Operation Black Thunder [May 1988]. Many were trapped inside Darbar Sahib and many were killed. Certainly, the allegations that people have been killed and tortured in Darbar Sahib are true. These things have happened; people were killed. We don't know who did this. To say that the movement is involved is ridiculous.

Labh Singh [Commander of the KCF until his murder in July 1988] would not agree to Rode's plan to have elections and so he and his associates started making plans to eliminate him. Gurjit Singh [former AISSF Convener] issued a statement against the Panthic Committee and we condemned him. When it became clear to all the groups that Rode and Gurjit Singh were not supporting the struggle we disassociated ourselves from them. Only the Babbar Khalsa kept their channels open and received money for one whole year afterwards. We reorganised the Federation after Gurjit's departure with Gurnam Singh Buttar [a medical doctor, since killed] as its head. When we assess the damage done by Jasbir Singh Rode, we can see that the whole organisation was nearly smashed. It had to be reorganised with a lot of hard work.

After Labh Singh's death the babbars announced a new KCF and a new Panthic Committee. Brahma [Avtar Singh Brahma, killed under mysterious circumstances on the border, August 1988] collected a few people together and they came to be known as the Khalistan Liberation Front (KLF). Such individualist behaviour was doomed. Only those forces will continue to remain that have an institutional base. Organisations based on the individual perish when the individuals perish. Many were working quite sincerely for the Taksal but when Rode came out of jail he saw to it that two prominent members of the Taksal were released with him [Mokkam Singh and Malkiat Singh] and they, on an individual basis, did much to disrupt the organisation. Likewise so did Manochahal. In 1987 Manochahal had to resign from the Panthic Committee because of demanding payments from a family. This had created ill feeling. He then set up on his own the Bhindranwale Tiger Force. After some time had elapsed we tried to work towards forgetting our differences and we brought him back.

Otherwise, we have good links with the workers in the Akali Dal and from the beginning have had a lot of dialogue with them. They look after the victims of the struggle and many of them have been severely tortured for their support. Their families have suffered terribly.

We are associated with Sikhism. Guru Nanak taught us how to raise our voice against injustice. He himself raised his voice. From the beginning, the Brahmin ideology opposed him. Sikhs declared themselves as a nation in 1699. Our ideology is clearly intended to bring about our liberation as individuals and as a people. There is no need to follow any other alien system of thought. We have our own values. Our history and *bani* inspires us. As far as Brahmanism is concerned, its object is to exploit people by sucking the blood of the poor. The Brahmins themselves do not work. Always they have divided people into static units. By contrast, in Sikh ideology, none of this hierarchy exists. There is equality, no matter what one's work and background. Each individual is required to be involved in the labour process and he must share what he produces with others. There can be no compromise with the Brahmins because they sit idle. Whatever government we set up in Khalistan will have to be based on the principles of Sikhism as contained in the *bani*. We will not create a society where one human being is poor and sleeping on the street and his neighbour is in a palace or luxurious building. We shall eliminate any remaining feudal or monopolist forces.

In the Indian state many nationalities are being oppressed and attempts are made to destroy their cultures. We want them to be free as well. We appeal to them to give us their full support and we will give them support. We would like to see all these peoples attaining their rights. In our struggle, the young people involved come from every background. Mostly, they are the sons of small farmers but there are also students in the forefront as well. The contribution of urbanite Sikhs – though few in number – is certainly equal to their percentage of the Sikh people. However, the maximum brunt of the oppression is borne by the small farmers and the landless in the villages. They give us the most support. The professional Sikhs have always given us ideas as to how to organise ourselves and many of the lawyers who fight the cases of those in prison do what is possible under present conditions. Ninety per cent of the people are indirectly or directly supporting us now. As far as Sikhs in the army are concerned, they are our people. They are our *taya's* [father's elder brother's] son or other relative, not some outsider. But all the officer class of the Punjab police are from outside. The police at lower level have sympathy for us, but there is very little they can do as they don't make the decisions.

Guru Gobind Singh gave us a democratic structure. Ours has to be a struggle organised deomocratically, and later so has our goverment. A structure cannot be imposed by any one individual. It is the people who elect their leaders in the Sarbat Khalsa. In the Sarbat Khalsa each has a right to express his views. As far as the Sikhs are concerned, they set up democratic structures in 1699, and throughout our history only those which have had the people's support have survived. On 26 January 1986, after almost 150 years, we rejuvenated the Sarbat Khalsa tradition, whereby the people express their collective will through the *gurmata*. Those who say we are not democratic are wrong. In the Sarbat Khalsa convention people can question their leaders. Many Sikhs had forgotten the tradition of the *gurmata* and it is according to a *gurmata* that we want an independent country called Khalistan. The Panthic Committee was established to lead the struggle. After the formation of this committee we put all the groups together to wage a joint struggle and the KCF was the armed wing of the Panthic Committee under the authority of the Akal Takht. The Federation had the duty to impart political education in the villages. Here, Kahlon made a very valuable contribution. We functioned from the Akal Takht from the end of January 1986 to the end of April of the same year. All the programmes we had formulated we could not implement because of Jasbir Singh Rode's betrayal and operation Black Thunder. Two months afterwards, Jasbir Singh came back to the Golden Temple with government bodyguards. It is a very ironic situation that a man who claims to be a leader of the Sikh people gets armed protection from the Delhi government, the enemy. He has totally sold out, that's why he gets protection. After Operation Black Thunder he made a march from Faridkot to the Golden Temple to liberate it. People were stoning them and swearing at them. Only sixty people were with them.

After Operation Black Thunder we lost contact with our groups, but after a time started reorganising. What saved us were the individual groups loosely affiliated to us. They would carry out operations as they were the only ones with the supply lines intact. When these individuals came in, I'd supply them with weapons and they would inform the units cut off that arms were still being supplied [in other words that I was not a traitor]. Each individual group leader is now responsible for creating his own supply lines and as from January 1990 all our old groups have been recovered.

Our new policy is to make all our groups independent, though they do have links and association and they do sit together, discuss and sort out rumours and misinformation until such time as clarification is reached. Each leader is given a free hand as to operations. Specific instructions are given as to the rules of the struggle: never to issue letters demanding money; never to intimidate. Those who join the struggle must do so out of love or through persuasion. Hindus, *per se*, are not the enemy. But if they want to stay in the Punjab, they must support the struggle. Their rights will be protected but whether Sikh or non-Sikh, we will not protect collaborators of the Delhi Darbar. All sections of the Sikh community are participating, farmers, carpenters, weavers, shopkeepers. We are not asking the non-Sikhs to join the armed struggle; but at least they shouldn't support the enemy. We have no antagonism to them. In our rule book we clearly specify that the enemy is the Delhi Darbar and the collaborators of the Delhi Darbar. We've given specific instructions to our groups not to act on misinformation and rumour but to ascertain properly if a person is a collaborator.

When the British left India in 1947, the leaders of the Hindus made certain promises to the Sikhs: that the Sikhs will be given an area where they will experience the warmth of freedom. Defence, foreign affairs and communications will be under the control of a central government, and all other authority would be given to state governments. And in the case of the Sikhs we had special promises that the centre would allow them to pursue their own way of life. For these reasons the Sikh people decided to enter the federal structure of India. After independence, instead of giving the Sikh people the freedom they had promised, they started discriminating against Sikhs in their struggle for a Punjabi-speaking state. When all of the states were reorganised on a basis of language, only Punjabi-speakers were denied that right. And in order to get this state, Sikhs had to sacrifice. It is unfortunate that the Hindus betrayed Punjab in the most shameful manner, by supporting the policy of the central government. They wrote in Punjabi that their mother tongue is Hindi! They played a fraudulent game on the Sikhs and still do so today. If they do not accept the language of a state, they should not live in that state.

Over a period of time the rights of states were taken away and power was concentrated in Delhi. Our development policies also were controlled by the centre. Even our local tax collection was transferred to the centre. The state government was a state government only in name. And this was why the Anandpur Sahib resolution came to be formed. And when it did not manage to redeem the various promises made to us in 1947, a peaceful agitation was begun in 1982 for self-determination. More than 100,000 people went to jail. The end result was that they sent the troops in to Darbar Sahib. We would like to ask the democratic and peace-loving countries of the world what we should do now, since all peaceful channels have been blocked. Our struggle is not only for the creation of Khalistan. We would support the struggle of the other nationalities within India so that everyone can be free. In this sense, our struggle is not separatist.

Sukhwinder Singh Gora (deceased)

Former mechanic. General of the Majha region (KCF) and deputy commander of the KCF until his death. Ancestral village Dadiala, District Gurdaspur. Background: artisan, born 1964,with eight years' schooling. He is one of four brothers and has four sisters, one of whom is younger to him. One brother is a motor mechanic, another works as a welder, a third is in the bank and their father farms five acres. Circumstances of death: killed 27 January 1992 in a shoot-out with the police and army in which he killed one SP, 3 sub-inspectors of police plus six others, before he himself was killed.

First interview

Due to the continuing struggle, my sisters were married very quickly and I left school early. Only my elder brother was educated properly and we had to pay quite a lot to get him a job. Seeing this I became quite disenchanted. It seemed that education alone was pointless. Even though my brother was educated we still had to pay to get him a job. We tried to get him into the BSF, but they wanted 5,000 rupees. I hated them for that. My brother said to them, 'I'm handing over my body to you and on top of that you're wanting 5,000 rupees. Better to stay at home than do *your* government service!'

After leaving school, I became a trained motor mechanic [for tractors]. I had taken *amrit* at the age of twelve but I've taken it again, subsequently, for the struggle [i.e. for a conscious reason]. There is a *gurdwara* near our house and I used to go there to recite the scripture every day, in the evening. A *granthi* there used to recite about our national heroes.

I was twenty in 1984 and running a small machine-tools shop. In 1984 all the *amritdhari* Sikhs started being arrested and cruelty inflicted upon them. I was affected by what I saw. So in 1985 at a big gathering in Mehta Chowk I took *amrit* there. I started wearing the *kesri* [saffron] turban and the clothes of the Khalsa and because of doing *sewa* [voluntary collective work] in the *gurdwara*, the BSF chaps in the village [there was a police picket in the village] labelled me a terrorist. My uncle's [father's elder brother's] sons were involved in the struggle and they were beaten up. This made me mentally committed to the struggle. However, at that stage, I was not personally involved in any way. However, the BSF questioned me where I had taken *amrit* and whom did I see. On hearing these sorts of questions I realised our honour and status was challenged and I joined the struggle. At that time I was arrested five or six times but, with the grace of God, not beaten. I got peace through reading *bani*. My thoughts stopped wavering, my earthly desires were eliminated and I stopped thinking of the family. The intoxication of prayer gives me strength and direction. Then I can face all difficulties. Our Guru Gobind Singh and his Khalsa went through problems and today we are grateful we can go through the same problems and serve the Panth. Our Guru Granth Sahib is there to guide us. This government therefore cannot challenge us in any way.

My sisters had encouraged me to join the movement. Sukhdev Singh Jhamke [a noted guerrilla killed in May 1989] used to come to the house and the family used to feed him and those whom he brought. In the early days I went to Darbar Sahib and met some Singhs there. We sheltered them at our tube well. My family never stopped me serving the nation, but warned me to be careful. All of my family have been taken to prison by now. I was influenced much by the local President of the Sikh Student Federation who was from our village. The meetings that he organised filled those who attended with strength. We village people don't go out much, but after 1984 we went to Darbar Sahib and the political meetings of the Federation. Soon I became an activist, supplying them with information. For two years I was underground. I mean by this I was not on the run, for I had joined the movement openly and hence was free. I joined the KCF. At first I was supplying information and hiding their weapons. No one had done any organisational or political work in my family before, though father had been a *sarpanc* [head of the village council] and he used to go on Akali *morchas*. My own political education came from my attendance at Federation meetings. I came to realise that Sikhs were not Hindustanis. I learned there of our ambitions and the reasons for our ill treatment.

There are many ways to join a struggle, why did you choose the armed struggle?

I simply fell in love with the *shastras* [weapons of Guru Gobind

Singh].[9] Then, in 1982, I had attended the very big convention called by Bhindranwale at Mehta Chowk. Bhindranwale announced before his arrest that the gathering must be peaceful. But some *agent provocateur* among the Sikhs fired at the police. The police returned the fire. There was a mother killed in that shooting. She died while trying to escape and her small child was still clinging on to her. One can protect oneself and others only by being armed.

After taking *amrit* in 1985 I no longer was interested in the household. I took a pledge that whenever the Sikh nation needs my head I shall give it. As I saw the intensity of the violence and of the grief and suffering increase there was therefore only one way to go. A Sikh cannot be oppressed. That is imprinted on his heart. The life of a Sikh is like the water flowing in a stream, each time you utilise it, it will replenish itself.[10] But when you try to stop this flow, the water will become stagnant and its level will rise. Similarly, if you heat water to boiling point it will spill over. And if, on top of that, you contain it as well, it will turn into steam and explode. First, the government heated us up, and now we are hot and have joined the struggle, they are increasing their oppression, killing innocent Sikhs and arresting many from their homes. Now we've been turned into steam! How can you contain steam?

How are targets picked?

Some people in the village spy on us to the police. We find out, after a while, who they are. More Sikhs [than Hindus] are touts now. You often hear, these days, that an innocent Sikh has been killed in a village. He's not innocent; he's an informer. We do warn them to stop their activities. Many of them do stop. One of our difficulties was that when people had their own personal rivalries they would inform against each other. So it became very important for us to be sure who we were hitting. Some Hindu informers still remain. But they are not the very poor Hindus. There's only one group among them who are informing – the *banias* [traders, merchants]. Only these informers were chased out of our villages. Our struggle is not a sectarian one against any particular group of people.

The KCF has a Punjab wide network but the government has infiltrated into armed organisations at every level and they are fomenting dissent among us. Fortunately our Sikh soldiers bring in a lot of information and reports which we check and verify.

Is there any truth in the allegations that the KCF forces villagers to feed them?

In our struggle we are making a home for all Sikhs. We have a lot of sympathy from the villagers. But there is much police infiltration of the guerrilla movement. They send out letters in our name demanding money in order to discredit us. They intimidate *amritdharis* and the general public. We call such people black cats. They carry the same weapons as we do, the AK-47, for which we have another name – *ant-karni* – it brings your end. In fact we get a lot of support from the public. When we go and knock at someone's door and they don't help us, it is only because they are worried about whether we are cats. If people do give food to the cats they are killed by them. In the morning they are all arrested. With some villagers we have long chats to win them over. Our Sikhs will tell you about the background of the struggle, Sikh history and the *bani*. However, these cats cannot do that. They are recruited from criminal elements and know nothing of our history. We do try to warn the people about them.

For a Singh [a baptised Sikh, one who is committed to the cause] who is on the run, it is essential to read *bani*. Reading history is now not so very relevant – that is for free men. Now is the time to create history. We live outdoors in the tall grass and among the sugar cane. On cold nights, as we lie awake, we read the *bani*. Also, some people who give us shelter in *deras* [out-houses] would get the impression we were not true Sikhs if we did not. It's difficult to form links with others because we're constantly on the run. I've been on the run for two and a half years, since the time I went to kill a police informer. My identity was leaked. I had to leave. They destroyed our house. They broke our tractor. When the police came to the village the villagers hid our family. Usually, when family members get arrested, not only the people from our village but also the nearby surrounding villages as well, surround the police station and they wait outside until the detainees are released.

To a large extent we've been successful. We've stopped the Central Reserve Police Force (CRPF) moving around the villages and confined them to their pickets and they therefore don't trouble the villagers so much. They don't move out of their posts at night. Ninety per cent of the problem is caused by informers. The few cats who do work for them are under close protection. They live in the Hindu cities and not in the villages. It is easier in the village to propagate our struggle from the gurdwara as we've got speakers. Now our plan is that the underground government [a reference to the Panthic Committee] must issue policies and we, the KCF, as its armed wing, must see that they are implemented. Sympathisers of the movement ask us to implement certain policies such as stopping the teaching of Hindi. We've done this! Then, too, lots of Sikhs were cutting their hair for jobs. This was happening to many boys from ordinary landowning families. They were selling their honour. We've brought changes in that respect, too. Now people are returning to their identity and not stooping so low to get jobs.

What precise help comes from the military?

I don't know. However, there are police people who inform us in advance of raids. There is no need for us to make links with army personnel because they come and talk to us on their holidays and they ask us what they can do for us. The soldiers themselves make efforts to form links with us. And, when we do any action in towns, we live in the houses of the *Bhapas* [a term rural people use for urbanite Sikhs]. As far as I am concerned, Khalistan is already achieved [because of this solidarity of feeling]. All sorts of people from many different social groups are making sacrifices. All are fighting and dying equally. And we will live together equally. If one has the qualification for a job one will get it in a future Khalistan. And we will help other movements who are struggling like ourselves once we attain independence. As to helping the poor and the needy, there is no question that we shall do that, as whoever lives in Khalistan must subscribe to the principle of equality.

[He was asked about help needed from the outside. He replied that the movement needed help in all fields.] We ourselves are looking after the orphans and we have to remarry the widows. We need weapons. Now we need rocket launchers to attack jeeps and pickets and we shall need constant monetary help to buy them. Additionally, there certainly has to be a political movement working alongside the armed struggle.

'As to our present life, what can I say about that? When we have weapons we are free and independent! All these forces that have been despatched to put us down, have surrendered in the end. All we need now is some international lobbying for our struggle, for we ourselves never get demoralised. Every time one dies, four join. We don't take them directly into the force; we make them work underground for a while. We're happy. We've made a pledge, and that's why we're fighting for the nation and will sacrifice our head for the nation. So what is there to worry about? We have to make every effort to achieve Khalistan. Only within Khalistan can our rights be secure. The central government has, at present, a programme to persuade us to come back within the constitutional fold, promising that they'll give us jobs. However, before we never got any jobs. This is just a ruse to tempt some of us away from the movement, divide it, and destroy our way of life. When we boys meet, we hug each other, because we haven't seen each other for such a long time. Such comradeship is more important to us than anything Delhi can give us. There is much affection binding us together. [He confides to the interviewer details about his actions against the CRP and the various supply lines.]

When we go to tke villages all the small children come running towards us asking us for guns which they call *ta-ta-ta* [an expression for the sound of the AK-47 going off]. Even ten-year-old children, when they find us, beg us to let them come along. We always persuade them not to come and to continue with their studies. It's not the right time, we tell them. However, we find that many of them want to join us.

How would you describe an underground Singh?

Someone who is not on police files. We are not underground in the usual sense of the term. We have weapons just as the paramilitaries have. We are the Sikhs of the 10th Guru and we don't hide when we fight. We forewarn our enemy that we're there. Those who are underground are those who work quietly and confidentially. Actions in the urban areas would not be possible for example, if we did not know beforehand who was with us and where we could go. We need food and directions when we are carrying out actions in urban areas. Urbanites help us in planning and the targets are those who are obstacles to our freedom and those who are informers. Our struggle is not with any sectarian or caste groups. For example, there are some Brahmins in the villages who are not obstacles. However, whoever is blocking our freedom – even if it be my own father and he is a tout – I cannot spare him and thereby give him a special favour. Now, there are very few informers in the village for we have been successful in getting the support of the people. We don't harm the poor because for our success we need the support of very ordinary people. Once I had kidnapped the relatives of five policemen. I did so because the police had arrested seven innocent villagers and tried to convict them of being engaged in an armed action. Each time the villagers applied for their release the SHO would say they were terrorists. We sent letters to the police constables' homes and we sent one too, to Gobind Ram[11] which said 'Son! If you want to kill our brothers, go ahead. We want them released without bail. If the government of India agrees to release them, the relatives of the five policemen will be returned unharmed. If not, the five constables – they were all Sikhs – must resign. If they do that, we'll also release their relatives.' For six days they carried out very intensive searches. By the Guru's grace and the support of the villagers they were not found. Then the seven villagers were released. But we knew that Satwant Singh and Kehar Singh[12] were going to be hanged and we knew four police touts. We hanged the four the same day.

Second interview

Meeting a year and four months later (April 1991) his voice reverberated with excitement at what he took to be an upturn in the KCF's fortunes. The interviewer asked him how they had managed to reorganise and expand the KCF.

This time last year our links went only as far as our district. They were limited. Now we have units operating all over the Punjab at tehsil and district level, and in other states as well, for example Haryana, UP. Mainly this expansion took place through relationships. There are those of us who have kin in Patiala and Chandigarh. Then there are the networks of relations in schools and colleges. Young people need no persuasion to join. We use the withdrawal of weapons to discipline groups and their personalities. One of our biggest problems has been that each group wanted to fight on its own. I think they see now that victory cannot come in that way. It can only come about through co-ordination.

What do you say to reports accusing the KCF of intimidation?

For the last three years our policy has been not to take money from the Sikhs. We're not worried about this propaganda. If Sant was a *badmash* then we're all *badmashes* as well. In any case at village level we counteract this propaganda. You cannot take money from any poor person, ever. We're clear on that. However, we impose a tax of the Khalistan government on the wealthy. We don't force money out of them. We tax them. We persuade Hindus and Christians to join the struggle. We must protect them. They are minorities. At first when we went to Ludhiana district people were not helping us. Now they trust us considerably more. Previously they were victims of government propaganda, and thought us to be thieves, and they were intimidated by criminal elements. Now we've developed a system of codes so that they know who they are dealing with. Their doors are now open. We've killed a lot of the criminal element. We also ask people to get in touch with us if they are being troubled by the police. Many have approached us. Government agents in the garb of freedom fighters have been the main problem. The KCF boys carry identity cards now. We shoot only criminal elements, not other *kharkhus* [fighters]. Should a KCF boy be doing something wrong, it is up to other guerrilla groups to inform Zaffarwal as the head of our organisation. Likewise if one of them is doing wrong, we should report it to their head. A lot of these killings take place to give us the image of being murderous and violent. This will stop support from overseas Sikhs and demoralize those at home. I'm not saying we don't kill. We kill informers. However, we have got nothing to do with this cultural policy of interfering in each and every person's affairs, as have some organisations [a reference to the Babbar Khalsa]. Our struggle is with the government and if we get involved in condemning those who drink or who make other small mistakes, people will not support us, and indeed will turn against us. Certainly we would not shoot anyone on these small matters. Our struggle is against the government of India. If we get involved in small things such as the killing of immoral men and women, this will harm our national struggle. This is accepted by all our soldiers.

There are very few informers from the public now. There are only informers infiltrated by the police and intelligence. Now our force is in all parts of Punjab, reaching into every home and down to each little child. So everyone knows about us. When we have a new recruit we trace him. People in his village inform us, through our networks, whether he loves the movement, or is an infiltrator. Whoever loves this movement, keeps an eye on what's going on, for us. If someone has a bad reputation in his village, those in his village inform us. Due to the support coming from the people we feel safe and protected. Much support these days is coming from UP and Rajasthan because the Sikhs there know that they stay there by grace of the Delhi government and that should anything happen they'll all be murdered.

Baljit Singh (deceased)

Ex-soldier. Ordinary member of the KCF. Ancestral village, Rasulpur Kalan, District Amritsar. Background: small farmer, matric. pass. Father previously in a Sikh regiment in the army. He is one of three brothers. One brother has an MA, but having failed to get a job, works for the Committee looking after the gurdwaras. A second brother, who is only a matriculate, farms their fifteen acres. He has two sisters.

After passing my matriculation I joined the Sikh regimental centre. I had completed my training just before the attack on the Harimandir Sahib. We learned of the attack on Sunday 10th June while we were gathered in the regimental *gurdwara*. There we learned that this *kadr dhari*[13] government had destroyed the Golden Temple and that our mothers and sisters were being insulted by the army of these *kadr dharis*. [Insult is the polite word for rape.] We couldn't bear this, so we collected arms from admin. company and recruitment company and killed Puri [the regimental commander] because he was stopping us from coming to Punjab. They deserved this as they disliked us anyway and were thinking badly of us. We deserted due to their enmity. The attack on the Harimandir was just the final crunch. This we could not tolerate.

After killing Puri I and other companions almost reached Lucknow before we encountered troops loyal to the government.[14] After a battle there, some became *shahid* and others were captured, as our ammunition was depleted. I was imprisoned for one month and spent nine months in Garhwal. After that I was again sent back to the regimental centre. Before I had been handling weapons, but now they gave me general duty as a servant. I had to clean and polish shoes, which I did not do even in my own home. I protested and then I again deserted and came back to the village. Then in the village the agents of the *kadr dhari* government started harassing me. Watching them, I realised I had to do something to preserve not only myself but also our way of life.

I had first joined the electricity department and then I joined the army, without paying any bribe. I didn't know much about Sikhism but

I listened to Santji's lectures and through him I learned a lot that I hadn't been taught before. We used to go to the Sikh festivals and listen to the *dhadhis* but the real understanding of our situation started when I began to listen to Santji. I visited him many times to listen to him. I used to go at night. He used to lecture us on Sikh principles and on how to protect them. He mentioned a lot about government discrimination against the Sikhs. He would tell us that when Darbar Sahib is attacked, that act will lay the foundation stone for Khalistan. On the question of discrimination he told us that when the Indian opposition Janata Party came to power the Pande brothers hijacked a plane in support of Mrs Gandhi. Later on they were rewarded with parliamentary seats. But when Sikhs did the same, for their ideology, they were treated like convicts. He used to talk about economic exploitation. We had been listening to all of this, but we did not make up our minds in any way. But when the Harimandir Sahib was attacked we were hurt. I was in the army centre at Ranchi at the time. There is a congregation in the Temple every Sunday. The *granthi*, who was a *hawaldar* [sergeant-major], conveyed the news of the Punjab situation. We felt there was no use our remaining in the regiment. We had joined for the service of the country. If the same country attacks our home, it is a very bad thing. It was quite an emotional meeting. Everyone there decided to desert.

In the Garhwal regiment, only ten out of eight hundred survived the attack on Darbar Sahib. Those that did survive were put in charge of those of us who had deserted and at the time of Mrs Gandhi's assassination especially, they treated us very badly. I was given general duty after a while, though usually those who are matric. are given jobs such as gunners and drivers. We were refused such posts. So I applied to the Sikh commanding officer for discharge. He told me I could not be discharged. That was a decision that could only be taken by army HQ. Certainly we had planned what we did. We planned it to serve the nation [the Sikh nation]. We will serve the nation in whichever way we can. No family likes to lose a person to the underground, but my elder brother said if that is my wish, go ahead and do it. He had connections with them and in fact they got him his job. Mother was OK, too, about my joining. But my Father warned me it would be a long struggle. There was great worry about the police, since I was a deserter, but after some time the army itself dismissed me.

I've seen torture first hand in our own village. Innocent people – but usually always *amritdharis* – were arrested frequently. Their families used to discourage them from travelling into town for fear of arrest on the way. Eight or nine from our own village were arrested like that and two never returned. Their whereabouts is not known. When someone was arrested we wouldn't come back for a few days. Many people were tortured during the days when there was curfew and ladies used to be harassed by the CRP when they came to visit relatives who were under trials in Amritsar jail. They would be searched by them, then by women police, and electronic devices put in objectionable places. There were many people arrested from the villages and I suppose the movement has had more support in rural than in urban areas. Nevertheless, urban Sikh families who know us always give us shelter.

We had started realising our position within India as we listened to Bhindranwale's lectures. After Operation Bluestar it became even more clear what our status is. For this reason, I've been openly with the struggle for the past six months. In each and every village to which we go now, they always say 'Give us time to serve the Panth'. They are anxious to join because they know they will be killed sitting at home or walking on the road. Then no one will know where they are. All sorts of searches are common now. We send those who are not marked by the police round the countryside with information. They also have a role in motivating political discussion. Women help us a lot. They inform the people about the current situation and initiate dialogues with them about its solution. The help of the villagers is crucial for us and without them we would have no shelter, no food and no places to move to. They do it out of their good heart and out of sympathy. Usually they are very happy to see us; especially their small children. The kids greet us with real love and affection and they want guns. 'We want a "ta" [an AK-47]' they say, 'to kill the CRP.' Not only do people give us information, we listen to their complaints. We are making contacts with other deserters. For there were many. Town Sikhs help us a lot, especially if they are in government service, and even some police too. They tell us about when there is going to be a raid. Also, those who are working for the electricity board can give us messages easily as they have security cards. The Electricity Board is very helpful.[15] The college students are all with us and if any women are arrested, they strike. People on buses and truck-drivers carry our weapons. The targets at this moment are the paramilitary forces because they humiliate the villagers. Killing is one thing, but the way they do it is another. They beat you to death. They electrocute you; pull out your arms and legs. During all this the constables give you milk and support you. When you are on the run, the villagers conceal one; deny one's existence. Whenever anyone is arrested, they surround the police station. There are now very few village Hindus left and the ones who are, are not our enemies. Only the Hindus in towns dislike the Sikhs.

As to our future in an independent Khalistan, we must put a curb on the activities of people like smugglers and those earning high interest from doing very little work. We must place limits on wealth, stop exploitative interests and establish fair price control.

Jasvinder Singh
(deceased)

Graduate and AISSF organiser. Ordinary member of the KCF. Ancestral village in District Gurdaspur. Background: small farmer's son, born 1968. He is one of four brothers and two sisters and is the youngest in the family. Jasvinder Singh was killed crossing the border, 1 January 1990, two days after this interview was held.

I was about seventeen when Bluestar happened. The government, for whom our people had done so much, betrayed us. We were, ourselves, aware of our *shahidi* [martyrdom] and sacrifices but we always thought India to be our country. We never questioned it! In childhood we were conscious of Sikh history and in the village we used to sit near elders in the evenings listening to their tales. They related the stories of Guru Gobind Singh and the *sahib zadas*. Also, one of my father's elder brothers was religious and through him we learned the *kirtan*. The government had stopped religious teaching in its schools. We could not obtain such teaching there. However, every year, near our village, on the birthday of Guru Gobind Singh there was a festival where we used to go to listen to the ballads of the *dhadhis*. From there we learned about the *misls*, the division of the sub-continent, the period after partition, of Master Tara Singh and Sant Fateh Singh. We learned that the British had offered our leaders our own country because we had a state during Maharajah Ranjit Singh's time and of how the boundaries of that state had been altered so many times by government conspiracy. At partition, we Sikhs could not match the cunning of Nehru and Gandhi. All of Nehru's family were cunning. This was discussed a lot at home and certainly it made an impact on us. Our leaders had blundered at the time of the division of the country and all of these sacrifices that are occurring now are due to their blunders. Young people are getting killed and suffering fake encounters from the police because of the mistakes of a few leaders. We listened to all of this and at the time didn't react much. We let it go because, we thought, we live in this country, India. But the time came when Indira Gandhi made a statement, either at the UN or somewhere else, that Sikhs are not a separate nation in India, but are part of Hindus. I took this to heart. Our Guru Gobind Singh had created Sikhs as a separate nation; he had blessed us with a separate identity. All the sacrifices we made for India, we made as Sikhs.

At the time of Operation Bluestar I was 16, nearly 17, and was studying. Suddenly all our villages were surrounded by the army. We could get no news, and the army all around made us feel bad. We started realising we are not safe – neither ourselves nor our religion.

Later, when we went to Darbar Sahib, we saw the marks of the bullets. Bloodstains were still visible. They could not even wash them away although it had been closed for so many days. The Sikh Reference Library, which had historical paintings and documents, was burnt. Nothing was left. We went into Darbar Sahib and listened to the *kirtan*. All its splendour was gone! There were bullet marks all around and the Akal Takht just opposite – our political centre – was ruined. The government wanted these places to remain only as religious centres. They ruined them in order to rid the Sikh mind of the notion that they are a nation. Many buildings around were destroyed simply to destroy the culture. I and many other young people began to think, on seeing this, that neither we nor our religion could be safe in a country that did this. There had been mass killing during the martyrdom day of Guru Arjun [the day of the invasion of the Darbar Sahib]. Many devotees had been killed. Also, there had been widespread cruelty by the army and police in the villages. So after passing the first part of my BA, I joined the AISSF in Hoshiarpur in 1985. Every young person I knew was discussing the situation in Punjab and felt that for our survival we must have our own home. After all, it is very common that if four brothers quarrel, they separate. We need a separate home. The students elected me President of the AISSF in Hoshiarpur. In that capacity, I used to tour the villages to find out what was happening and to prepare lists of *shahids*. I met most of their families and brought them together. Some of those who had been assassinated were innocent. For example, they would arrest some innocent boys whose only fault was that they were wearing traditional Sikh dress. They would then kill these boys in false encounters. The police started harassing me while I was preparing this list. On 28 February 1987 at a large district gathering, I honoured the parents of these *shahids* for their sons' sacrifice. On 31 March 1987 I was arrested and taken to Talwara police station. There I was tortured. I was also taken to the CIA [Central Investigative Agency] staff at Dasuya and given the same treatment there. Approximately twenty-five people were held at the centre and we were all taken out, one by one, into a certain room, and then sent back after an hour or so. They were questioning us as to why we were separatists. Stay with India and do as you are told, they were saying. There was a DSP there, among them, I don't remember his name, a Hindu. They couldn't get anything out of us and we were there for ten days. I was then taken to Garshankar CRP HQ. There they administered electric shock. I was thrown to the floor and blindfolded and had many currents passed through me. Any officer who passed by would kick us. I was eventually charged under certain sections of the Indian penal code, accused of waging war on India, and sent to Hoshiarpur jail. After three or four months I was given bail. I was along with 150 others. Most were innocent, from both village and town, and some were barely sixteen. They had all been tortured. There were better educated people in the jail also.

I had rejoined my university course when the police came to arrest me again. I ran off on my motor bike but they stopped me and re-arrested me. I thought I might be safe if only I could get back to the college, as I had attended in the morning and was marked present. I ran there leaving my shoes behind. I ran into the Principal's office. I told him they were arresting me. According to rule I could not be arrested without his consent. But he gave it. After my arrest the Vice-President of the AISSF organised a demonstration. He stopped the buses and the road traffic. Police lathi-charged and wounded many of the participating students. Our parents and family members had learned what had happened to us, but they were also harassed. They were quite happy about our joining the AISSF. Everyone understood that if it meant saving Sikhism, one had to sacrifice. No other family member was involved save myself. None of us had applied for the services either, as we knew we would not be successful. Even if they offer us a job, it will be that of a slave and we won't accept. There's widespread discrimination against the Sikhs. I have passed my Diploma in Civil Engineering. All of the Hindus have jobs, but the three or four of us who haven't are Sikh. All the young people of my year had not ever been in any political movement but Operation Bluestar affected them so much that they decided to join the Federation. Those in the Federation are not just from the rural areas. Many young, urban Sikhs are helping as well. Even before Bluestar they had joined the Federation and after the Delhi riots, still more joined. As the Guru said, *jab ban laggi tabi ros jaggi* [when the arrow strikes anger is aroused].

In Delhi we had been burnt alive, our women had been raped, and whatever wrong could be committed, was committed. Sikhs had to stand up for themselves after this. The Sikh youth in the cities is with the movement. Wherever the government finds out about their activists, they arrest and torture them. This struggle for nationhood is going on in other parts of India as well. We need people to keep in touch with these other movements. I've been involved since 1985 and have complete faith in its victory. We already feel we've saved Sikhism. A debate has started within the Sikh nation. They have started thinking of themselves as a separate nation who can be safe only in their own homeland, although that is not what the pro-government press reports. We receive great cooperation from the people and are treated like their own children. They do not differentiate between themselves and us. More people in the struggle are from the villages because Punjab is a village society. Moreover, it is village society that has been suffering, economically. For example, eighty-two lakh tons of wheat are taken away at a very cheap rate each year. This is direct discrimination, for we are, after all, small farmers and cannot store. They purchase from Punjab at a cheap rate and they sell back to us dear. Our state, which is a Sikh state, supplies food to the whole of India.

We must end this exploitation in the future and see to it that the labourer gets proper wages and the farmer gets a fair price for his wheat. In this struggle, we are bringing people into the movement through political means, not through terrorism. People are consciously joining us for a separate state. They voted for those MPs who have not taken an oath to the Constitution! They are supporting the Panthic Committee in the struggle for Khalistan. We have links in the civil and armed services and they do help us financially. Whatever they can do for us, they do. Our targets are the CRP, in order to incapacitate the machinery of the Indian state so that we can start afresh with our new ideas. We have chosen our path now and any one or any obstruction in our way becomes our target, our enemy. We will not pardon any informer, whosoever he may be. Any informer is our target as well as those CRP and BSF who have come from outside and are oppressing the people.

We have thought much about a future Khalistan. We wish all human beings equally to have the same rights. All poor people should have their living standards raised, so that there is no poverty and no gap between rich and poor. We have to restore the rightful equality of the human being. We shall have to have a new constitution and new structures guaranteeing that equality, and a return to justice, so that our sisters and daughters may be safe. All Hindus will be welcome to remain if they subscribe to that new constitution.

We have a sense of well-being, and now that we have dedicated our lives we are without anxiety. We pray morning and evening and remember our *shahids* who have joined the Guru. I feel better than when I was living my earlier life. For what sort of Punjab is it where boys younger than me have their legs broken or are shot? For independence we have to make sacrifices and certainly we have difficulties and problems. However, I am happy, and without worries close to my heart. I am marching towards my goal.

Do you want to give any message to the world?

Our voice should be heard at the UN. Internationally we are not getting justice. Sikhs everywhere should help the struggle in whatever way they can. Without such help the movement will lose momentum.

Anup Singh (deceased)

Young businessman. Graduate. Ordinary member of the KCF. Place of birth and residence: Gurdaspur City. Background: born 1969, of artisan origins. He is the younger of two brothers and has one sister. His father is retired from the army. Anup Singh was killed crossing the border, two days after this interview was held.

It was only when I was in BA Part I that I developed connections with the movement. Before that, because we were young, we knew nothing about Sikhism, rather we were all atheists. We used to go to the *gurdwara* just for the sake of it. We knew nothing about what was happening to the Sikhs and Sikhism, despite all of us being *keshadari* Sikhs [Sikhs with uncut hair]. We used to go to the Temple and listen to the lectures of Santji. I was 15 at the time. I'm 21 now. The first time I listened to Santji I couldn't understand anything of what he said. Then, through going and listening often, his message slowly dawned. My elder brother also started going to listen. Still we didn't participate in anything, but we became conscious of certain discriminations through Santji talking about them. For example, now I'm a graduate, if I apply for a job I'll not be given one due to being a Sikh; a Hindu will be preferred. The small farmers work so hard in their fields for which they do not receive their proper reward of a square meal at the end of the day. Hindus get better jobs. For example their *chamars* [untouchables] are posted as SSPs.

It was during the attack on Darbar Sahib that the extent of the discrimination became clear. If Darbar Sahib can be attacked, anything else is possible. After the attack, myself and my elder brother got baptised. It changed our lives. We began to pray and lead a religious life. Mentally we are convinced we are Singhs, though we are not complete Singhs yet. [He means they do not fulfil all the criteria to be regarded as good Sikhs.] We became vegetarian and gave up alcohol. Father previously had taken alcohol often. The whole family began reciting hymns each morning and evening. We met people in the movement and developed links with it and slowly got involved, gradually understanding what we couldn't understand at the beginning.

I speak Punjabi only. I read English and Hindi and can speak English a little. I would never use Hindi. I find that as a Sikh I am discriminated against. For example, once when my brother was in some sort of trouble, his friends visited the house. Obviously they had to be looked after well. Yet when the police found them in each other's company, they wanted to know why. My brother was tortured. This made us very emotional and I and some others started reorganising the Sikh Students Federation in our area. We were five or six *amritdhari* students. We started organising it in a Shiv Sena [an organisation of armed Hindu vigilantes] area because they were scaring the people. We used to organise strikes after the killing of innocent people, and protest against fake encounters. The Shiv Sena used to counter this. On one occasion there was a quarrel and the police arrested two of us, and then released us. The *lalas* [Hindu shopkeepers] gave money to the police to harass innocent students who were then killed in fake encounters. We were underground for over a couple of months for fear of being eliminated in a fake encounter. Then I was re-arrested and brought to Gurdaspur. Somehow my family got me released. However, I had hardly slept when the police came to my house. They said I was wanted by the SSP. My family didn't produce me. I was frightened and fled. They insulted our sister and our mother with bad language and took Father away in a jeep, saying that my sister and mother would also be taken to the police station. Then my elder brother came to where I was hiding and said to me that they could not live with these abuses and that I should give myself up to the police and if they shoot you, well …

In prison, I could not bear to see the condition of my class fellow and what he had been through. I was young and very scared. His legs were completely crushed and they had turned black. I was taken the next day to Dina Nagar and repeatedly accused of having connection with the underground movement. 'Tell us who you have killed and who you are friendly with,' they repeatedly questioned. I was tortured there and then transferred to Pathankot. The family meantime were searching for me and after four or five days I managed to send a message through a *hawaldar*. The family came and promised to get me free. Then I was brought back to Dina Nagar and I was tortured yet again by the same DSP. They used to place an iron pipe across my legs and two people – one on either side – would stand on it for five to seven minutes and roll it over my legs. They used to hang me upside down for a long time. We were three in that place – two other students and myself. Then there was also an old man whose only crime was that someone said they had seen the boys sitting with him at a shop. They used to put chillies in his eyes. He was a married old man with children. He could not get up and walk, he was tortured so badly.

Eventually my family managed to free me. They paid 20,000–25,000 rupees in bribes and that was even with someone influential speaking for me. The DSP himself told us that had he not been approached I would have been dead. For no crime whatsoever I had been ordered to be shot. I returned home and then every week used to have regular visits from the police. They took me to the police station on three or four occasions for interrogation. At first I thought if I ran away the police would interrogate and torture my family. My family also got fed up with me and they assured the police they would set me up in a small business. After some time my elder brother was also interrogated. They registered some case against him and he was sent to jail where he remained for five months. Again, on his release, I was called several times to the police station. I became convinced that they were going to kill me in the end. So, if this were so, I thought, why not join the struggle and die for the nation. Why be beaten up unnecessarily? I stayed on in the college studying, but I was being harassed all the time. However, by that time I was involved and that was better than sitting at home waiting to be killed. After a while I left my studies. I didn't apply for government service because we are not going to work for the government when we don't accept the Constitution. We don't expect jobs from them. They won't offer jobs to the Sikh youth, in any case. They only want to exterminate them. Even if they offer jobs to the Sikhs in the police force they will post them on the border so that they get killed. When my family had seen the condition of my body they told me not to worry about them and that they would get through things somehow. The family fully supported me in going underground.

Initially, I had not joined any organisation, despite the fact I had listened to Santji and had admiration for him. I joined the struggle only after being tortured. We had been shocked at the attack on the Akal Takht. We used to discuss it in meetings. Then the Delhi massacres occurred. At that stage we thought we must be slaves to experience such treatment. Two of my father's sisters are in Delhi. They told us about the atrocities, and this made up our minds. I know very little about the other movements in India that want their own home. I only know they want to be separate. This government is such. In any case we cannot as yet bother about these other movements when we are ourselves slaves. We have plenty of our own worries. I have now been in the struggle for the last one and a half years. In 1984 everyone was awakened and all the Sikhs are with us now in the struggle for freedom. The Sikh nation was asleep, but now the 1989 parliamentary elections have shown us the extent of our support. As long as we remain part of India we shall remain slaves. So we are trying to establish links with army and civil service people. Sikhs everywhere are very emotional about what happened. The people we have met are all of the view that the movement should be sharpened. The military will join at the proper juncture. Operation Bluestar showed that there could be desertions. We often meet army people and discuss everything with them and they assure us that they will join at the right time. Villagers help us in many ways – sheltering us, donating money. Some innocent villagers are tortured for this. It will be a long struggle for Khalistan, but in Khalistan there will be no discrimination. Everyone will be equal. Hindus can stay; it's up to them. We're not against them. Our fight is against the central government. Anybody who obstructs us is our enemy. Khalistan is our goal and anyone who opposes us – be they civil servant or supporter of the Akali Dal – is our enemy. In Khalistan the poor will be given their rights and if the son of a poor person is properly qualified, he will get the job. At present only the children of the rich, or those who pay a bribe of a lakh rupees, can get good jobs. Such discrimination will have no place in a future Khalistan. We are very happy in the struggle because we feel we are fighting for our independence. Whatever we are doing is for the best. We have no bad intentions towards anyone. It is only our enemies we kill. We are very happy. We are not worried about losing our lives. We are interested only in the freedom of the nation. We have not joined a marriage party! [In other words, we expect difficulty.]

Influential nations should raise our case in the UN and come here and see for themselves the real conditions of our people. If they have any humanitarian feeling they should come and see how our young people are killed by the police. Even the lone son of his parents is taken away to the border and shot. Nearly 200–250 students whom I knew two years earlier have been shot by police. I personally know this. They belonged to the Amritsar-Batala area and those who have survived have been given dirty police jobs so that they'll kill us. For example, it is quite typical for someone who has passed an engineering degree to be offered a policeman's job. You can imagine that under compulsion he takes the job, for his family's sake. I have travelled throughout districts Amritsar, Gurdaspur, Hoshiarpur, Patiala and Rupar. There is complete support for the Khalistan movement there. People as a whole don't believe they can get justice and freedom in India and this is why they fight for Khalistan. We can't understand what the Hindus of the Punjab want. Some Hindus support and finance police killing of Sikhs. Only a few are wise and acknowledge the discrimination against us.

Beant Singh (deceased)

Farmer. An area commander of the KCF. Ancestral village, Sukachira, tehsil Batala, District Gurdaspur. Background: married with two girls and four boys. Beant Singh was killed in internecine fighting between guerrilla groups in 1990.

I had gone to Amritsar to pay homage to *Bababji* [a term for the Guru Granth, the Sikh scripture]. There I met Bhindranwale. He had challenged me, 'You are not the son of your father if you do not take revenge for the wrong doing to our nation.' He told me that one must draw swords with those who push one against the wall. After listening to his speeches, I became increasingly troubled. From the beginning of my life, I have never cheated, never betrayed a friend or my community. So, by the grace of Waheguru, after the attack on Darbar Sahib I managed to forge close links with the boys, taking food and messages to them. Through this I gained some personal experience of them. But I also saw torture with my own eyes. The police would arrest the mothers and sisters of those boys who were on the run. There was one chap – Avtar Singh Rupawala [now dead]. He killed many BSF people and his *nanake* [maternal relative's home] was a mile from my own village. He was caught there. The police viciously beat his entire family. They shot dead his maternal grandfather after torturing him. He was 100 years old. They also beat up his virgin granddaughter. Rupawala had killed five or six policemen. When caught, he apparently said, 'Long live Khalistan' and then, since he was surrounded by police, shot himself in the stomach and in the head. They tortured his maternal uncle as well. When I saw all this, I thought of my own life as shameful.

A second incident had a personal effect on me. I had one of these old village guns. Someone informed the police of this. They took me to Batala and demanded I hand it over. I said to them I'm an ordinary common villager. I cut my fodder to feed my cattle and nothing more. (Though I did have the gun in fact.) The police said, 'You're all bastards. You kill people. Then you run to Darbar Sahib.' Three days they hung me up and beat me. Then they would give me a rifle and tell me to put the bits together. 'I've never seen such a weapon,' I would say. 'Don't you know how to eat your food?' the policeman would say. 'Of course I do, my mother trained me. Oh you stringer of pearls [*mothianwala,* i.e. wonderful man][16] I have no weapon.' On the fourth day I told them, 'You may as well kill me. If you really want to register a case against me for possessing an illegal weapon, I'll mortgage my land, bring some money for you, so that you can purchase a weapon for me.' My people in the village collected 6,000 rupees and I was released. Others were also tortured. They helped me. For example, when I was being tortured really badly and was about to confess, one of them persuaded me not to, as 'they only ask for further information as to associates and then in the end they kill you anyway and you'll then die the death of a dog. So be your father's son,' he told me, 'and continue to bear the pain. After a while they'll stop.' Other inmates also helped me. 'They've tortured you for one or two days. They'll go on for another two.' They did. They tied me up again and blood started pouring from my nose.

Can you describe in detail what sort of treatment was meted out?

They string you up naked. They don't even leave your *kachcha* [underpants] on. They open up your hair. They put salt and chillies on a stick and put it up your rectum. When they do this to you, the man in you is no longer alive. *Waheguru ji ka Khalsa* [wonderful is the Lord]. [He is unable to continue to relate details of his torture. After a while he resumes.] When they tortured me again, I was beaten with a slightly bigger stick.[17] I thought my present way of life is not worth living any longer. I realised that until we become free we must continue with the struggle. Then all the blood of the martyrs will not be wasted. With this in mind, I walked away from my family, my two girls and my three boys. Another son has since been born.

There was a *sarpanc*, called Darshan Singh, and he used to go with the police and get Sikhs martyred. This tout was producing alcohol illegally and the police gave him protection. Baba Jhamke [Sukhdev Singh Jhamke] said that some Sikh must get up and eliminate this unjust man. I was ploughing my fields and a little boy came and told me 'Uncle, Darshan Singh is in the village.' I left my plough. My wife knew the consequences and she pleaded 'We've got little children' (the eldest was nine). I said to her, 'Go and sit down. I've become a Singh of the Guru and my life is now dedicated to the Panth. I'm not yours any more and you are not mine.'

When Darshan Singh was about to leave his own village I was informed. I threw my bicycle in front of his motor bike. On this particular day he didn't have his bodyguard and he started running to the BSF picket. I pulled him from his motor bike and chopped him at 12 o'clock. Some people saw me and it became known. Police used to come looking for me and I'd be hiding here and there. Then they demolished my house. They took all my in-laws and friends to police stations. They still, even now, arrest and beat them up. My wife has been beaten up twice. Once she was arrested just before bringing my food to me in the fields but she didn't confess. This harassment is continuous. Since Gobind Ram's son has been killed we've had little peace. They took all the tube-well pumps from my farm.

Does that affect you?

Not at all! I don't feel anything at all. I'm working for the Guru's cause.

Can you give me more detail about your life?

I've crossed the border many times. I'm neither happy nor unhappy. This is Sat Guru's [the one and only true God's] work! The sacrifice will bear fruit. The enemies are the police and the Brahmins. They are like a snake, wherever they get an opportunity they will sting you. Our present targets are the BSF and CRP, blowing up their bridges and destroying their vehicles. When Sikhs come from the army, we meet with them. They discuss strategies with us and they give us training. They, too, are also telling us that their life is *haram* [shameful] but they have to wait for the right moment to redress their grievances. They don't let us go near their weapons as they say that we Sikhs in the army are not trusted. They are in a very unhappy position in the services.

We consider those Sikhs in other services as demons. For example, every time the local Punjab police gets paid and given rewards, they are very happily carrying out the government's work. So why shouldn't they kill us? They are our target. They are demoralised. Every time one Sikh is killed in action, so many of them will be killed. So they are very reluctant to attack us now. Only a very unfortunate *jhujharu* gets killed by the security forces. But the real fighter, who has the grace of Sat Guru [the True God], no matter how surrounded by paramilitary forces, he escapes. In the early days of my life I heard much about Shahid Bhagat Singh and Baba Dip Singh[18] in *dhadhi* gatherings. Wherever there were such gatherings I used to attend. I've always listened to their songs. Listening to them gave me a lot of strength. Listening to our people's history is important for us. In a future Khalistan our country and our people will be safer, they will get jobs and there will be no poverty. There won't be any atrocities on the innocent. But look at what happens today: police arrest the poor and weak and criminals get away with all the killing that they want. They beat up our old people and they plunder our daughters and sisters. At night they go out on robbing sprees and blame it on the *jhuhjaruan*.

Rachpal Singh Bhola (deceased)

A lieutenant-general in the KCF. At one time described as the best guerrilla they had found so far. Ancestral village, Tur, District Amritsar. Background: born 1968. They are a family of three brothers, of which he is the youngest. He has three sisters, two of whom are married. One brother is in Germany, and one is farming. He attended five classes at the village school.

When I was young I learnt much about the Singhs from the *dhadhi darbars*. I fell in love with the Singhs. I also listened to Sant Jarnail Singh's speeches, although I went to Darbar Sahib only after its attack.

What were the effects of the 1984 invasion of Darbar Sahib on you?

When one's brothers and sisters [he means fellow Sikhs] are killed, it does affect one! One becomes restless and can no longer sit at home in peace. It was such a sad thing that happened. My *chachca* [father's younger brother] had been with Bhindranwale's people. He was twenty-five when he was martyred. Hindus celebrated the attack on Darbar Sahib and were distributing sweets. *Chacha* attacked them and he in turn was attacked by the CRPF. He became a martyr. I had learnt much about the struggle from him, so shortly after his death I started getting involved in border activities. While *chacha* had been alive, I had been feeding and sheltering his friends. After his death, the police visited our house many times, as they do in all such other cases, insulting our daughters and sisters many times and dragging us to police stations. After such insults I could not just sit around. I left home. When 'our House' was attacked [a reference to Darbar Sahib] it had made all of us very sad. I went to see it. I was overwhelmed by grief. Since I left my home the police have incessantly troubled my family. I went to my sister's. She is married near Khem Karan (District Amritsar). Her husband's brother would often accompany the Singhs on their exploits, when he was on leave from the army. On one of these trips he was killed. He had been giving much secret help, carrying weapons from the border to the villages, then burying them. Someone informed on him, me and his brother, and we were all on the run. They were both killed. They were martyred. Now we cannot sit at home, ever.

After their killing I came to see Zaffarwal. Then I myself started taking goods across. I have been a lieutenant-general for the past four months and have twelve area commanders beneath me. I have selected them. Usually they have come to join us after repeatedly being in prison and tortured. There is nowhere else for them to go. I started working in Faridkot because of family links there. My recruits are from nearby villages in Amritsar. They have their own networks of reliable people on whom they can depend for food. Otherwise if we are not near homes we know, we simply ask the people for food. They feed us voluntarily. The local people who feed us give us quite a bit of information on the police and police pickets. We never take anything from anyone in the villages. No rich person stays in a village. We pick one of these big wealthy *lalas* [traders] or rob the banks. Sometimes we pick them up from their shops during daytime. We get our money from them very quickly.

Very few police help us in gathering information. The Sikh police are only concerned with killing us. However, we have close links with some in the Home Guard. We give them some money from time to time. When they're on guard they'll help us by stealing weapons. Some join us. There are also some sympathetic soldiers. However, at the moment there is not much active support coming from the army, though they say they'll join the struggle when there is a war. We are not close to urbanite Sikhs. Nevertheless they'll give us information as to who has what, or tell us when large sums of money are going to be deposited in the bank. They are sympathetic to the cause. We've got certain homes in towns that we go to. When we are injured we usually receive treatment at village level. If we cannot get better there, we approach some city doctors. Some are happy to treat us and others do it out of fear.

Jassa Singh Santuwal (deceased)

Chief of the Malwa region of the KCF. A lieutenant-general. Ancestral village near Zira, Ferozepur District. Background: born 1967. One older brother who is a farmer. Studied to matric. level. Circumstances of death: arrested by police and subsequently killed in a false encounter in mid-July 1991.

I joined the movement in 1984. I participated in a protest march to oppose the storming of the Darbar Sahib. We were arrested *en route* to Amritsar. I was in Ferozepur jail for six months. I had met Sant Bhindranwale prior to 1984. He had been to our village once. However, I only became involved when Darbar Sahib was attacked. During my six months in jail I met many committed Sikhs, many of whom have since been killed. When I came out of jail, I decided to participate in the struggle with arms. At that time we were working in small groups. I was with Harbhajan Singh Mand, president of the Ferozepur Sikh Students Federation. During early 1986 and early 1987 I was doing secret work for the movement. I was also involved in some actions as well. On 28 February 1986, I was re-arrested and taken for three months to Ferozepur and Faridkot CIA centres. Throughout this time I was tortured. My legs are still torn. These centres were full of young Sikhs. It was government policy to intimidate us. However, the more we were tortured the more mental clarity we gained and our sense of direction remained uppermost. It hardened us. Ten cases were registered against me. I was sent to a high security government jail in Sangrur and I was sentenced to remain there for two years. My only visitors were my parents, who encouraged me not to betray the Sikh people. They had no evidence for all the cases registered against me. They provided only false witnesses. The court was held within the prison itself, though I had access to a solicitor. No sooner had I been released than I was re-arrested again. After re-arrest I was moved around from jail to jail, blindfolded. Then I was bailed out by another judge. On release, I went on the run. I joined Gurnam Singh Wadala's group [president of the Sikh Students Federation, Gurdaspur]. I didn't see much organisation of the armed struggle. Only later did I learn he was following Gurjit Singh's instructions. So in 1987 I joined the KCF (Zaffarwal).

To support ourselves we steal from banks and Hindu industrialists. They give us money. We give some of this money to very poor Sikhs and to support the families of the many innocent boys who have been killed. We protect people if they are threatened with robbery. The people are our jungle. If we win, it will only be because of the support of the people.

As a lieutenant-general I know that the KCF is organised in all districts of Punjab at tehsil level. Most of our contacts were made in jails. I used a person in my *ilaqa* [local area] and Zaffarwal also, to study the border. I organised my own group and its supply lines. I travelled in every district, meeting all the lieutenant-generals. All lieutenant-generals keep a link with each other. They form a high command and take operational decisions. For any actions to occur, the leaders of the various groups have to come together and agree to whatever has been proposed. They then go back to their various cells, with their own supply routes and safe houses. Infiltration destroys only one cell. If one of the groups is not operating according to rule, we discipline its leader and then, ultimately, if this continues, disarm him. Literate people are now prepared to give us support by participating in military action. The new young recruits are used to send messages and carry weapons. For example, if we want a press statement delivered, they'll do that. Only after they've done that sort of thing for quite some time will they be directly recruited.

It is a policy of our organisation to forge links with the armed forces. We would prefer if they would give us support from within and not leave the forces. Lawyers, intellectuals give us their ideas regarding our struggle. After discussion, if we like some of these ideas, we adopt them. Intellectuals have advised us for example against bothering too much with cultural reforms. The eating of meat and the drinking of alcohol is irrelevant and if we put out a call for a ban on these, people are bound to go against us.

We are very reluctant to get close to the Sikh Student Federation boys. In the past they have done us a lot of damage. They use us for their own popularity and as a bargaining tool. After that they draw close to the government. Our policy is to expand our organisation to the other states so that we create hell for the government from every direction.

Do you have any message for the outside world?

This government destroyed our beloved Darbar Sahib. Every day it kills people in false encounters. We need help for our true and lawful struggle. We have a vision of Khalistan as a place where we can live in freedom and where our way of life can be preserved. Minorities will have their own special rights safeguarded.

Jarnail Singh Hoshiarpur

Lieutenant-general of the KCF and Panthic Committee member. After the death of Sukhwinder Singh Gora, Deputy Commander of the KCF. Ancestral village Sathiala, tehsil Baba Bakala, District Amritsar. Background: born 1966, the second youngest of five brothers, of whom one works for the Electricity Board, another for the bank, while a third farms and the youngest is a student. He has two married sisters. He has studied beyond matric. level. The family has six acres.

I gained my knowledge of Sikhism from my Father. It seemed to me that Sikhism is like a date palm – if you reach the very top you experience its sweetness but if you go only halfway, you fall and break your bones. In Sikhism you have to be mentally clear to enjoy it. Father – an *amritdhari* from the very beginning – participated in the *jathas* to the Darbar Sahib. I had a lot of discussion with him and with one Dr Mohinder Singh of our village, who was a member of the SGPC for Baba Bakala. I was very interested in the *vars* [heroic odes] of the *dhadhis* and father used to read many books from the Sikh Missionary College. I was too young to fully understand Bhindranwale's speeches.

When Darbar Sahib was attacked my father was in Mehta Chowk Gurdwara with one of my elder brothers. There was a curfew and the officers came and informed Baba Thakur Singh, the head of Dam Dami Taksal, that Sant, Amrik Singh and Shubeg Singh had been killed and that they should come to collect their remains. However, half an hour later, the army said they would be unable to release the bodies. During the attack and in its immediate aftermath the army did not allow any movement on the GT road going to Amritsar. However, people reached through the *galis* [lanes and small streets]. When we saw the destruction, the flames of fire burst in us. We felt we were walking dead. I had gone to Darbar Sahib with my paternal cousin just before 3 June. On that day, there was an exchange of fire from both sides. We were part of the crowd outside and quite a few people were injured. When we came back to my village, which is near Rayya, people were saying, 'they have snatched the turbans from our heads'. They were very despondent. People were up all night. The next day there was a surge of people heading towards Darbar Sahib. It was stopped. They remained demoralized until the killing of Mrs Gandhi. To some extent this saved our honour. As a family we kept on going to Mehta Chowk and to Anandpur Sahib on Kar Sewa. There were a lot of political discussions taking place. The main conclusion of all of them was that we should have our own separate home. Three trucks went from my village to attend the Sarbat Khalsa in 1986. People were delighted that the *qaum* [nation] was together, acting in unison. Slowly I resumed my visits to Darbar Sahib during 1987. I gradually became close to two known militants. Then they started coming to see me in the village. I gave them shelter. When Rode came to Darbar Sahib and gave the slogan of *puran azadi*, so many Singhs – you could not count them – were infuriated. They asked him why he was confusing the issue, and told him that if he were afraid for his skin then why did he not just sit at home. There was much rumour circulating that bad things were going on inside the Darbar Sahib. I didn't see anything. However, keep it in mind that Darbar Sahib is the home of our people. Therefore thieves come, as well as those doing *gurbani.* I tend to think, nevertheless, that it's government propaganda, for we were keeping a watchful eye. I left before Operation Black Thunder for my village. Some of those I knew got killed; others surrendered. After that, I got cut off. I was never arrested or tortured. I had the Guru's protection. But one of my elder brothers was arrested by SSP Gobind Ram and was lodged in Gurdaspur jail for eight to nine months. They registered some false cases against him. Mainly they wanted me to give myself up and they kept on coming to the farm. All of us would have to leave in advance of the police. Villagers could warn us they were coming. We had to leave my mother behind to take their insults. Since the police were constantly looking for me, I took to arms. I joined the KCF, Jhamke group. Jhamke's group split after he was killed and then I made direct contact with Zaffarwal. In 1989 I started getting involved with direct actions. When the message came that they had made me a Panthic Committee member I thought to myself that this sack of hay was too heavy for me! They said I must do my *sewa* [duty]. So I prayed that I may keep my pledge and offer my head to the Panth.

Ours is a national struggle. It is simply that people want to be free. We want to get rid of Brahmanic imperialism. They eat our Punjab. To this end I've attacked many economic targets and many army vehicles and depots. However, I doubt if recruits are joining us now, if only because of the torture to which they've been subjected.

Regarding those in the Sikh Students Federation, all I can say is that they talk of Khalistan! [rather than doing anything about it]. Police do nothing to them. By contrast when we talk about Khalistan both we and the families who help us are brutally tortured. We have no links with the Federation now. Gurjit Singh was constantly snatching our boys – buying them, breaking them or killing them. If he had been truly committed to the cause he would not have done that. Also, we never go near the other *jathebande* because we know they are infiltrated. We have met a number of Manochahal's lower-level boys. On one occasion, while discussions were going on, he killed two of our boys. One of the boys killed – Ahail Singh from Delhi – had lost all his family members in the massacre in 1984. Manochahal said he had been killed because he had come to steal their weapons. But I ask you, would this be the act of someone who had lost all his family members, save for one sister? Rather it would be the act of a criminal. People are wicked! He was an educated boy and it was unfortunate he came in their way! Even the security forces can't get at our boys. But Manochahal and the Babbars can. We have not retaliated. For they are very discredited now. People are saying that they may possibly be linked to the security forces in some way.

Panjwar has killed many KCF boys. He takes responsibility for those killings. The purpose of Panjwar and of the Babbar Khalsa is to destroy us, control the struggle, and do a deal with the government. We are aware of what they are doing and we have no discussions with them about unity. We've given instructions to our boys not to meet them in any way. You cannot have unity with those who fight against Khalistan.

I met Mann in July 1990. I had a long discussion with him and he told me we were involved in a very righteous struggle. He said he held Zaffarwal in high regard. My team keeps in touch with him and we have a good understanding with him. He said to me 'if I can't do anything good for the struggle, I won't harm it'. He has a lot of respect in the villages. However, the policy of people becoming leaders because they have suffered and particularly the policy of martyrs' widows becoming political leaders, will not continue. For in every home there is a *shahid*. And there will be many more. For each day, at sunrise, Sikhs have garlanded the nation with their heads.

Many of the killings and robberies of innocent people are done by government forces so that our freedom fighters can be discredited and lose the people's support. Entire families have been wiped out. Once we caught four policemen red-handed. They had given a family notice that they would come to collect money. After interrogation we found they had Babbar Khalsa notepaper on them. In another case, in village Buttar, near Mehta Chowk, two families [he names them] had received letters demanding two lakh rupees. They gave the time when they were coming to collect the money and warned the families that they would be killed, if they informed anyone. These families informed us, and we went there to guard them and their houses. These letters were from the Dashmesh regiment (Matthewal). We read in newspapers about killings in buses and trains and Panjwar taking the responsibility. Panjwar told me these are all 'false responsibilities'. He denied killing Sandhu. The police killed Sandhu and took responsibility in Panjwar's name.

As to the Taksal, we are keeping some boys over there and we still talk to Baba Thakur Singh. Nothing much happens there. When one of us goes there we're just there for fifteen minutes. Baba gives money to the families of the *shahids* and attends their *bhogs*. There are also quite a few students there. Otherwise the *taksal* has nothing to do with Sikh nationalism. However, he gives the village families a lot of moral support by doing *kirtan* and *ardas*, giving them confidence that Khalistan will come about soon.

The people who are really useful to us are the Kar Sewa people. They draw their strength from volunteers from all over to renovate and rebuild *gurdwaras*. It's a good camouflage for us. At night they give us food. Someone who's not involved with the movement brings it out to us in the fields. The *gurdwaras* are like forts for the movement. Most villagers are full of anticipation of what will come from the struggle. We tell them that our goal is to destroy the structure of government, to remove Brahmin rule from our land forever [the actual words used are 'to roll up and remove the bedding of the Brahmins from the house']. We remind people of all the promises made to the Sikhs by the government. Ours is a history of betrayal. Whatever we have, they want to snatch it away from us. We talk about all of these things to the villagers in the heart of their homes, and we produce leaflets for the schools and gurdwaras to boycott the system. We do not do this directly; we have another network for this, relying on old people and young boys. Our jungle is the people. The struggle of the ordinary people is stronger than the bullet. They recognise that the Punjab police are mercenaries and that they are paid to kill us. Some villagers will leak out information to us on raids and ambushes.

How would you describe your present life?

We pray to the true God that our nation and people can experience the warmth of freedom. At the moment our youth, our women and our old people are slaves. We are very happy fighting. Yet sometimes we do get affected when we think that in times gone by we protected the honour of our Hindu daughters and sisters and yet they in return now humiliate our women, and rob our families' honour. It is not ordinary Hindus who do this. They have no guts. Its the security forces. And some Sikhs participate along with them in that. We urge all Sikhs to give one final push to the Brahmin government to achieve Khalistan. [His actual words were: to put their shoulders to the plough together, with force.]

Notes

1. Punjabi Suba means a Punjabi-speaking state. This was achieved in 1966 after a long, peaceful and non-violent campaign. However, certain Punjabi-speaking areas were excluded from the new state and Chandigarh, the state capital, was not handed over to the Punjab.

2. Bhartiya Janata Party. A right wing Hindu party which believes that minorities have no place in India unless they subscribe to the Hindu way of life.

3. The Arya Samaj was an organisation which sought to bring Hindus who had converted to Sikhism, and Sikhs as such, back into the Hindu fold. Hindu–Sikh relations became embittered as a consequence of that.

4. Brahmanism, for the Sikhs, is synonymous with the division and discrimination characteristic of a hierarchical society based on the rules of purity and pollution.

5. What is implied is that a life of dignity and harmony can only be achieved

if one has honour. When one's honour is stolen, the very continuance of one's life is shameful.

6. These are the words of the tenth Guru, Guru Gobind Singh, in the *Zafarnama*.

7. One of the founders of the movement. He was killed in police detention.

8. It seems that Baba Joginder Singh was trying to cash in on the fame of his stepson's name. Dilbir Singh, who was close to the Sant and to whom the Sant had requested at the end of his life 'Be loyal to our friendship', reports that Baba Joginder Singh and the Sant had a distant relationship. 'His share of the property had been eight acres yet he lived in one room thirty-feet long. In one corner there was dried fodder and in another dung cakes. He did not bother about his poverty and he was not close to his wife and family. Particularly he never had a harmonious relationship with his stepfather. Whenever he visited the Darbar Sahib, he never bothered to see him,' Dilbir Singh recalls.

9. This phrase has a religious reference which I cannot locate. It means that the very weapons which others use to violate your rights can also be used to defend your legitimate rights. It refers to the general notion that one can only secure one's protection and implement just rule for all with the aid of morally motivated force.

10. This is an indirect reference to the Sikh principle *wand chako* (share). He means that if you give and keep on giving, you in return will receive.

11. Gobind Ram was a notorious police chief who as SSP Faridkot and subsequently SSP Gurdaspur was responsible for many acts of terror, quite a number of which are on record. Gobind Ram was killed by a bomb in January 1990. One of his sons was killed in October 1989.

12. Satwant Singh and Kehar Singh were hanged in January 1989 for the murder of Mrs Indira Gandhi. The latter was an innocent man.

13. He means, literally, wearers of *kadr* – homespun white cloth – and, by association, those for whom the wearing of this cloth is a trademark, namely members of the Congress Party.

14. Two thousand Sikh soldiers were committed to General Court Martial following this incident. In a letter to the then President of India, Giani Zail Singh (quoted in Nayar and Singh, 1984: 160–3) certain high ranking military officers attempted to explain the mutiny of the Sikh and Punjab regiments in the following words.

> The Sikh soldier is nurtured today, as in the past, on his religious tenets and traditions which have been fully approved by the Army and the government of independent India during the last 37 years … Before being inducted into the Army as a trained soldier he takes the oath of allegiance at a ceremonial parade by physically touching with both hands the Guru Granth Sahib which is displayed on parade for this purpose. Thereafter he is led to the Regimental War Memorial [which embodies the Chakra and the Khanda – the coat of arms of the Khalsa] and ceremonially adopts as his own the vow taken by Guru Gobind Singh at the time of taking up the sword of righteousness against Moghul oppression. The vow reads:
>
> Grant me oh Lord this boon
> That I may not falter from doing good

May I entertain no fear of the enemy when confronted by him in battle
And may I be sure of my victory!
May my mind be so trained as to dwell on Thy goodness
And when the last moment of my life should come
May I die fighting in the thick of battle

The official motto of the Regiment 'Nische Kar Apni Jeet Karon' [Be sure of victory] is taken from this vow. And it is enjoined on every soldier, officer of the Regiment to memorise this vow and to act upon it. We wish to point out that it is the duty of the commanders to ensure that no conflict arises between the observation of military duty and the religious faith, practices and susceptibilities of the individual soldier. Signed Lt. Gen. M.S. Wadalia, Lt. Gen. Harbaksh Singh, Lt. Gen. J.S. Dhillon, Lt. Gen. J.S. Aurora and Lt. Gen. Sartaj Singh.

15. Those working for the Electricity Board have official identity papers. They are relatively free to pass messages. The Electricity Board frequently does not disconnect the power when accounts have not been paid. Partly this is because meter readers in the Majha region as well as junior land revenue officers (*patwaris*) were among the first to be got rid of.

16. By using this term he is trying to flatter his torturers. Most boys hurl abuse ceaselessly at their captors.

17. He uses the word *tahuni* to belittle his experience of pain. *Tahuni* is a word describing the mild thrashing one might give to a child. The appropriate word reflecting the severity of the torture inflicted is *tashaddar*, which indicates a level of cruelty and terror of greater magnitude than *zulm* (oppression).

18. Baba Dip Singh was a legendary figure in Sikh history who fought against the Afghans knowing he was outnumbered, to prevent the desecration of the Darbar Sahib. Legend has it that he continued fighting with his head on his left palm, wielding a sword in his right hand, only just able to reach the Harimandir.

8

Concluding Remarks

Chaliand (1980: 8–9) has remarked that '[p]aradoxically human beings as groups turn out to have fewer rights than individuals unless they form a state ... it has been easier for a country to achieve formal independence from an ex-colonial power than for a minority to obtain a measure of effective autonomy within a Third World state.' One reason explaining the Sikh difficulty in achieving such a state has been their structural integration into the wider Indian polity and their position on an open plain. Had Sikh society managed to preserve intact 'its own religious, cultural and legal institutions' as the Scots have done (Nairn, 1977: 106) and had there been a thriving civil society, it would have mattered little that any form of political sovereignty they had had previously had gone. In any case, what was often called the Kingdom of Ranjit Singh was in fact the kingdom of Punjab and it was not run in accordance with Sikh principles. Throughout the years since the independence of India and Pakistan, Sikhs had to fight to retain Punjabi. Had the Punjabi language disappeared as a medium of instruction, so too would their access to the Guru Granth. Additionally, the highly centralised nature of the Indian polity had succeeded in siphoning off most of Punjab's wealth and making inroads into the identity of the Sikhs. Aside from the dependence on the state for jobs, the nature of allegiance in the rural areas, a subject to which I shall return, played its role in defeating the politics of principle which Bhindranwale and the Sarbat Khalsa resolution epitomised. All alliances in the rural areas have some limited strategic purpose in mind and hence, ultimately, they create fragmentation. Thus, while most interviews with the KCF guerrillas have commented on support levels among the population, I was to witness personally these support levels falling away during 1992 as farmers experienced an intensification of the terror and their allegiance swayed. On a visit to the Punjab in September and October 1992 it seemed that the farmers had retreated into privately held convictions in the face of ever growing police dominance and repression. By January

1993, such dominance was assured for the time being, though this in no way implied that the public regarded the police to be guardians of their liberty, albeit that they had eliminated extortion and allowed people the freedom to once again wander safely on their own land. In January 1993, a spirit of defeat hung over the villages and their inhabitants; a certain silence in their inner selves about the events of the past 8½ years. The population were looking to who exhibited the most power and their loyalties were wavering. Both friendship and enmity hovered in the same pair of eyes. And no one is perhaps more dangerous than when they are uncertain of their own allegiances. This fluidity was classic for situations of occupation and civil war, but this desire to be on the winning side aided the fall of the guerrillas by exhibiting so very little faith in them. Given this sort of atmosphere in the countryside, it was a miracle that the committed were remaining together, their ideals and connections unaffected by the repression. Certainly their families were fleeing or in hiding. Their children were being hounded out of school and the process of rounding up those who had given shelter and food or who were still giving it and who were thought to have militant sympathies, had begun. However, as one landlord in Amritsar District stated, this was merely 'the spring weeding'.

The problems which have occurred within militant ranks, many detailed in Chapters 4 and 5, and which enabled a successful counter-insurgency to be launched, have a number of sources. The nature of Pakistani support for the Sikh insurgency, as well as Jat Sikh social structure and political culture, have been significant factors in undermining the movement.

Some KCF fighters who survived were based in Pakistan. In the pre-1986 days, arrangements for them depended on the local population. Quite spontaneously the latter fed those who managed to cross the border, and they were to continue to do so through the years. They had tremendous sympathy for the Sikhs, because they fought the Hindus. They donated their trucks and allowed their homes to be used for storing weapons. At checkpoints, police, without being instructed, would let Zaffarwal's arms through. However, according to informants, the local population and its attitudes were rather different from some officers in the ISI. Some fighters were armed more than others. For as one field officer in Pakistan intelligence remarked of the CJJ fighters, 'they were the real fighters coming through, strong and healthy. Zaffarwal's boys were so skinny.'

Funding to the CJJ increased not only because of the above perception of them but also because 'Pakistani field officers took money from the *jhujharuan* for themselves' and the CJJ could pay better. (Informant's name cannot be disclosed.) There were those within the ISI dedicated to the continuance of the CJJ for personal reasons. Its policy was to create chaos in Punjab, rather than to concede sovereignty to the Sikhs. Thus, due to the personal corruption of field staff and the apparently considerable control over the CJJ exercised by Indian intelligence, the latter were able to penetrate Pakistani networks. Gill's statement on p. 133 records that.

However, neither the chaos created by indiscriminate arms supplies from Pakistan, nor the chaos created by police tactics as described in Chapter 5, would have been possible had it not been for the socially and culturally sustained ambition of individual guerrilla leaders and the resultant political fragmentation.

It appeared to be difficult to combine the ideals of the Sarbat Khalsa, with its emphasis on the Sikh principle of the welfare of all, with the actuality of family vendettas in the rural areas. These always involved more than the family, that is, a network of persons strategically placed in all branches of administrative life. There was an inordinate respect given to the powerful, rather than to principles of legality and, correspondingly, a use of the powerful for unlawful ends. A member of the Council of Khalistan recalls that he'd been approached innumerable times 'by decent people', as he put it, requesting him to do them a favour by getting rid of their opponents. Equally, he also had people coming to him from the militant side saying 'don't worry we'll get your land back for you'. He was clear that the struggle was not about the elimination of personal opponents and the reclaiming of one's land, but about bringing into being a society where laws would take care of private vendettas as well as illegal land seizures. One can safely assume that if people were prepared to approach him when his group were powerful, likewise, when the police turned the tables on the guerrillas, they would approach them also, with equal ease and as though there were no differentiation. That indeed is happening. This use of whichever group was in power to further one's own very limited goals did not bode well for the building of organisations to achieve long-term political goals, nor for issues of ideological principle to achieve salience. The powers of the state were greatly enhanced by this flexibility of allegiance and the temporary, situational character of all allegiance. From this emerged the unprecedented loneliness of the present Sikh position internationally. This was the story of the tragedy of modern progressive values being corrupted, betrayed, if not destroyed, by pre-modern forms of allegiance and mentality. The state was attacking the Sikhs as a people. It did not face, in Turton's terms (1984: 43), a subjected people, 'people already formed as social subjects'. However, feuds and factions within rural society divided the resistance to the state, aiding and abetting their own elimination. Jat social structure could not 'carry' Sikh values. An additional difference of perspective, between those in the rural areas and a rich urban class among the Sikhs, aided the repression process. Urbanites in Delhi and in the Punjab frequently told me that they did not want to live in a Jatistan (though in fact there were many artisans and labourers in the guerrilla movement). Quite a number of Sikhs from an urban background worked for Indian intelligence to defeat the movement, while other Sikh urbanites, who favoured Khalistan, worked to dilute it by suggesting that it cover a wider area than the Sikh majority areas, so that they would not be dominated by the Jats.

Two challenges emerge from this period. The interviews with the guerrillas show that Sikh principles are seen as a protection against economic injustice, and a spiritual resource when faced with cruelty and oppression, as well as an explanation for injustice. However, I am not suggesting thereby that militant activity had a religious reference. It was a political militancy reacting to recent circumstances brought about by the Indian state. The Sarbat Khalsa resolution provides a challenge to create from Sikhism a political model for the running of a modern state. Sikhism has ideas of social and economic injustice but it does not, in itself, have a blueprint for a state. Kramer (1987) has noted the same for Islam. This is one focus which required the concentration of all in the movement.

A second challenge, equally as important, is the necessity of changing the patterns of allegiance in the rural areas. Never, traditionally, have allegiances been stable. They remain similar to the *misls* of two centuries ago as described by Gupta:

> Most of the followers of a particular *sardar* considered themselves not as his subordinates but as his associates and partners ... in each enterprise undertaken, and thus regarded the lands acquired as the common property of all in which each claimed his individual share according to his quota of contribution. Hence the term *misl*, a confederacy of equals under a chief of their own selection. One could always transfer to another chief (1952: 135).

The position of an individual in an alliance was equal to all others. It was certainly not permanent and it was meritocratic, in that he got what he worked for and no more. All writers have stressed that leaders were acceptable because of their innate qualities and that none could neglect the needs or wishes of their followers. These needed constant care and readjustment. As in tribal Afghanistan, power is granted by consensus and it is not necessarily given to a man for life (Roy, 1986: 22). Meritocracy, rather than hierarchy, governed, and this affected the relative permanence of political allegiances. Then, too, the individual's relationships to others, and his status in relation to them, seem to have been affected by the religious precepts that 'serving mortals is a sin at par with untruth', and that no Sikh is a subject except of God. The individual twisted this firm rule of religious tradition, which is one guaranteeing social non-enslavement, bending it to ensure his own private and selfish dominance over others.[1] It has been converted into non-cooperation in civic life. It was used as a cover for indiscipline. The social and political implications of this behaviour, in the present context, and the consequent violent competitiveness that has undermined the social fabric, are that Sikhs have become nothing but an aggregate of individuals when facing the state. This actual fact of life contradicted Sikh tradition. For Sikh traditions have been collective, displaying a concern for the condition of society. Nayar (1979: 72) says 'On Guru Gobind Singh's death ... the Khalsa were authorised to take collective decisions. There was no difference between *sangat* [congregation] and Sat Guru [the one and true God]. The first decision they took was to replace Moghul authority by their own.' The *sangats* were described 'as an orchard containing ... thickly grown fruit' and as Bhai Gurdas, an interpreter of the Sikh scripture, says: 'the depth and value of *sangat* is unfathomable. It is *sach khand* [the true or immortal realm] in itself where God is worshipped' (var 29 pauri 13).

This collective tradition stresses cooperation. Yet present Sikh politicians knew nothing of the first Sarbat Khalsa held after 150 years, or about the decisions it reached. The Sarbat Khalsa resolution was passed at the Akal Takht and is thereby binding, according to Sikh institutional practice in the period preceding Ranjit Singh's rule. The Sikh political factions, in caring little or nothing for this resolution, have perhaps shown a flexibility towards their own institutions that tempts others to disregard them also. Clearly this pure – in the sense of authentic – tradition converges with many others, as would be expected in an area that has been a corridor for centuries. Other idioms have broken into the Sikh tradition. One of them has been the state tradition whereby many families have been happy to serve Indian state institutions. Secondly, Sikh tradition has been more than a little touched by Jat culture, with its emphasis on the individual in all respects: individual leadership, individual character, individual bravery, etc. The flexibility of allegiance and the lack of co-operation with one another, except for strategic considerations, so characteristic of Jat political practice are associated, in their eyes, with their personal freedom and independence. And readers will have noticed the proliferation of personalities mentioned in the text, each having their own following, and the ensuing innumerable divisions. This form of political practice has undermined the movement, and there are no signs that the dangers of this behaviour for the Sikhs as a collectivity have been appreciated, except on the level of tactical error. A guerrilla movement, if it is to be run properly, must be responsive to issues concerning organisation, ideology and tactics and must free itself of cultural and historical constraints. Patterns of behaviour and organisation that are submissive to cultural history will lead to inadequate functioning and will be known in advance. For the security services, also manned by Jats, are the product of the same traditions. The different guerrilla units must have known the reality of the state power facing them, even while acting as though they were in the *misl* era. Making their own separate truces, certain guerrilla units would win local and temporary pre-eminence. Such behaviour ultimately weakened the movement. The anarchy of the *misl* period was recreated, and just as farmers had been ruined then by those demanding revenue, whether they be government troops or plundering bands of robbers, so, too, in the post-1988 period they were ruined by extortionists, both police and militant alike. Thus two guerrillas of the Khalistan Commando Force (Zaffarwal) speaking to an army officer who was a captive of a guerrilla leader in the Tarn Taran area told him 'Uncle, don't think you'll see Khalistan in either your generation or ours. Everyone is in the movement only for the money and for the rivalry.'

Questions of exposure

1. A mixture of traditions has weakened the movement for independence. The 26 January 1986 Sarbat Khalsa elevated an old tradition of the Sikhs. However, the elevation of the Gurmata and Sarbat Khalsa tradition does not necessarily consign Sikh nationalism to the realm of 'culture spiritualised' to quote Kapferer (1988: 2). It was not a nationalism that made culture 'into an object and thing of worship' (Kapferer, 1988: 209). Rather the resurrection of old traditions has to be seen in the context of the assault on the Sikh faith and people in 1984, since '[e]thnocidal state policies imply ethnogenesis' (Wilson, 1991: 57).

Even serving officers in the police and civil administration viewed militancy over the issue of sovereignty as having come about only as a consequence of injustice. Amongst the fighters, a degree of entrancement with culture and past history was certainly apparent. This was most noticeable through the influence of the songs of the *dhadhis*. These songs, containing the ideals of a people, provided motivating spirit and hence had capacities for mobilization. They recorded reality and dignified the resistance to it, but had no further message to young people except sacrifice. It was the harsh realities of day-to-day existence on an open plain, amidst enemies from one's own people and from one's own village, that most determined the path the resistance took after the first three or four years. The intention to have a society run in accordance with their own values neither implied fundamentalist tendencies nor the spiritualisation of culture. It was merely a means of asserting the Sikh tradition over the state tradition of individual collaboration and the Jat tradition of individual dominance, both of which had the family and its networks as their core rather than the Sikh principle of 'the welfare of all'.

In an article regarding Peruvian peasants who support Sendero Luminoso, Degregori (1991: 244) remarks, 'It is not strange that people should long for ... the society of great harmony since they have been terribly damaged by the movement of history in Peru.' In the Punjab, the intrusion of the state into all aspects of Sikh life, created an awareness among Sikhs of their egalitarian and democratic ethic and their different social and political institutions. These contrasted with the hierarchy of the state which they served. Equally, the ongoing guerrilla movement made visible all the excesses of Jat society: that force rules; that one must always keep a group around one, for one's protection and advancement; that jealousy greatly affected their relationships *vis-à-vis* each other and the life of any of their organisations. Schoeck's (1969: 96) remark that 'What embitters and corrodes the jealous man is a kind of emotional fiction ... that the other has, so to speak, taken the fame away from him' explains much of the behaviour that destroyed the KCF as an organisation and the militant movement as a whole.

Among the committed, both the state tradition and the Jat tradition were seen as contrary to the Sikh spirit. Hence the vision, in the Sarbat Khalsa document, of a society where there will be social peace for all. The Sarbat Khalsa document voiced Sikh tradition. The distinct Sikh tradition always came to the fore when the climate of tolerance had been foregone in the wider society. For example, Kahn Singh Nabha's proclamation 'We are not Hindus' was set in circumstances of economic dislocation preceding the Land Alienation Bill and of proselytisation. Likewise the economic and political centralisation, following the reorganisation of Punjab in 1966 and the genocide of 1984, led to the assertion once again of core tradition. Such an assertion occurred at moments of danger.[2]

The Sarbat Khalsa document was the antidote to the irrelevant personal ambitions that flourished among both the warring parties: the guerrillas and the police. I say irrelevant because clearly when the state is bent on finishing off the Sikhs as a people – which is how matters are perceived in some quarters – behaviour which does not adapt to that situation is out of context. Yet because of family feuds, or for reasons of personal pride and ambition attached to a service career, or a guerrilla career, much behaviour could be labelled as belonging to that category. In his own terms, the Director-General of Police was doing his job superbly well. He was the one credited with finishing off militancy in the Punjab. He regarded this as the crowning glory of his IPS career. In the process many youth were killed, not all of them militants, but some completely innocent. This none too selective killing was occurring when right-wing Hindu nationalists had become a growing force in Indian political life. His pride in doing his job well was inappropriate when it was a common enough view in Delhi that it would be a good idea to finish off the Sikhs by starting a war with Pakistan. Gill was a primary example of the state tradition, which would be hard for service personnel in Punjab to abandon. 'Would you like to be ruled over by a Mann or a Badal?' he asked me, laughing. All Sikhs wanted government jobs. The Zaffarwal interview records how he tried to get into the army while the brother of his deputy, Sukhwinder Singh Gora, attempted to get a BSF job.

Through the years, serving the state has been an important part of rural life. Resistance to the state also has been significant. The guerrilla groups were captured by a different part of the Sikh past and just as inappropriately organised to combat state power. Viewed traditionally, they were like the *misls*, disputing over operational areas. Similar to the constituent parts of the Dal Khalsa, the eighteenth-century Sikh army, with each guerrilla leader remaining in command of his followers, they were dissimilar to it in that they rarely joined their forces for collective action. Each of these forces, as well as each person within them, had the right to pursue his own alliances. Malcolm wrote favourably of such decentralisation, viewing it as preserving the Sikhs as a people. In contemporary times, the consequences of decentralisation as a principle of organisation was havoc, anarchy and killing on a hitherto unprecedented scale. It no longer performed the same function as it did in Malcolm's day. The impact of a large and accumulating number of deaths of young people over the years was defused by the tradition of serving the state and by what, in the Punjab, may be termed as the Jat tradition of using others within state structures to rid oneself of one's personal enemies.

2. A mixture of personnel within each guerrilla group was damaging to their operations and long-term success and contributed to the exposure and elimination of their members. In their composition, groups covered the full spectrum of rural life: the uneducated, the bandit, the religious person and the political nationalist. Although all in the guerrilla movement – at least until 1988 – were aware of who were in their groups, nevertheless many young guerrillas who died thought some sort of Utopia would be ushered into existence just by the mere achievement of Khalistan, and this too even when the cruelty inflicted upon them came from their own people. Such treachery from within could have been anticipated, but was not. All the interviews, for example, show a pride in their history rather than a critical look at it. Those who were committed were undoubtedly trapped by the fear and envy aroused by the person of principle in a land of compromise. The ones who survived the longest were the successful gunrunners, like Panjwar[3] – in effect no more than bandits – who received extensive political patronage. After

Labh Singh's murder he had turned into a mercenary for his own safety and then, to give him some measure of financial independence, had become a gangster. The state reconstituted his gang to work in co-operation with police and paramilitary units until it outlived its usefulness.

The mix of personnel within guerrilla ranks was damaging due to an absence of ideological training. Without such a training recruits had no ideological discipline. Hence the necessary polarization between those who were for and against Sikh sovereignty could not emerge. The absence of such a training may have resulted in the cell system being smashed. Equally, perhaps, the Sikhs needed to have a more sophisticated cell system.[4] Carelessness resulted in the deaths of individual guerrillas and the penetration of their networks. For example, guerrillas would be permitted to be involved in multiplex relationships which diverted them from their stated goal. Thus Nishan Singh Makhu (not a KCF member) was involved in the transport business and when he claimed money owed to him by his partner, who didn't want to pay, the latter took the police to exactly the spot in the fields where he was sleeping.

3. One can never know the full range of connections of guerrilla movement at any stage of its history, unless one has access to intelligence sources. However, even then, the very varied nature of the help given to a resistance movement prevents comprehensive knowledge. One *can* say that this particular resistance movement has been especially exposed, owing to having to thrive on an open plain, though I mention this last of all since those reporting on the views of those engaged in such resistance (for example Regis Debray on Che Guevara, 1975: 88) are of the view that 'It is not the topography which in the final analysis determines whether or not an area presents conditions favourable to ... the armed struggle; it is the presence or absence of sufficiently antagonistic social contradictions.' None the less, the open plain imposed limitations on the functioning of the movement from its very beginnings, one of which was the early pocketing of the movement by Pakistan as young Sikhs fled across the border during Operation Woodrose. Guerrilla connections on a worldwide scale remained undeveloped. Unlike the Basques (Douglass and Zulaika, 1990: 245) the Sikhs had few contacts with other movements for national liberation. In turn, an almost total absence of such ties – barring the Afghans and the Kashmiris – allowed their political front (which, in the case of the KCF Zaffarwal, was located in London) to cultivate ties with respectable sections of society in Punjab, mainly professionals having affiliations to human rights groups and to international human rights bodies. In the short term, human rights groups were able to inform international opinion

about the condition of society in the Punjab, though, of course, they could not change it. They did not come from those sectors of society who were critical of their own system. Indeed had such persons and their associates come to power they would have found themselves occupying he same role *vis-à-vis* the militants as the government of India.

After the open resistance to the state collapsed in the autumn of 1992 and the winter and spring of 1993, tremendous effort was being put into human rights activities by the Council of Khalistan, the international wing of the Panthic Committee. They justified the publicity that some of the cases received in terms of the shield that it might provide to other similarly placed individuals. However, had it been possible to fight the guerrilla war without huge civilian losses and had the nature of the terrain – jungle, a nearby sea or high mountains – put the odds in their favour, the need for continuous monitoring by local human rights groups and the dependence on continuous international publicity would not have been so critical. Human rights groups do not have a high profile among either the Tamils or the Afghans. For the Sikhs, connections with such bodies was a route forced onto all sections of the resistance movement by their position on an open plain but also by the devastatingly negative impact of the state and the Jat traditions on the nature of allegiance. At this historical juncture, the area did not present the right conditions, either natural or social, for sustained growth of a guerrilla movement.

In the light of the foregoing, the words of Edward Said (1986: 159) take on special significance: 'Having had the experience of limits, we [the Palestinians] are thrown back on ourselves in this period of political indecisiveness and forced to raise the issues of whether we have learned what it is that has brought us this fate ... Can we put on knowledge adequate to the power that has entered and dislocated our lives so unalterably?' The guerrilla groups presented conflicting voices to the outside world. The latter was interested in what framework the Sikhs were going to use to rule. However, not only did those who kept in touch with the militants through their political organisation not develop the implications of the economic programme outlined in the Sarbat Khalsa resolution for twentieth-century Sikh society, but doubt also developed as to whether they, and indeed the Sikhs as a whole, favoured sovereignty. The cost of the confusion over aims and how to achieve them, of organisational indiscipline among all groups, of penetration of some, and, within the KCF, of the existence of so many private armies, was the loss of innumerable young lives. Conservative figures appearing in the *Indian Express* indicate the number of deaths in the past five years to be as follows: 3,074 (1988); 2,729 (1989); 3,775 (1990); 3,700+ (1991); and in 1992, 5,000 and more.[5] A substantial majority of these were the lives of young persons. Both the state and the militant groups have been involved in this violence and, for reasons specified in Chapter 5, could not, or would not, provide protection for the individual against the ravages of each other. Normal coexistence in the rural areas among families was disrupted by the seizing of young people and the deaths of young people at the hands of other young people.[6] The threat hanging over families with teenage children was such that, whenever they could, they sent their sons abroad. Even the son of a former IG, I.B. Punjab, remarked, 'Those who can are sending their children out, the terror is such!' Society had become atomised, though, throughout the struggle, civic associations, primarily of lawyers and village *pancayats*, have been performing a role that protects and shields the individual. Ultimately, members of these civic organisations knew that the state was prepared to destroy those who offered defence to the unprotected or who organised their own protection against the police. None the less, *pancayats* in particular have played a role in preventing rural society from disintegrating. Whether they will continue to do so remains to be seen, for the January 1993 *pancayat* elections were rigged.[7]

The present situation in the Punjab is described precisely in Elizabeth Colson's words (1992: 279): 'If violence is used to destroy the bases of community life and undermine trust in any social relationship with young people as the objects of violence and as instruments of atrocities ... then, they will find it difficult to re-enter society even if peace is eventually re-established. Violence let loose in this fashion can destroy the future. It can also force its victims to settle for any form of government that gives them freedom from attack.'

Notes

1. Grewal (1988: 24) points to this tendency when he says, 'the equality of the individual member built into the doctrine [of Sikhism] gave him the right to fight and conquer'. I would suggest that the latter is a Jat tradition.

2. I therefore disagree with Harjot Oberoi when he writes that Kahn Singh Nabha's statement in 1897 brought 'almost four centuries of Sikh tradition to an end' (1988: 136).

3. Here it is appropriate to mention Anton Blok's point (as quoted in Brown, 1990: 263) 'that bandits are likely to be involved not with the peasantry but with notables and officials'.

4. Sendero Luminoso's cellular structure is maintained up to national level. 'At all levels there are political and military commands [but] the political command exercises control' (Harding, 1987: 191). The Vietcong (Pike, 1966: 235) had two types of cell, a three-man cell structure and a special activity cell. They had, additionally innumerable functional liberation associations all of whom pulled in the one direction. Indeed their mode of preparation and training of each guerrilla cell, and their overall planning, were of such an advanced nature that, despite the differences of terrain, it could have been emulated. Pike's book and

Fall's introduction to Troung Chinh's writings are fascinating illustrations of the amount of thinking and effort necessary to win a guerrilla struggle. None of this was in evidence in the Sikh struggle which was controlled by its military wing.

5. The daily *Jagbani*, 23/10/92, cited the higher figure of 7,349 for 1991.

6. Bourque and Warren similarly write (1989: 16), regarding Peru and its civil war situation, 'the sons of peasants are conscripted to kill the sons of other peasants'.

7. The *pancayat* elections were designed to consolidate politically the gains achieved through terror. A 13 January report in the *Hindustan Times* 'Pancayat Poll Fever Grips Punjab's Villages' says 'voters are promised big sums of money for their vote ... Liquor is free, abundant and of good quality'. A report in the *Tribune* of 22 January, p. 11, 'Massive Rigging Alleged', says that the Congress Minister of State for Transport had interfered in the poll process in several areas of Amritsar District, and that the police had prevented many people from filing their nomination papers by planting arms on them. They were temporarily incarcerated. The report mentions the case of one SHO breaking the seal of the ballot box and putting votes from one ballot box into that of the favoured candidate.

Appendix One

The Murder of Sleep and the Wonder of the Shahid[1]

Nation at the Guru's door
I was asleep after prayer[2]
The witch slithered like a thief
A great thirst overpowering her.
Time's hands are limitless and strong,
They suffice to stab such witches,
The martyr's blood boiled, burned
In all dimensions of time.

On the martyrdom day of the Guru
Listen you shrew
The innocent children of my nation
Were killed by you [when they were]
deep in sleep
The General [Sant Jarnail Singh]
at the Guru's door
His old watchman
having all-powerful time on his side
A rider poised for victory.
Unaware, innocent, children you devoured,
you cruel witch.
Time was like the bridge between two worlds, [earth and heaven]
below
was the (serpent like) creeping river.
You will be thrown around like an insect
when the Limitless [Beant Singh] wreaks vengeance
Breaking the doors of your empire, he
will push you into a dark hell.

Hordes of ungrateful people thronged
at the doors of the Harimandir

You spilt the blood of Mian Mir[3]
And made the Temple lake red.
Far away in times womb slept
the seed of innocent forests,
The ungrateful one's eye fell on them,
singed them in seconds.

The female serpent laid a creeping siege
to Sri Harimandir
The eatables fit for saints [in the *langar*]
were put to the torch haplessly.
In the hearts of the image worshippers
slept the wretch
to burn whose venom
came the arrow of the Limitless.

In the vicinity of the injured Harimandir
Beant suffered spasms.
The afternoon sun like a hot plate
was burning away.
But in the dream of Mian Mir
flows the gentle Ravi.
In this flow a hand was raised (a Divine Hand). All the waves
turned to engulf Beant.

Notes

1. Translated for me by Gurtej Singh Brar.
2. Sikhs were unaware of the pending attack on the day of the fifth Guru's martyrdom.
3. This line means, you destroyed the foundation of communal harmony.

Appendix Two

The famous notices announcing the martyrdom of Labh Singh on 18, 19, 20 and 21 July, 1988. These were printed in Ajit, *for which the editor, Barjinder Singh, was accused of sedition.*

In the struggle started by Sant Baba Jarnail Singh Bhindranwale to cut the chains of slavery from the neck of the Sikh nation, to this end and for this cause a precious diamond of the Sikh nation General Bhai Labh Singh sacrificed his life on 12 July 1988. *Bhog* ceremony for his spiritual peace, the peace of his soul, will take place on 18 July 1988 at 1pm in Thanda and on 21 July 1988 in village Panjwar at 1pm. Bhai Labh Singh's sacrifice will give inspiration to the Sikh struggle. The federation appeals to the Sikh Sangat to reach in large numbers on 18 and 21 July.

Convenor of the AISSF Daljit S. Bitoo

Martyrs Gathering

Keep your feet on the religious path and don't shirk sacrifice.

Labh Singh sacrificed his life while struggling with government forces. The *bhog* ceremony and *Akhand path* for the peace of his soul will be held on 21 July 1988 in village Panjwar, district Amritsar.

Hari Singh Baba, Nakodar

Martyrs Gathering

In the struggle begun by Sant Jarnail Singh Bhindranwale to liberate the Sikh nation, General Bhai Labh Singh sacrificed his life. The *bhog* ceremony and *Akhand Path* will take place in his native village Panjwar, near Jhabal, on the 21st. We appeal to all *sangats* to attend the *bhog* ceremony in large numbers.

Wassan Singh Zaffarwal, Gurbachan Singh Manochahal

Martyrs Gathering

'One who dies in the battlefield is great. One who runs away takes birth again and again.'

General Bhai Labh Singh acted on the words 'In the end one has to sacrifice one's life in the battle field when all other means have failed'. The *bhog* ceremony and *Akhand path* will take place today in his native village of Panjwar 21 July 1988. We appeal to the *Sarbat Khalsa* to attend the last *Ardas* of this brave soldier.

Avtar Singh Brahma, Sukhdev Singh Babbar

Bibliography

Amnesty International 1988, *India: Review of Human Rights Violations*, London.

— 1989, *India: Some Recent Reports of Disappearances*, London.

— 1991, *India: Human Rights Violations in Punjab: Use and Abuse of the Law,* London.

— 1992, *India: Torture, Rape and Deaths in Custody*, London.

Aron, R. 1972, *Progress and Disillusion*, Harmondsworth, Pelican.

Banga, I. 1978, *The Agrarian System of the Sikhs*, New Delhi, Manohar.

Barrier, N.G. 1966, *The Punjab Alienation of Land Bill of 1900*, Monograph and Occasional Papers Series no. 2, Duke University Programme in Comparative Studies on Southern Asia, Duke University.

Benjamin, W. 1973, *Illuminations*, Glasgow, Fontana/Collins.

Bhalla, G.S. and Chadha, G.K. 1982, 'The Green Revolution and the Small Peasant', *EPW* XVIII, 15 May, 826–33 and 22 May, 870–7.

Blok, A. 1972, 'Social Bandits: Reply', *Comparative Studies in Society and History*, 14(4), 494.

Bourque, C. and Warren, K.B. 1989, 'Democracy without Peace', *Latin American Research Review* XXIV Part 1, 7–34.

Brown, N. 1990, 'Brigands and State Building: The Invention of Banditry in Modern Egypt', *Comparative Studies in Society and History* 32, 258–81.

Chadha, G.K. 1985, *The State and Rural Economic Transformation, The Case of Punjab*, New Delhi, Sage.

Chakravarti, U. and Haksar, N. 1985, *The Delhi Riots*, New Delhi, Lancer International.

Chaliand, G. 1980, *People Without a Country*, London, Zed Press.

Clutterbuck, R. 1980, *Guerrillas and Terrorists*, Columbus, Ohio University Press.

Cunningham, J.D. 1966, *History of the Sikhs*, Delhi, S. Chand and Co.

Colson, E. 1992, 'Conflict and Violence', in *The Paths to Domination, Resistance and Terror*, Nordstrom, C. and Martin, P. (eds), Berkeley, CA, University of California Press.

Das, Veena 1985, 'Anthropological Knowledge and Collective Violence', *Anthropology Today*, 1(3), 4–6

— 1990, 'Our work to Cry, Your work to Listen', in Das, V. (ed.), *Mirrors of Violence*, 345–98, Delhi, Oxford University Press.

Debray, R. 1968, *Che's Guerrilla War*, Harmondsworth, Penguin.

Degregori, C.I. 1991, ' How difficult it is to be God', *Critique of Anthropology* 11(3), 223–50.

Dhillon, G.S. 1992, *India Commits Suicide*, Chandigarh, Singh and Singh.

Douglass, W.A. and Zulaika, J. 1990, 'On the interpretation of Terrorist Violence: ETA and the Basque Political Process', *Comparative Studies in Society and History*, 32, 238–57.

Dunkerley, J. 1992, *Political Suicide in Latin America*, London, Verso.

Economic and Political Weekly (*EPW*) (news reports) 1986, 'Self Reinforcing Circle', 3 May, 758–9

— 1987, 'Crackdown without a political strategy', 3 May, 837–8.

— 1988, 'Preparing the Ground for Emergency', 16 April, 757.

— 1988, 'Tiwana Commission's Findings', 23 April, 813.

— 1990, 15 October, 2136

— 1990, 'Criminals into Heroes', 15 September, 2024

— 1990, 'Hesitating to Act', 6 January.

Fall, B. 1963, *Primer for Revolt:* A Facsimile edition of *The August Revolution* and *The Resistance will Win* by Truong Chinh, New York, Praeger.

Feldman, A. 1991, *Formations of Violence*, Berkeley, CA, University of California Press.

Foucault, M. 1979, *Discipline and Punish: The Birth of the Prison*, New York, Vintage.

Geertz, C. 1975, 'The Integrative Revolution: Primordial sentiments and civil politics in the new states', in *The Interpretation of Cultures,* C. Geertz (ed.), 255–310, London, Hutchison.

Gill, S.S. 1988, 'Contradictions of the Punjab Model of Growth and Search for an Alternative', *EPW*, 15 October, 2167–73.

— 1989, 'Changing land relations in Punjab and implications for land reforms', *EPW*, 24 June, A79–85.

Gramsci, A. 1971, *Selections from Prison Notebooks,* ed. and translated by Hoare, Q. and Nowell Smith, G., London, Lawrence and Wishart.

Grewal, J.S. 1988, 'Legacies of the Sikh Past for the 20th Century', in *Sikh History and Religion in the Twentieth Century*, ed. O'Connell, J.T., Israel, M. and Oxtoby, W.G, 18–31, *South Asian Studies Papers* 3, Toronto, University of Toronto Press.

Grewal, S.S. and Rangi, P.S. 1989, 'Wheat Cultivation', New Delhi, *Economic Times,* 26 August.

Guha, R. 1983, *Elementary Aspects of Peasant Insurgency in Colonial India*, Delhi, OUP.

Gupta, D., Banerjee, S., Mohan, D. and Navlakha, G. 1988, 'Punjab: Communalised beyond Politics', *EPW*, 13 August, 1677–84.

Gupta, H.R. 1952, *A History of the Sikhs* Vol. 1, Simla, Minerva Book Shop.

Harding, C. 1987, 'The Rise of Sendero Luminoso', in *Peruvian History*, ed. R. Miller, 179–99, University of Liverpool, *Institute of Latin American Studies Monograph* no. 14.

Hill, P. 1986, *Development Economics on Trial*, Cambridge, Cambridge University Press.

Juergensmeyer, M. 1993, *The New Cold War*, Berkeley, CA, University of California Press.

Kahlon, A.S. and Kurian, J. 1981, 'Rising Wheat Costs', *The Times of India*, 25 May.

Kapferer, B. 1988, *Legends of People, Myths of State*, Washington, Smithsonian Institute Press.

Kaur, H. 1990, *Bluestar over Amritsar*, Delhi, Ajanta International.

Kedward, H.R. 1978, *Resistance in Vichy France*, Oxford, Oxford University Press.

Kiernan, V. 1979, *Poems by Faiz*, Karachi, Oxford University Press.

Kitson, F. 1971, *Low Intensity Operations*, London, Faber.

Kramer, M. 1987, *Shiism, Resistance and Revolution*, Boulder, CO, Westview Press.

Kriger, Norma J. 1992, *Zimbabwe's Guerilla War*, Cambridge, Cambridge University Press.

Kumar, R.N and Sieberer, G. 1991, *The Sikh Struggle*, Delhi, Chanakya Publications.

Mahboob, Harinder Singh 1990, *Jhanan di Raat*, Adda Tanda, Jullundur, Swan Printing Press.

Malik, H. 1987, 'Mishra Commission Report, Salt on Raw Wounds', *EPW*, 25 April, 738–43.

Nayar, G.S. 1979, *Sikh Polity and Political Institutions*, Delhi, Oriental Publications.

Nayar, K and Singh, K. 1984, *Tragedy of Punjab*, Delhi, Vision Books.

Nairn, T. 1977, *The Breakup of Britain*, London, New Left Books.

Oberoi, H.S. 1988, 'From Ritual to Counter-Ritual: Rethinking the Sikh Question, 1844–1915', in O'Connell, J.T, Israel, M. and Oxtoby, W.G. (eds), *Sikh History and Religion in the Twentieth Century*, 136–58, Toronto, University of Toronto Press.

O'Neill, B. 1990, *Insurgency and Terrorism*, New York, Brasseys.

Pettigrew, Joyce 1991, 'Betrayal and Nation Building among the Sikhs', *Journal of Commonwealth and Comparative Politics* XXIX no. 1, 25–43.

— 1992a, 'Songs of the Sikh Resistance Movement', *Asian Music* XXIII–I, 85–118.

— 1992b, 'Martyrdom and Guerilla Organisation', *Journal of Commonwealth and Comparative Politics* XXX no. 3, 387–406.

Pike, D. 1966, *Vietcong*, Cambridge, MA, MIT Press.

Rao, A. 1987, 'To the Government's Satisfaction', *EPW*, 11 April, 625–7.

Roy, O. 1986, *Islam and Resistance in Afghanistan*, Cambridge, Cambridge University Press.

Said, E. 1986, *After the Last Sky*, London and Boston, Faber and Faber.

Schiff, Z. and Ya'ari, E. 1990, *Intifada*, New York, Simon and Schuster.

Schoeck, H. 1969, *Envy*, London, Secker and Warburg.

Scott, J. 1975, *Weapons of the Weak*, New Haven, CT, Yale University Press.

— 1986, 'Everyday Forms of Peasant Resistance', *Journal of Peasant Studies* 13 no. 2, 5–35.

— 1990, *Domination and the Arts of Resistance*, New Haven, CT, Yale University Press.

Seale, P. 1993, *Abu Nidal: A Gun for Hire*, London, Arrow Books.

Shiva, V. 1991, *The Violence of the Green Revolution*, London, Zed Books.

Singh, Daljit 1992, 'Punjab River-Waters Dispute', in Kharak Singh (ed.) 1992, 196–228.

Singh, Gopal (ed.) 1987, *Punjab Today*, New Delhi, International Publishing House.

Singh, Kapur 1971, 'Sikhism and Politics', *The Sikh Review*, August, 38–51.

Singh, Kharak *et al.* 1992, *Fundamental Issues in Sikh Studies*, Chandigarh, Institute of Sikh Studies.

Singh, Surendar 1991, 'Some Aspects of Groundwater Balance in Punjab', *EPW*, 28 December, A146–55.

Statistical Abstract of Punjab 1990, *Small-scale Industry*, Economic Adviser to the Government, Chandigarh.

Therborn, G. 1978, *What Does the Ruling Class Do when it Rules?*, London, Verso.

— 1980, *The Ideology of Power and the Power of Ideology*, London, Verso.

Tully, M. and Jacob, S. 1985, *Amritsar*, London, Jonathan Cape.

Turton, A. 1984, 'Limits of Ideological Domination and the Formation of Social Consciousness', in *History of Peasant Consciousness in South East Asia*, ed. Turton, A. and Shigehuru, T., National Museum of Ethnology, Osaka, Japan, p. 1973.

— 1986, 'Patrolling the Middle Ground: Methodological Perspectives on Everyday Peasant Resistance', *Journal of Peasant Studies* 13 no. 2, 36–47.

United States State Department 1993, 'India: Country Report on Human Rights. The 1992 Country Report on India as it was presented to Congress on January 19th', Unclassified State Department Document 018642/17.

Van Den Dungen, P.H.M. 1972, *The Punjab Tradition*, London, George Allen & Unwin.

Wilson, R. 1991, 'Machine Guns and Mountain Spirits', *Critique of Anthropology* 2(I), 33–61.

Wolf, E. 1955, 'Types of Latin American Peasantry', *The American Anthropologist* 57, 452–71.

— 1973, *Peasant Wars in the Twentieth Century*, London, Faber.

Index

Ajnoha, Gurdial Singh, 34
AK-47, 63, 64, 69, 73, 105, 160, 161, 166
Akal Takht, 4, 8, 30, 34, 35, 37, 45, 64, 76, 82, 152, 153, 155, 168, 191; attack on, 14, 173; damage to, 38
Akali Dal, 20, 33, 43, 44, 47, 111, 143, 145, 154, 158, 174; split in, 40; Women's, 49
Akali Dal (Badal), 121
Akhand Kirtani Jatha, 71, 72, 107, 129
Akhand Path, 151, 201, 202
Alam, Izhar, 23, 104, 109
alcohol: addiction to, 58, 72, 73, 129; consumption of, 151, 180; illicit production of, 74, 75, 176; prohibition of, 74, 75
All India Sikh Students Federation (AISSF), 11, 15, 30, 36, 43, 48, 45, 86, 92, 93, 139, 146, 153, 158, 167, 168, 169, 171, 179, 180, 182
Amar Das, Guru, 31
amritdharis, 10, 11, 36, 71, 89, 94, 144, 157, 158, 159, 165, 181; attacks on, 139
Anandpur Sahib Resolution, 6, 7, 30, 40, 44, 129, 145, 149, 157
Arjun, Guru, 31, 168
army: contacts with, 160; Sikhs in, 144, 147, 155, 164 *see also* ex-servicemen
Arora, Suresh, 109

Babbar Khalsa, 48, 65, 70–8, 86, 93, 94, 104, 120, 127, 129, 133, 153, 163, 182, 183
Babbar, Sukhdev Singh, 67, 71, 131, 132, 202
Badal, Parkash Singh, 33, 34, 121, 133
Bains, Ajit Singh, 42, 44
bank robberies, 82, 151, 178, 179
Barnala, Surjeet Singh, 43, 44, 151
Behla incident, 62, 118–19
Behla, Gurminder Singh, 118, 119
Behla, Manjinder Singh, 118, 119
Behla, Surjit Singh, 118, 119
Bhindranwale, Sant Jarnail Singh, 6, 22, 32, 33, 34, 35, 36, 38, 47, 55, 58, 59, 70, 71, 77, 83, 85, 86, 90, 97, 113, 115, 139, 145, 146, 159, 165, 166, 174, 177, 187; family of, 46
Bhindranwale Tiger Force for Khalistan (BTFK), 82, 85, 86, 87, 91, 118, 126, 154
bhogs, 85, 107, 108, 111, 115, 121, 123, 126, 151, 183, 201, 202; attendance forbidden, 43
Bhola, Rachpal Singh, 177–8
Bhullar, Gur Iqbal Singh, 128
Bibi Kahan Kaur incident, 121
Billing, Ram Singh, 42
Bittoo, Daljit Singh, 42, 48, 77, 86, 94, 132, 201
Bobby, killing of, 18–20
Border Security Force (BSF), 4, 12, 16, 76, 98, 105, 112, 123, 130, 157, 158, 170, 176, 194; attacks on, 93, 175
borders: crossing of, 112; importance for guerrillas, 66
Brahma, Avtar Singh, 83, 84, 154, 202
bribery, to obtain jobs, 147, 174
Budsinghwala, Gurjant Singh, 67, 86, 116, 122, 123, 133; killing of, 120–1, 131
Bulara, Mrs, 41
burning of Sikhs, 9, 10

Buttar, Gurnam Singh, 48, 93, 153

Car Jhujharu Jathebande (CJJ), 49, 70, 74, 75, 76, 83, 85, 87, 92, 93, 100, 105, 106, 112, 130, 131, 132, 133, 188, 189
cell structure of guerrilla organisations, 63, 88, 98; smashing of, 195
Central Investigative Agency (CIA), 15
Central Reserve Police Force (CRPF), 4, 12, 15, 20, 21, 61, 76, 83, 85, 105, 108, 115, 119, 123, 160, 166, 170, 176, 177; attacks on, 93
Chaheru, Manbir Singh, 45, 67, 82
Channi, Charanjit Singh, 83,
Chattopadyay, S., 109
Chauhan, Jagjit Singh, 71
Chhandran, Rachpal, 67, 91,
Chhina, Satnam Singh, 91, 94
Congress Party, 9, 37, 46, 66, 107
Council of Khalistan, 41, 137, 153, 196
counter-insurgency, 103, 106, 113, 130–3; effects of, 114–26

Dam Dami Taksal, 31, 32, 38, 47, 82, 97, 107, 181
Darbar Sahib, 44, 47, 71, 146, 151, 153, 165, 182; invasion of, 3, 4, 8, 30, 31, 35, 36, 40, 55, 57, 60, 140, 153, 165, 168, 171, 175, 177, 178, 179, 180, 181 (death toll during, 35)
Dashmesh regiment, 86, 183
death toll among Sikhs, 35, 78, 196
dhadhis, 9, 32, 165, 167, 177, 181, 192
Dhillon, Hardeep Singh, 105
disappearances, 11, 14, 111, 174
drugs: addiction to, 58, 72, 73, 129; prohibition of, 74; use of, 151

eating: customs, 71; of meat, 72, 180
education, 36, 62, 77, 113, 121, 129, 137, 138, 143, 146, 147, 157, 169, 174
electric shock torture, 16, 68, 69, 166, 168
electricity supplies, 5, 33, 56, 96, 148
Escort Agencies company, 128

ex-servicemen, 14, 19
extortion, 11, 78, 85, 90, 95, 97, 103, 104, 114, 115, 117, 121, 126, 127–30, 132, 163, 183, 188

Faiz, Faiz Ahmed, 142
fake encounters, 45, 125, 131, 150, 167, 172
false cases, 14, 17, 39, 182; use of, 11
families, 150; harassment of, 11, 40; resistance of, 62; sufferings of, 17, 59–60, 123–6, 129, 140, 148, 175, 176, 184; support for guerrillas, 137, 141, 142, 149, 172; vendettas, 90, 189
family planning, 74
farmers, small, 56, 57, 61, 62, 66, 84, 116, 126, 138, 140, 43, 148, 154, 155, 156, 157, 164, 167, 187; union of, 67
Fernandes, George, 19
Food Corporation of India, 93, 96
food, given to guerrillas, 99, 116, 141, 150, 159, 166, 184, 188

Gandhi, Indira, 34, 165, 167; death of, 14, 31, 41, 112, 181
Gandhi, Mahatma, 146
Gandhi, Rajiv, 9, 15, 30, 45
Garcha, Devinder Singh, 75
ghottna, 68, 141, 149
Ghuman, Baldev Singh, 45
Gill, K.P.S., 11, 107, 108, 123, 133, 194
Gill, Rajinder Pal Singh, 66
Gill, Sucha Singh, 55
Gill, Sukhjit, 42
Gora, Sukhwinder Singh, 84, 89, 92, 105, 107, 109, 116, 141, 157–64, 180, 194; death of, 138
Granth, Guru, 33
Green Revolution, 55, 56, 129; effects of, 58
Grewal, Gurdarshan Singh, 13, 44, 58, 128
guerrillas, 12, 44, 46, 55–81, 89, 96, 97, 98, 99, 109, 110, 137, 192, 195; activity, 4, 61; and local populations, 103–4; disintegration of units, 91, 110; intelligence, 113; leaders of, 64; size of groups, 63; splits in movement, 104

Gupta, Sanjiv, 109
gurmata, 67, 94, 155, 192
Guru Granth Sahib, 64, 72

Hamammi, Said, 132
ul-Haq, Zia, 105
Hargobind, Guru, 31
Hind Samachar newspapers, 76
Hindus, 14, 35, 57, 73, 93, 99, 106, 108, 121, 123, 138, 144, 146, 147, 156, 163, 166, 168, 170, 172, 173, 174, 179, 184, 193; doctors treat guerrillas, 138
Hoshiarpur, Jarnail Singh, 84, 110, 131, 138, 139, 180–4

Indian Acrylics killings, 121, 122
Indian Administrative Service (IAS), 74, 112, 113
Indian Ex-Servicemen's League, 14
infiltration, 63, 97, 180
informers *see* police, informers
intellectuals, 97, 108, 113, 150, 180
Inter Services Intelligence (ISI), 105, 188
irrigation, 56; canal, 5; tube-well, 5

Jaijee, Inderjit Singh, 75, 108, 124
Janata Party, 165
Jats, 55, 62, 70, 108, 119, 150, 188, 189, 190, 191, 192, 193, 196
Jhamke, Sukhdev Singh, 59, 84, 89, 158, 176, 182
Jinda, Harjinder Singh, 45; hanging of, 41

Kahlon, Harinder Singh, 15, 36, 38, 39, 41, 77, 152, 155
Kahlon, Kuldip Singh, 36, 37, 39
Kairon, Partap Singh, 68
Kallia, Hardev Singh, 84, 86, 90
Kar Sewa, 183
Kaur, Bibi Darshan, 15
Kaur, Bibi Gurdip, 20
Kaur, Joginder, 124
Kaur, Pritam, 35
Kaur, Surjit, 18
Kaur, Sushil, 68
Khalistan, 3, 38, 46, 49, 71, 74, 76, 83, 95, 96, 99, 104, 111, 145, 152, 154, 155, 161, 165, 166, 173, 174, 177, 180, 183, 184, 190, 194; declaration of, 8, 37, 38, 44, 48
Khalistan Armed Force, 130
Khalistan Commando Force (KCF), 6, 31, 47, 48, 49, 56, 57, 61, 63, 64, 65, 67, 68, 75, 103, 110, 128, 138, 139, 140, 141, 143–86, 150, 152, 154, 157, 159, 164, 174, 177, 179, 183, 188, 195, 196; cell organisation of, 90; decentralisation of, 98; defections from, 90; losses suffered by, 98; organisation of, 82–102, 162; policy, 89, 110; rules of engagement, 99, 100
KCF (Rajasthani), 86
KCF (Zaffarwal), 70–8, 78, 85, 86, 95, 97, 105, 120, 133, 179, 192, 195
Khalistan Liberation Army (KLA), 130
Khalistan Liberation Force (KLF), 48, 65, 83, 84, 86, 120, 121, 133, 154
Khalsa, Bimal Kaur, 41
Khalsa, Harinder Singh, 106
Khera, Ajit Singh, 75, 137
Khudian, Jagdev Singh, 49
Khukhrana, Kulwant Singh, 121
kidnapping, 10, 13, 17, 115, 117, 127, 130
Kumar, Sajjan, 9

Lakhowal, Mr, 68
Lal, Chaman, 45, 104
Lala murder conspiracy, 34
Land Reform Act, 58
land: alienation of, 56, 193; ownership of, 5
Lenin, V.I., 145
looting, 78, 103, 104, 121, 130, 131; by police, 17, 18, 22, 118

Majha, 88; resistance in, 65–8
Makhu, Nishan Singh, 195
Malhotra, O.P., 19
Malwa, 88, 89, 90, 112; desecration of *gurdwaras*, 68; resistance in, 65–8
Manchanda, killing of, 132
Mand, Dhian Singh, 74
Mand, Harbhajan Singh, 179
Mann Akali Dal, 11, 12, 39, 40–2, 64

Mann, Simranjit Singh, 12, 20, 40, 41, 68, 86, 87, 91, 94, 115, 117, 120, 126, 131, 133, 182, 183
Manochahal, Gurbachan Singh, 21, 22, 59, 82, 103, 114, 201
Matthewal, Sital Singh, 84, 86, 89, 105; killing of, 91
Mehta, Rajinder Singh, 92
Mills, John, 22
Mishra, Judge, 9
misl, 190, 192, 194
money paid to obtain release, 140, 149, 175
Movement Against State Repression, 42–3, 108, 123, 124
Multani, Mr, 13
Muni, Sushil, 46, 47
murder, 129, 130, 131, 132
Muslims, 146; deaths of, 150

Nabha, Kahn Singh, 193
Nanak, Guru, 31, 147, 154
Narain, Lala Jagat, 34
National Security Act (1987), 13, 44, 151
National Security Guard (NSG), 120
Naxalites, 73, 77, 144
Nayyar, Gurbachan Singh, 37
Nehru, Jawaharlal, 147, 167
Nijjar Farms company, 128
Nirankari sect, 32, 34, 70

Operation Black Thunder, 47, 83, 84, 153, 155, 182
Operation Bluestar, 36, 37, 40, 63, 67, 139, 148, 166, 167, 169, 173
Operation Woodrose, 4, 36, 40, 105, 111, 126, 139, 195
opium, 66, 151

Pakistan, 66, 94, 98, 105, 106, 107, 115, 116, 127, 131, 133, 143, 188, 189, 194, 195; training of militants, 106
Pamma, Paramjit Singh, 68
pancayats, 76, 149; election for, 39; revival of, 12
Pande brothers, 165
Panjwar, Barjinder Singh, 93
Panjwar, Parmjit Singh, 84, 86, 93, 103, 122, 126, 183, 194
Panthic Committee, 39, 41, 43, 45, 47, 48, 70, 71, 82, 85, 86, 87, 89, 91, 95, 114, 130, 131, 143, 152, 155, 160, 170, 180, 196; second, 42, 73, 84, 130, 154
paramilitaries, 61, 127; violence of, 166
peasants *see* farmers, small
police, 20, 42, 43, 45, 61, 68, 83, 85, 94, 98, 103–34, 116, 149, 169, 177, 178, 184; attacks by, 20, 64; commando battalions, 109; confession to, 141; harassment of innocent people, 11, 14, 69, 124, 140, 172; informers, 116, 127, 159, 162, 170 (killing of, 160, 163); intelligence, 106, 108, 114, 129, 131; kidnapping of relatives of, 162; killing of, 118, 119, 122, 157; road blocks, 18, 109; role in creating militants, 59; tactics of division, 133; threats to witnesses, 13; view of militants, 105–10; violence of, 10, 11, 17, 69, 108, 113, 127, 140, 141, 174, 187 *see also* looting
Punjab Agricultural University (PAU), 66
Punjab Assembly elections, 75
Punjab Human Rights Organisation (PHRO), 36, 42–3
Punjab Union of Working Journalists, 39
Punjab University Chandigarh, 73
Punjabi language, 73, 75, 143, 145, 156, 171, 187; enforcing use of, 76

Ragi, Darshan Singh, 46
Rai, Buta Singh, 3
raids on houses, 17, 22, 39, 117, 118
Rajasthani, Gurjant Singh, 84, 86; killing of, 91
Ram, Gobind, 64, 73, 93, 162, 176, 182
Ram, Sita, 109
rape, 78, 103, 130, 148, 149, 164, 169
Rehet Maryada, 99
resistance of Sikhs: rise of, 30–54; nature of, 61–4
Ribeiro, Julio, 23, 45, 104
Rode, Harcharan, 152

Rode, Jasbir Singh, 38, 45, 46, 47, 49, 71, 83, 153, 155, 181
Rupawala, Avtar Singh, 175

Said, Edward, 196
Saini, Kulwant Singh, 11, 40
Sakhira, Sukhdev Singh, 45
Salarpur, Nishan Singh, 87
Samra, Pargat Singh, 84, 85, 87, 132; killing of, 73
Sandhu, Ajit Singh, 108, 117
Sandhu, Balbir Singh, 115
Sandhu, Harminder Singh, 30, 39, 47, 87, 93, 132; killing of, 49, 73
Sandhu, Kanwar, 111, 123
Sandhu, Mukhwinder, 36, 39
Sangha, Sukhwinder Singh, 59, 91, 92
Sant Sipahi Front, 15
Santuwal, Jassa Singh, 91, 179–80; death of, 138
Sarbat Khalsa, 67, 70, 71, 94, 151, 181, 189, 191, 192, 193, 196, 202; calling of, 37, 38, 44, 46, 82; democracy in, 155
Sarbat Khalsa resolution, 76, 77, 130, 131, 187, 190
Sataravala, J.I., 19
Scott, Jim, 61
Sekhon, Sant Singh, 112
Serai, Ram Das, Guru, 33
Shahabuddin, Syed, 19
shahids (martyrs), 60, 96, 97, 164, 167, 177, 183, 199; widows of, 151, 183
Shahpur, Balwinder Singh, 84, 86, 90, 91, 110
Sharma, A.K., 109
Shiv Sena, 172
Sibia, Gurdip Singh, 131
Sidhu, Ravi, 43, 128
Sikh library, burning of, 35, 168
Sikhism, 72, 144, 145, 146, 147, 154, 171, 181; as vehicle of liberation, 74; principles of, 31, 38, 46, 56, 57, 97, 140, 150, 154, 187, 190
Sikhs: non-integration of, 8; tied to cannons, 146
Singh, Ahail, 182
Singh, Amrik, 59, 181
Singh, Anup, 138, 171–4
Singh, Baba Dip, 177
Singh, Baba Thakur, 90, 181, 183
Singh, Bai Kanwar, 131
Singh, Balbir, 16, 17
Singh, Baljit, 164–6
Singh, Balwant, killing of, 73
Singh, Barjinder, 201
Singh, Beant, 31, 122, 138, 174–7
Singh, Bhai Sukhdev, 107
Singh, Bharpur, killing of, 18–20
Singh, Dara, 119
Singh, Darshan, 176
Singh, Dilbir, 32, 33, 34, 35, 36, 37, 38, 39, 59, 77
Singh, Gagandeep, 151
Singh, Giani Kartar, 128
Singh, Gurbaksh, 6, 7
Singh, Gurjit, 45, 46, 47, 48, 71, 83, 84, 86, 91, 153, 179, 182
Singh, Gurmit, 124, 125
Singh, Guru Gobind, 21, 32, 115, 145, 155, 158, 167, 191
Singh, Harbhajan, 60, 85
Singh, Harinder, 32
Singh, Harjabh, 83
Singh, Harjit, 196
Singh, Jagir, 47
Singh, Jaspail, 42
Singh, Jasvinder, 138, 140, 167–70
Singh, Jathedar Lakha, 11
Singh, Joginder, 151, 152
Singh, Kanwaljit, 49
Singh, Kanwarjit, 59, 60, 83
Singh, Kapur, 97
Singh, Kehar, 112, 162
Singh, Labh, 47, 48, 82, 83, 84, 86, 89, 111, 143, 153, 154, 195, 201
Singh, Maharajah Ranjit, 37, 57, 65, 167, 187, 191
Singh, Malkiat, 48, 154
Singh, Man, 125
Singh, Manbir, 151
Singh, Mangal, 19
Singh, Maninderjit, 20
Singh, Manjit, 68
Singh, Mohinder, 181
Singh, Mokkam, 48, 154
Singh, Narinder, 36, 44, 65, 72, 97
Singh, Narinderpal, 22, 109
Singh, Navkiran, 42
Singh, Nishan, 85

Singh, Rachpal, 35
Singh, Ram, 70, 71, 72
Singh, Randhir, 126
Singh, Sarabjit, 59, 65, 66, 106, 127
Singh, Satwant, 111–12, 162
Singh, Sewa, 147
Singh, Shahid Bhagat, 177
Singh, Shaminder, 121
Singh, Shamsher, 130
Singh, Shubeg, 35, 181
Singh, Sirdar Bachittar, 15, 16
Singh, Sirdar Kapur, 30
Singh, Sohan, 38, 40, 46, 48, 73, 77, 94, 132
Singh, Subedar Gurdip, 18–20
Singh, Sukhwinder, 140
Singh, Surinder, 14–18
Singh, Surinderpal, 15, 16, 17
Singh, Swaran, 19, 48, 108
Singh, Wadawa, 71, 77
smuggling, 66, 94, 107, 111, 113, 115, 116, 166; of weapons, 106, 194
Sohian killings, 121, 122
Special Courts Act (1984), 12, 44
Sri Lanka, invasion of, 148
strikes, 147, 172
Sukha, Sukhdev Singh, hanging of, 41
Sursinghwala, Harbhajan Singh, 59, 84, 85, 87, 132; killing of, 73
Sutlej Yamuna canal link, 44

Taksal, 37, 46, 48, 83, 89, 151, 154, 183
Tarn Taran area, 114–20
Taura, Gurcharan Singh, 34
terror, 107, 108, 130, 197; creation of, 11, 78; police policy of, 104
Terrorist and Disruptive Activities (Prevention) Act (Tada), 12–13, 15
Tiir, Gurnam Singh, 71
Tira, Manohar Singh, 121
Tiwana, C.S., 44
torture, 10, 11, 12, 16, 22, 39, 40, 58, 68, 69, 111, 116, 121, 125, 138, 140, 141, 150, 166, 169, 171, 172, 173, 175, 176, 179, 182; severity of, 141
trade unions, 140, 144, 145; leaders killed, 147
train massacres, 77–8, 121, 122
trans-Jumna, attacks on, 9
tube wells, 158, 176

Vaidya, General, 31

Wadala, Gurnam Singh, 179
Waheguru, 137, 149
water, supplies of, 5, 30, 33, 44, 56, 96, 148
Wavell, Lord, 20
weapons: of Sikhs, seized, 9; supply of, 64, 66, 94, 105, 106, 107, 115, 127, 149, 162, 163, 175, 178, 188, 189, 194
weddings, 75; limiting size of, 75; waste in, 74
wheat, 4; price of, 4, 33, 55, 148, 169
women, 99; help for guerrillas, 166

Zaffarwal, Wassan Singh, 31, 47, 48, 57, 64, 82, 83, 84, 87, 89, 92, 107, 112, 130, 137, 138, 140, 141, 143–57, 163, 178, 180, 182, 183, 188, 194, 201
zulm, 10, 46